P9-DGP-478

HELLO, AND WELCOME!

HI THERE! We're Liz and Jen, and we co-own a candy company in Brooklyn, New York, called Liddabit Sweets.

It wasn't so long ago that we were home cooks with aspirations of working in food. After completing the Pastry Arts program at the French Culinary Institute (where we became friends), and after a couple of jobs in kitchens and candy stores, we struck out on our own.

Candy attracted us for different reasons. Liz loves the science behind the magic, the how-and-why of the transformation from raw ingredients to finished product. Jen loves to follow her well-honed instincts, putting the 2,000-plus cookbooks in her mental (and actual) library to good use while coming up with a brand-new recipe or improving on an existing one. What we *both* love about candy is the element of fun and nostalgia. We like to say that we take our ingredients and technique very seriously; ourselves, not so much.

It's this sense of wonder and playfulness that we want to share with you, dear reader! In this book you'll find comprehensive, down-to-earth explanations behind the theories and techniques particular to each subset of candy—for example, elegant chocolate candies, ooey-gooey caramel candies, and fluffy aerated candies—and to accompany them, a whole slew of clearly written, tried-and-tested recipes. We'll also be right there with you the whole time. No, we're not creepily stalking you; we mean in the form of Liz Says and Jen Says boxes, which will give you extra hints and tricks throughout. Instead of just telling you to brush down the side of the pan while cooking sugar syrup, we tell you *why* you need to—and what to do if something goes wrong. In this way, we hope to encourage you to be your own troubleshooter, to minimize frustration, and to foster a love for all things sweet in your kitchen. Once you have some knowledge of the basics, you'll be able to improvise and add your own flair—and that's where the real fun comes in. Consider this the starting point to your personal confectionery journey.

Why Bother? Or, the Magic of Homemade Candy

Ah, candy. Children's fondest desire, dentists' bane (and boon); incentive for doing chores and homework, filler of Halloween pillowcases and holiday gifts; cheap, readily available (in fun sizes, too!), and there whenever you need it.

Here's the thing, though. Most mass-market candy you get these days is . . . well . . . crap. (Pardon our Français.) When was the last time you really looked at a candy bar before you ate it? Weighed it in your hand, examined the center, read the ingredients? How lovingly did you savor your most recently consumed peanut butter cup, or gummi worm, or butterscotch drop?

Chances are you tended to ignore it. To pretend it wasn't there. Candy is so often thought of as taboo, bad for you, forbidden, that we often convince ourselves to ignore it *as we are eating it*. And we're in this unique position because candy *is* very cheap, and it's ubiquitous. Why treat as special something you can get at any corner store, gas station, or supermarket?

It wasn't always this way. Sugar used to be worth more than its weight in gold, as did chocolate. Confectioners' shops kept jealously held secret techniques and recipes, passed down through generations; and many of these techniques are dying arts today.

It needn't be so extreme. There is a happy medium between All and Nothing. And we encourage you to dwell in that happy medium when you start making candy at home.

Homemade candy is a lot easier to pull off than many people think. Yes, you usually need a thermometer; and yes, you need to be precise with your measurements. But that's just until you get the basics down. Within the foundational recipes—such as caramels, brittles, and marshmallows—there's all kinds of room to innovate and improvise, and that's the real fun of it. Well, that, and the fact that everyone is always SUPER IMPRESSED when you bring homemade candy to a party. In this section we'll outline how this book works and give you a few things to keep in mind, so you have a general idea of what you're getting into and can step boldly into your bright candy-making future.

Things to Know Before You Go

Before you set out on your magical, mystical journey through this book, arm yourself with the following delicious morsels of information. Behold the wonder:

1. Our goal in writing this book is to get you to understand some of the essential techniques and theory behind making candy, and then to take the damn thing into the kitchen and make some damn candy. Don't worry about getting it dirty; don't worry about keeping it wrinkle-free. If there's a blank space on a page, write down some notes. We want you to *use* this book. Mmmkay?

2. It's extremely helpful if you have a sense of humor. It doesn't have to be finely tuned like a sports car, or expansive like the Serengeti, or erudite like a college professor. It just needs to be present and available, and functional under stress.

3. Now pay attention, because this is the *most* important thing to remember: MAKING CANDY IS FUN. (Well . . . the most important thing might actually be "don't stick your hand in the 300°F lollipop syrup," but you get the idea.) Don't be afraid to make mistakes; even if something doesn't turn out perfectly the first time, chances are it will still be tasty.

How to Use This Book

We'll give you the benefit of the doubt and assume that you know, in the most literal sense, how to use this book: Open it at the front page; read top to bottom, left to right; string words together to form sentences. However, the following is a part you should read right now, before you read those other parts, so that you know how to use the other parts when you read them. It includes sage advice, Dos and Don'ts, and even some pretty pictures! Look!

READ THOSE RECIPES!

Before you decide to take a running leap into one of the recipes, read it through, beginning to end. Read the introduction, and read all the notes that go along with it. Read any other sections we refer you to. Knowledge is power, people! Remember: You're working with extremely temperamental substances that have the potential to injure you. The more you know before you start anything, the better your chances of sweet, scrumptious success.

MISE THE HECK OUT OF THAT PLACE

Here we're referring to the French culinary phrase *mise en place* (MEEZ-on-plas), which means "everything in its place." This phrase will change the way you cook. All professional cooks have everything ready to go before they start cooking; that's how they can cook on a line, that's how they can turn out consistent food time after time, that's how they make sure they're not missing the baking powder when it's time to add it (and that they don't forget to add it altogether). So do what the pros do and measure everything out first! We cannot stress this enough. (Actually, pretend we're still stressing it.)

As a general rule, you'll want to measure out all the ingredients into individual bowls, in the order you will be using each one. However, if you see several ingredients grouped together in the steps—for example, "add the pennies, chopped celery, and beaver tail to the mixture"—you can go ahead and measure the pennies, chopped celery, and beaver tail into the same bowl. As much as possible, we'll guide the way you set up your ingredients; we'll also point out when you can measure something right into the vessel you're going to use, like, "combine the bat milk and powdered honeysuckle in a small saucepan." (In this case, measure the bat milk and honeysuckle straight into the saucepan—no need to dirty another bowl.) Ditto a first step such as "place the alien goo in the bowl of a stand mixer": You're going to be whipping up that alien goo first thing, so no need to transfer it from one bowl into the mixer bowl.

Organization helps. It really does. (And we're telling you this as two extremely disorganized people—just ask our editor. Hi Kylie!)

SOME OTHER STUFF YOU SHOULD KNOW ABOUT THE RECIPES

We've listed ingredients in both metric weights and imperial volumetric measurements. We use weights for everything in our kitchen and we highly recommend you do the same, as it's more exact; however, if you just have your measuring cups and spoons on hand, no problemo.

You will come across specialty ingredients from time to time: citric acid, for example, or peanut flour. We provide resources for obtaining said ingredients (see—you guessed it—Resources, page 291), as well as substitutions when possible from more readily available sources. The original ingredients will work better; but hey, we're not here to tell you to go buy a kilo of passion fruit puree. Unless you want to, of course.

IMPROVISING DOS AND DON'TS

• DO be informed. We strongly recommend following the recipe exactly as written the first time or two around. Know that making any substitutions we haven't recommended, or that you're not used to working with, may result in a candy that is very different from what you expected.

• DO use your (metaphorical) noodle. Want to use kangaroo extract instead of pure kangaroo oil? Go for it! But make sure you know that you'll need twice as much extract.

• DO go boldly. We highly encourage experimentation—it's part of the fun of making candy yourself! Just remember to manage your expectations: Not everything will come out perfectly the first time, no matter what you're making, and this is especially true for putting your own spin on things. (Real-life example: It took Jen about 6 weeks to perfect the Snacker nougat recipe on page 256.)

• DON'T guesstimate. Make sure you measure out what you're substituting, and that you write the item and amount down somewhere. If you add ½ cup of carpet tacks to a recipe and it fails horribly, you'll want to know not to do that again (conversely, if it ends up a brilliant success, you'll want to be able to re-create it with precisely the same amount of carpet tacks).

• DON'T wait till the last minute to pull together your ingredients. If you're making a substitution because you got to the point where you're supposed to add baking soda and you're totally out of baking soda—sorry, but we can't really help you. This is why you need to read everything through. Always know what you're substituting, and why you're using it instead of what was called for in the recipe.

• DON'T fly blind. Taste as you go! If you're trying a new flavor combination and aren't sure about the proportions, try a little each time you add stuff (making sure to cool it down first, if necessary—a spoonful of hot caramel should never go directly into the mouth). We joke about having to taste everything for quality assurance, but the big secret is that it's actually true.

OKAY, OKAY, ENOUGH CHITCHAT. LET'S GET GOING!

SPEED DATE THE CANDIES

RECIPE	CHOCOLATY	CRUNCHY/CRISPY	NUTTY	CHEWY	FRUITY	MELT-IN-YOUR-MOUTH-Y	VEGAN	GLUTEN-FREE	DAIRY-FREE	NUT-FREE	BOOZY	QUICK ASSEMBLY	GEE-WHIZ SHOWSTOPPING	ARE THERE VARIATIONS?	SHIP IT, SHIP IT GOOD	NIFTY-GIFTY	MAKE WITH THE WEE ONES
Simply Perfect Dark Chocolate Truffles (p. 59)	✓					✓		✓		✓		✓		✓			✓
Simply Perfect Milk or White Chocolate Truffles (p. 62)	✓					✓		✓		✓		✓		✓			✓
Salted Soft Chocolates (p. 67)	✓			✓			✓	✓	✓	✓		✓			✓		✓
Buckeyes (p. 72)	✓		✓					✓				✓					✓
Wolverines (p. 75)	✓		✓				✓	✓	✓			✓					✓
Nonpareils (p. 77)	✓						✓	✓	✓	✓		✓			✓		
Chocolate Bark (p. 79)	✓	✓										✓		✓	✓		
Chocolate Mint Meltaways (p. 82)	✓					✓	✓	✓	✓	✓		✓		✓			✓
Cherry Cordials (p. 85)	✓				✓			✓	✓	✓	✓					✓	
Chocorrone (p. 89)	✓	✓	✓						✓			✓			✓		
PB&J Cups (p. 91)	✓		✓					✓						✓		✓	
Rochers (p. 95)	✓	✓	✓				✓		✓		✓			✓	✓		
Hip-to-Be Squares (p. 99)	✓	✓	✓									✓					✓
Pâtes de Fruits (p. 105)				✓	✓		✓	✓	✓	✓							

RECIPE	CHOCOLATY	CRUNCHY/CRISPY	NUTTY	CHEWY	FRUITY	MELT-IN-YOUR-MOUTH-Y	VEGAN	GLUTEN-FREE	DAIRY-FREE	NUT-FREE	BOOZY	QUICK ASSEMBLY	GEE-WHIZ SHOWSTOPPING	ARE THERE VARIATIONS?	SHIP IT, SHIP IT GOOD	NIFTY-GIFTY	MAKE WITH THE WEE ONES
Agar Fruit Jellies (p. 109)				✓	✓		✓	✓	✓	✓	✓	✓		✓			
Gummi Candies (p. 112)				✓	✓			✓	✓	✓		✓		✓		✓	
Candied Citrus Peel (p. 114)	✓			✓	✓		✓	✓	✓	✓				✓	✓		
Non-Evil Turkish Delight (p. 117)				✓	✓			✓	✓					✓			
Goody Goody Gumdrops (p. 120)				✓	✓			✓	✓	✓						✓	
Sea Salt Caramels (p. 123)				✓				✓		✓					✓	✓	
Salted Chocolate Caramels p. 125)	✓			✓				✓		✓				✓	✓	✓	
Fig and Ricotta Caramels (p. 127)				✓	✓			✓		✓			✓		✓	✓	
Brown Sugar–Coffee Caramels (p. 131)				✓				✓		✓			✓		✓	✓	
Beer and Pretzel Caramels (p. 133)		✓		✓						✓	✓		✓		✓	✓	
Turtles (p. 137)	✓	✓	✓	✓				✓							✓		
Vanilla Marshmallows (p. 141)				✓				✓	✓	✓				✓	✓	✓	✓
Classic European Nougat (p. 145)			✓	✓				✓	✓					✓	✓		
Marisa's Vanilla Bean Saltwater Taffy (p. 149)				✓				✓		✓					✓	✓	

RECIPE	CHOCOLATY	CRUNCHY/CRISPY	NUTTY	CHEWY	FRUITY	MELT-IN-YOUR-MOUTH-Y	VEGAN	GLUTEN-FREE	DAIRY-FREE	NUT-FREE	BOOZY	QUICK ASSEMBLY	GEE-WHIZ SHOWSTOPPING	ARE THERE VARIATIONS?	SHIP IT, SHIP IT GOOD	NIFTY-GIFTY	MAKE WITH THE WEE ONES
Salty Peanut Taffy (p. 152)			✓	✓				✓							✓	✓	
Maple Candy (p. 157)						✓		✓		✓							
Peanut Butter Pinwheels (p. 159)			✓			✓		✓				✓		✓			
Le Fondant (p. 162)						✓	✓	✓	✓	✓		✓					
Mint Patties (p. 164)	✓						✓	✓	✓	✓		✓		✓			
Spicy Pralines (p. 167)			✓					✓							✓		
Oh, Fudge! (p. 169)	✓					✓		✓		✓				✓	✓		✓
Fluffy Peanut Butter Nougat (p. 172)			✓			✓		✓	✓					✓		✓	
Five-Minute Marzipan (p. 175)			✓				✓	✓	✓		✓	✓					✓
Buttermints (p. 177)						✓		✓		✓		✓		✓	✓		✓
Tooty Frooty Lollipops (p. 183)					✓		✓	✓	✓	✓					✓	✓	
Barley Tea and Honey Lollipops (p. 187)									✓	✓					✓	✓	
Chai Latte Lollipops (p. 189)								✓		✓					✓	✓	
Peanut Brittle (p. 193)		✓	✓	✓				✓						✓	✓	✓	

RECIPE	CHOCOLATY	CRUNCHY/CRISPY	NUTTY	CHEWY	FRUITY	MELT-IN-YOUR-MOUTH-Y	VEGAN	GLUTEN-FREE	DAIRY-FREE	NUT-FREE	BOOZY	QUICK ASSEMBLY	GEE-WHIZ SHOWSTOPPING	ARE THERE VARIATIONS?	SHIP IT, SHIP IT GOOD	NIFTY-GIFTY	MAKE WITH THE WEE ONES
Cinnamon-Walnut Brittle (p. 195)		✓	✓	✓				✓						✓	✓	✓	
Honeycomb Candy (p. 197)		✓		✓				✓		✓				✓	✓		
Chocolate-Dipped Honeycomb Candy (p. 200)	✓	✓						✓		✓			✓	✓	✓		
Butterscotch Drops (p. 202)							✓	✓	✓	✓					✓		
Roni-Sue's Best Buttercrunch Ever (p. 204)	✓	✓	✓					✓					✓		✓		
Bacon Buttercrunch (p. 208)		✓						✓		✓					✓		
Tropical Toffee (p. 211)		✓	✓					✓			✓			✓	✓		
Dragées (p. 213)			✓				✓	✓	✓					✓	✓		
Praline Paste (p. 217)			✓				✓	✓	✓			✓					
Sesame Candy (p. 218)		✓		✓				✓	✓	✓				✓	✓		
Caramel Apples (p. 223)				✓	✓			✓		✓							
Candy Apples (p. 225)		✓			✓		✓	✓	✓	✓				✓			
Honey Caramel Corn (p. 228)		✓						✓		✓					✓	✓	
Pecan Turtle Caramel Corn (p. 230)	✓	✓	✓					✓							✓		

RECIPE	CHOCOLATY	CRUNCHY/CRISPY	NUTTY	CHEWY	FRUITY	MELT-IN-YOUR-MOUTH-Y	VEGAN	GLUTEN-FREE	DAIRY-FREE	NUT-FREE	BOOZY	QUICK ASSEMBLY	GEE-WHIZ SHOWSTOPPING	ARE THERE VARIATIONS?	SHIP IT, SHIP IT GOOD	NIFTY-GIFTY	MAKE WITH THE WEE ONES
Cake Amazeballs (p. 232)	✓									✓							✓
Butterscotch Sauce (p. 241)								✓		✓	✓	✓	✓	✓			
The Best Hot Fudge Sauce (p. 243)	✓							✓		✓		✓		✓			
Snacker Bars (p. 256)	✓		✓	✓				✓					✓	✓	✓		
Twist Bars (p. 260)	✓	✓								✓			✓	✓	✓		
Nutty Bars (p. 265)	✓	✓	✓										✓		✓		
King Bars (p. 267)	✓	✓	✓		✓								✓		✓		
S'mores Bars (p. 271)	✓	✓		✓						✓			✓		✓		
Passion Spice Caramel Bars (p. 276)	✓							✓		✓	✓		✓		✓		
The Dorie Bar (p. 279)	✓	✓		✓	✓					✓			✓		✓		
Coconut-Lime Bars (p. 282)	✓		✓					✓					✓	✓	✓		
Chocolate Toffee Matzo Crunch (p. 285)	✓	✓								✓		✓			✓		
Chocomallow Cookies (p. 287)	✓	✓		✓						✓			✓		✓		

COCONUT-
LIME BARS
PAGE 202

CANDIED
CITRUS PEEL
PAGE 114

BARLEY TEA AND
HONEY LOLLIPOPS
PAGE 187

Chapter One

CANDY 101

(OR, THE BEST COLLEGE COURSE YOU NEVER TOOK)

Here is what you *won't* find in this chapter: the history of wood chips, advice for successful clowning, and no-fail tetherball moves. Here is what you *will* find: a breakdown of candy's main components and their functions, a list of tools you'll need for your confectionery adventures, and master techniques for chocolate work, cooking sugar, and otherwise assembling your majestic creations.

While you should, in theory, be able to open this book to any recipe and be able to go ahead and start cookin', there are advantages to reading this section first, in full, in one sitting. (Okay, it doesn't have to be in one sitting.) Understanding the ingredients that go into your candy, what purposes they serve, and the ways they behave, will go a long way in helping you to nail the recipes on your first try. You'll have a better understanding of why problems might arise, and you'll be better equipped to come up with MacGyver-esque ways of dealing with them. Plus, the real fun of making candy at home—coming up with your own genius creations—is that much more doable when you know why there's *x* amount of sugar in this recipe and *y* amount of water. Now go forth and learnify!

CANDY: IT IS MADE OF STUFF

Mostly a few select kinds of stuff:

Sugar

Sugar plays an integral role in many of these recipes: It contributes sweetness, body, structure, and/or caramelization. It's the building block of confectionery, and none of these sweets could be made without it (sugar-free confectionery is a whole different ball game). At a molecular level, sugar (technically called sucrose) is made up of one molecule of glucose and one molecule of fructose. These two components of sugar act very differently—and if you know how, you can use them to your advantage.

FRUCTOSE is the sweeter of the two: about twice as sweet as table sugar. Fructose is the sugar found in fruits. Agave syrup is also very high in fructose, as are honey, molasses, and maple syrup. What's nice about fructose is that it's very good at inhibiting crystallization (important when you're trying to make caramel—see What's the Word, Caramel?, page 50). What's less nice about it is that it's incredibly sweet and generally has a fairly assertive flavor; it also browns very quickly when cooked, well below the browning point of sucrose. For these reasons, in this book we'll be using fructose a lot less often than our good friend . . .

GLUCOSE. This is a critical ingredient in any sugar candy. Since it's a syrup in its natural state, glucose inhibits sucrose from recrystallizing once it's been dissolved. This helps keep your caramels chewy and your lollipops clear. The most common form of glucose is corn syrup (before you start hyperventilating, see The Rant We've Been Working on for Five Years on page 5). Though glucose can be made from any starchy substance—potato, rice, wheat—in the United States it's almost always made from corn. It's about half as sweet as table sugar and fairly thick and gooey, which makes it a very versatile ingredient: It adds volume to recipes without adding too much sweetness; it has no flavor, so it won't compete with oils or spices; and it caramelizes only at very high temperatures—helpful in keeping clean flavors in lollipops and other hard candy.

When we call for glucose in this book, we'll indicate "corn syrup" or "glucose syrup." Though for home cooking they're generally interchangeable, corn syrup tends to be less viscous and commercial glucose syrup will produce a product that is more stable and less apt to crystallize. For everyday use, corn syrup is fine; if you anticipate making candy often, or are planning a lot of production for holiday gifts or an event, you might invest in a tub of glucose syrup. It's readily available online from places like Sugarcraft (see Resources, page 291) and through Amazon.

GRANULATED SUGAR. This is sugar that's in crystals or granules (natch); whenever we use the phrase in the recipes in this book, we mean your everyday, snowy-white, grocery-store kind. (Incidentally, white sugar is refined to the point where all of its molasses has been removed.) If we call for a special kind of sugar, such as brown, turbinado/raw, or confectioners', we'll specify that, too. Here's what you need to know in case you run across one of these other guys in a dark alley:

BROWN SUGAR. This is the same as white sugar, but with some molasses added back to it after refining. The molasses is what gives brown sugar its rich flavor and moist texture; dark and light brown sugar simply have different amounts of molasses. Make sure to store brown sugar airtight; if you don't, it will eventually dry out and form a frustratingly sturdy little brick. If it does brick up on you, you can put it in a zip-top bag, add a piece of apple, seal the bag, and leave it overnight; or, if you need it right away, nuke it on High in a bowl with a damp paper towel over the top in intervals of 5 to 10 seconds until it's softened up.

TURBINADO, DEMERARA, OR "RAW" SUGAR. Light golden in color, this is cane sugar that's slightly less refined than its white cousin. The molasses that remains in the cane juice when it crystallizes is what gives it its golden cast. **MUSCOVADO** sugar is made in a similar manner, but is even less refined, so it ends up being basically crystallized cane juice with much of the natural molasses still included.

CONFECTIONERS' SUGAR. Also known as icing, powdered, or 10X sugar, this is just finely ground white sugar with a little bit of cornstarch added to prevent clumping. We mostly use it in fondant (page 162) and frosting (pages 235, 238, and 240). When it comes to buying sugar, you can go organic or non-. It's totally your call.

THE RANT WE'VE BEEN WORKING ON FOR FIVE YEARS

While we're talking about ingredients, let us bring up one of our pet peeves: people freaking out about corn syrup. We totally understand that many of the articles written on the subject are boogeyman-tastic—some of that stuff is terrifying! However, there are a few things we'd like to say about corn syrup before that knee-jerk reaction sets in. Ahem:

1. Corn syrup is NOT high-fructose corn syrup (HFCS). Simple as that. They're two different products. Corn syrup is made by adding enzymes to corn slurry (cornstarch mixed with water) to break down its starches into component sugars: glucose and fructose. The glucose is packaged and sold as corn syrup (which, by the way, has been available to everyday consumers for more than 100 years; it's not exactly a novelty item). High-fructose corn syrup goes through another step of processing, where pure fructose is added to the mix to approximate the sweetness of sugar. That's it; that's the difference.

2. Corn syrup—high-fructose or no—will not kill you. We promise. Is it good for you? No. Should you be chugging a couple quarts of it every day? Of course not. Will you develop a raging case of radioactive brain worms tomorrow if you eat a fruit roll-up? Negatory. Our golden rule is "everything in moderation." Rome wasn't built in a day, and the health issues more and more people face as time goes on didn't pop up overnight. You shouldn't be eating candy all the time, anyway! Didn't your mother teach you anything?

3. Corn syrup's real nefariousness comes from hiding in packaged staple foods. Even if there were HFCS in candy you made at home, you know that candy shouldn't be a main part of your diet. What can be creepy about HFCS is that it shows up in things you don't expect: bread, crackers, peanut butter, and fruit juice, to name a few.

4. Brown rice syrup is essentially the same thing as corn syrup, only it's made with brown rice instead of corn. It is no more nutritious, virtuous, or natural than corn syrup. Ditto sorghum, barley, etc.

As far as GMO/organic worries go, that we can't really help you with; GMO regs are hazy at best right now, though if you want organic, just check the label.

Whew. Okay, down off the soapbox. For those of you still interested in whether you can substitute brown rice syrup (or malted barley syrup, or honey, or molasses) for corn syrup, the answer is, again, generally: no. Sometimes you can—brown rice syrup in caramel, for example, might be passable—but it will change the flavor, and we haven't tested with it, so we have no idea what the results will be like and don't recommend it. In honey's case, well, that's basically pure fructose, so it'll make the end product that much sweeter (and runnier). Ditto agave syrup; ditto maple syrup. To start, go by the book—that's why we're here!—and as you get more comfortable with techniques and recipes, you can start messing around with substitutes.

JEN SAYS: Make sure to check the ingredient label on your corn syrup; some are now made with HFCS as an ingredient (I don't even know how they do that), and if you're looking to avoid it, you'll have to be vigilant. But if you were concerned about HFCS to begin with, you were probably already checking ingredient labels like a champ.

ILLEGAL SUBSTITUTION

We often get questions about substitutions, especially for sugar. Can I use raw sugar? How about evaporated cane juice? Or possibly a sugar substitute? The answer, in short, is no. In some applications—brittle, for example, or caramel, where you want a nice toasty flavor—using turbinado sugar would be acceptable (though not recommended). But for any aerated candy, like nougat or marshmallow, it just has to be refined sugar. The candy doesn't turn out the same way otherwise, and recipes adapted for turbinado sugar would require a whole different book. Subbing syrup for granulated sugar is out of the question; it's a chemical thing.

Salt

Whenever folks ask us the secret of making really great, delicious candy, we always tell them: salt. Salt has the amazing property of elevating whatever it's near, giving extra oomph to rich flavors like caramel and peanut butter. We call for several different kinds of salt, and for the purposes of this book some of them are more or less interchangeable—note the handy-dandy chart opposite. Just please, please, pretty please, *don't* use standard table salt in these recipes. There's nothing wrong with it in general; it's just processed in a certain way that makes it taste . . . well, flat. Sea salt has a sparkle that you just can't replace.

FINE SEA SALT is the closest analog to table salt we've found, and there are so many store brands that in many cases it's as cheap as table salt. Fine sea salt is best when you want to add an overall flavor boost without discernible crystals, as in Buckeyes (page 72) or in Chocolate Mint Meltaways (page 82).

COARSE SEA SALT adds the fireworks to the Sea Salt Caramels (page 123) and the Fluffy Peanut Butter Nougat (page 172). It can be used in much the same manner and proportion as the more delicate—and pricey—fleur de sel. But if you can spring for the fleur, it's worth it.

FLEUR DE SEL ("flower of salt") is a highly prized, hand-harvested French sea salt characterized by moist, irregularly sized, complexly flavored granules.

MALDON SEA SALT consists of large, delicate flakes and is really a specialty salt—the priciest one listed here. It's often used for garnish because it's so dang pretty, and we use it only a couple of times—on top of the PB&J Cups (page 91) and the Turtles (page 137)—but hey, the more you know . . . (Cue PSA jingle and shooting-star rainbow . . . *now*.)

KOSHER SALT. If you can have only one kind of salt, get kosher salt; you can use it for any of these recipes in a pinch (HA! get it? pinch? . . . get it?). It has nice hollow pyramid-shaped crystals that crush easily between the fingers for recipes that call for fine salt; and they can be left intact for any recipes that require more of a fleur de sel or coarse salt feel. We like Diamond Crystal; Morton's is also great. (Kosher salt is our favorite to cook with at home, too, and economical to boot; we bet you'll never go without it again once you've tried it.)

SALT TYPE	TEXTURE	SUBSTITUTE
Fine sea salt	Fine, dry, sandlike granules	Kosher salt
Coarse sea salt	Coarse, dry granules; solid crystals	Fleur de sel, Maldon sea salt
Fleur de sel	Mustard-seed-size, moist granules; can be crushed between fingers	Maldon sea salt
Maldon sea salt	Large flakes; easily crushed	Fleur de sel
Kosher salt	Sesame-size hollow crystals; can be crushed	Fine sea salt

Fat

Fat contributes flavor to candies, and changes the texture as higher proportions of it appear in the ingredients. Consider the difference in the texture of the Cinnamon-Walnut Brittle (page 195), which has a lower fat content and shatters cleanly and crisply in your mouth, and Roni-Sue's Best Buttercrunch Ever (page 204), which has a higher fat content that imparts a tantalizing scrunchy, munchy

quality that is really quite difficult to put into words. (You know what it's like when you're walking in fresh dry snow? Kinda like that.)

For the purposes of this book, fat will mostly be dairy: cream, milk, butter. *Always use unsalted butter* in these recipes! Salted butter makes it difficult to control the salt content yourself. Salt is also a preservative (that's why salted butter exists in the first place), meaning that salted butter can be left sitting on a supermarket shelf longer than unsalted, so it's not always as fresh.

TRUTH OR DAIRY

A note for our nondairy buddies: Unfortunately dairy is irreplaceable in all of the recipes that call for it (again, it's a chemical thing). Luckily, there are many dairy-free recipes in this book, such as the Coconut-Lime Bars (page 282), Honeycomb Candy (page 197—just grease the pan with cooking spray instead of butter), and Wolverines (page 75). For the complete dairy-free lineup, see the chart on page xiii.

Gelling agents

Gelling agents are used to help thicken the liquid in candies like gummies, agar fruit jellies, and pâtes de fruits. The final texture of the candy depends on which agent is used, and how it's incorporated in the recipe.

GELATIN is the most widely used gelling agent. It's derived from animal tissue, so it's not vegetarian-friendly. Gelatin is what you find in Jell-O, gummi candies, and marshmallow, among other things. It has a pleasantly chewy consistency and is very temperature-stable (though boiling it compromises its gelling power, completely aside from producing a profoundly nasty smell). It's often available in ¼-ounce packets; keep in mind that each ¼-ounce packet = roughly 1 tablespoon = 3 teaspoons = 7 g.

AGAR is simply powdered dried seaweed. It's vegan-friendly, and it produces a "short" (breaks if you try to bend it) and slightly granular texture. Fruit slice candies are often made with agar, and it's used as a thickener and stabilizer in mass-produced foods. Agar jelly candy has the distinction of tasting extremely fresh; this is because the juice or puree flavoring is added after the syrup has finished cooking, so the zingy flavor is preserved—equally great for really puckery-tart flavors, like citrus and passion fruit, and delicate ones like cucumber, fresh herbs, and melon.

PECTIN is derived from citrus fruits and apples, and is the main thickener in most jams and jellies. It produces a chewy, jammy candy with a distinct cooked flavor—in fact, Pâtes de Fruits (page 105) are basically tasty little overcooked jam squares. (Although saying that just makes us want to put them on tiny toasts with a smear of butter and have them for high tea.)

Chocolate

Chocolate is fairly straightforward—if you don't know what it is yet, well, thank goodness you bought this book! To make your life easier, we'll be specific when we refer to it.

"Unsweetened" is pretty self-explanatory—no sugar added. The terms "semisweet" and "bittersweet" are more or less interchangeable, and both fall under the category of "dark" chocolate (Officially Defined as having 35 percent or more cocoa solids). We'll specify white, milk, or dark chocolate in the recipes, but the percentage is up to you. If there's a specific percentage we recommend, we'll list that, too (for more on percentages, see page 23).

Summer coating (also known as compound coating or *pâte à glacer*) is chocolate that's had some or all of its cocoa butter replaced with vegetable oil. This has the benefits of reducing chocolate bloom (see page 30) and eliminating the need to temper. The main disadvantage is the mouthfeel: the vegetable oil can leave a waxy slick on your tongue (you know that greasy feeling in your mouth after eating those pink-and-white iced animal cookies?). That said, if you need to dip something in a flash or during a warm or humid day, it's an acceptable alternative to real chocolate. You can buy it online—in dark, milk, and white (or colored) varieties—at Sugarcraft (see Resources, page 291) or in specialty pastry stores. Another, tastier, unwaxy option: Make your own Cheater's Chocolate Coating (page 32); if you start with great chocolate, you'll end up with great coating.

A FEW OF OUR FAVORITE (CHOCOLATE) THINGS

We've used many kinds of chocolate in the past, and there are pros and cons to each. Currently we use Cacao Barry for most purposes; it has a strong chocolaty flavor and stays relatively thin when tempered (which helps create a nice thin shell when you're dipping). However, it does tend to be pricier than other brands that are still very good, like Callebaut (Trader Joe's house brand chocolate is made by Callebaut, and you can buy it in big chunks for a very good price). Guittard also makes a high-quality chocolate, and it is available online in disk form in large boxes—useful if you plan on doing a lot of dipping! Just keep in mind that chocolate chips won't work as a dipping chocolate; they contain stabilizers and stay frustratingly thick when melted.

Vanilla

We feel very strongly about vanilla. The word is often used to describe—as Webster's dictionary defines it—something that is "lacking distinction; plain, ordinary, conventional." We beg to differ, Noah. Vanilla is actually a flavor, and a wonderful, gorgeously nuanced one at that. Not only does it shine on its own, but it enhances any flavor it's paired with, bringing both to new heights. Did you know that vanilla beans are actually the seedpods of a particular genus of orchid? That, before hand-pollination became a feasible option in the mid-19th century, the cultivation of said orchid and pods depended on a symbiotic relationship between the plant and a distinct species of bee? That it's the second most expensive spice in the world, just behind saffron? That it requires an insane amount of skilled human labor to grow, tend, harvest, cure, and sort the beans? Well, now you do. And DON'T let us hear you take that tone with vanilla again.

Vanilla is available in several iterations:

PURE VANILLA EXTRACT is an infusion of vanilla beans in high-proof neutral spirits. It's widely available, and can be used in every single recipe in this book. Proportionally, you'd use twice as much of it as the next strongest vanilla contender, which is . . .

VANILLA PASTE. Available at some specialty food stores and online, vanilla paste can be pricey (about $10 for a 4-ounce bottle). But you use less of it per recipe, and you get all the good stuff that lives inside a vanilla pod—*without* having to scrape the pod and fish it out of whatever you're infusing. We like Nielsen-Massey, which is available at Williams-Sonoma and online.

VANILLA BEANS. All this being said, there's no substitute for real, whole vanilla beans. Pricewise, they're steep—75¢ to more than $1.50 per bean, depending on how many you're buying—but for some recipes, the Sea Salt Caramels (page 123) for one, you really have to make the candy with a whole bean at least once. All the little crunchy seeds, plus the extra punch of vanilla from infusing the bean in the caramel . . . it defies description.

Make sure to save your spent beans! Rinse them and dry them; then either stick them in an airtight jar with granulated sugar to impart a lovely vanilla scent, or put them in a small bottle with some high-proof vodka (about 1 spent bean for 2 ounces liquor). Allow that to steep for 2 weeks, shaking it occasionally, and—hey, presto!—homemade vanilla extract. (Thanks to our buddy Allison Kave of First Prize Pies for that little tip.)

Watch out for imitation vanilla! Real vanilla extract is entirely affordable for the purposes of this book, and we find that the fake stuff has a chemical aftertaste that can be off-putting.

Booze

Alcohol flavors candy in two ways. When it's added at the beginning of a recipe, like in the Butterscotch Sauce on page 241, the actual alcohol evaporates during the cooking process, just leaving the flavor behind. (This is why many extracts are suspended in neutral alcohol.) When it's added after any cooking has been done, like in Papa Gutman's Eggnog Truffles on page 66, the boozy kick is left intact—good to keep in mind if you're a teetotaler (or just don't like the taste of alcohol).

Oil

Oil is used mostly for keeping sticky stuff off of things you don't want sticky stuff attaching itself to: knives, baking sheets, mixing spatulas. Occasionally it will show up in a recipe for that same purpose (like in the Dragées on page 213). The most significant recipes that feature it as an actual ingredient are Chocolate Mint Meltaways (page 82), to which coconut oil contributes a lovely cooling effect, and Cheater's Chocolate Coating (page 32), in which oil helps stabilize normally temperamental chocolate.

Eggs

Used almost exclusively for making aerated candies (like Classic European Nougat, page 145, and Vanilla Marshmallows, page 141), egg whites can do some amazing things. Their proteins form a delicate foam when whipped; and when hot syrup is poured into the whipping whites, the proteins cook and form a more stable foam. To further stabilize any egg foam—such as meringue, nougat, and so on—add a small amount of cream of tartar (see page 119) or distilled white vinegar in the early stages of whipping, when the whites are just starting to look foamy (you'll need about ⅛ teaspoon cream of tartar or vinegar per white).

Eggs also help bind baked goods together, and the yolks help emulsify anything they're added to (they contain lecithin, which, when extracted from soybeans, is often used as an emulsifier in chocolate. Put THAT in your salad dressing and smoke it). For the purposes of this book, it doesn't much matter what temperature the eggs are when you use them; but if you're taking them straight out of the fridge, maybe let them sit uncracked in hot water for 10 minutes to disperse the chill a bit. *Important:* Never add sugar or salt to fresh yolks and let them sit without whisking them together; the proteins in the yolks will coagulate and "burn," leaving your final product lumpy.

Flour

The flour in these recipes is almost always all-purpose—again, unless otherwise specified. Why is that, you ask? Well, flour is used in only a few of these recipes (the candy bars and cake balls, mostly), and all-purpose works best in all of them. It's also the easiest to procure.

LIZ SAYS: Nerd Alert! Ever wonder about the difference between cake flour, all-purpose flour, and bread flour? You might think that it has to do with how fine the wheat is ground, but you'd be wrong (good guess, though). It actually has to do with the amount of protein in the flour. When you mix wheat proteins with water and knead them, you form gluten—the stretchy substance that gives structure to baked goods. Sometimes you want a lot of gluten, like when you make bread: The gluten gives the loaf its shape and traps the air bubbles produced by the yeast, allowing it to rise. Sometimes you want as little gluten as possible: for a delicate pastry like a shortbread, say, or a tender cake like angel food. All-purpose flour falls in between these two, offering the perfect middle-bear amount of tenderness and stability.

Coloring

Think of food coloring as being along the same lines as vanilla (*sans* the existence of a magical Pigment Plant from which they're distilled): The most widely available versions are liquid (the kind you find in any grocery store) and gel, which is available at specialty cake shops and online (see Resources, page 291). We specify amounts for liquid food coloring; if you're using gel, start with a single drop and go from there. As for natural vs. artificial, we'll let you make your mind up about that one (though natural colors will be less vivid than artificial).

MEET THE EQUIPMENT

We've divided this list of candymaking tools into two sections: the *musts* (as in, you really, really need these things and there is no way around them) and the *coulds* (as in, these would be quite helpful if you have the ability and inclination to acquire them—see Resources, page 291—but you will not die without them). We will offer alternatives as much as possible with all of the *coulds,* but you probably already have some *musts* lying around your kitchen.

Now, let's say you recently returned from your tour in the Peace Corps, having given away all your worldly possessions in a fit of altruism right before you left. Starting from absolute zero, you can get a candy thermometer, a sturdy 4-quart saucepan, a heatproof spatula, a 13 × 18-inch baking sheet, a roll of parchment paper, three mixing bowls, a can of cooking spray, a good-quality knife, and a strainer for about $125. Throw in a hand mixer and you'll still keep it around $150.

Conversely, if you're Julia Child's great-grandniece and you own a whole collection of copper pots, three or four stand mixers, whisks in several sizes, and a six-burner stove, you won't need to buy anything at all. Congratulations!

Since both of these scenarios seem fairly unlikely, let's just say you have the basics: a few saucepans, a couple of mixing bowls, a sharp knife, your granny's old hand mixer, and some vegetable oil. You can make almost every recipe in this book with an investment of about $30 for an analog thermometer, a 13 × 18-inch baking sheet, and a new roll of parchment paper.

You in? Of course you are!

Musts

HEAVY-BOTTOMED NONREACTIVE SAUCEPANS. You'll need several sizes of these. Two-, 4-, and 6-quart saucepans are the ones we use the most—and in the recipes, these generally correspond to small, medium, and large. The pans don't need to be made by any sort of fancy manufacturer, but they really should be well constructed and weighty; chances are you already have them. If you don't, Winco Winware is a fantastic, inexpensive, and incredibly sturdy option, available on Amazon. Hot sugar syrup can be extremely dangerous, and you don't want to have to worry about whether or not your pan is going to melt. And by "nonreactive" we mean "stainless"—aluminum doesn't agree with baking soda, and copper is unnecessarily expensive unless you're a pro (also potentially toxic if you're cooking anything acidic in it).

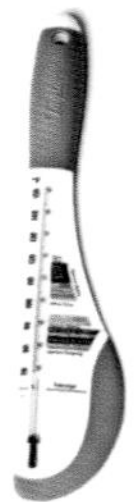

TEMPERING THERMOMETER. If you plan on doing a lot of chocolate tempering (see page 23) for dipping candy bars and such, it might be worth investing in one of these. After you get the hang of the process, you probably won't need it anymore—but it's helpful to have around when you start to learn, so you can get a better sense of what the different chocolate temperature stages look and feel like.

CANDY THERMOMETER. You absolutely, positively have to have (at least) one of these. They come in all kinds of shapes, sizes, and price ranges, including digital and programmable with alarms and presets and creepy robot voices, but you can also get a solid, reliable analog candy thermometer for about $10. It has to be marked "candy" or "deep-fry"—the temperature ranges you need while making candy are far above those on standard meat thermometers. Anything ranging from about 200°F/93°C to 325°F/163°C will be just dandy.

Analog thermometers are perfect to start out with; they're inexpensive, easy to clean, and sturdy. That said, they're not the most precise; sometimes you really need to know the temperature of your candy to the very degree, and in that case you'll probably want a digital thermometer. Great digital thermometers are available for about $25; they're invaluable for fruit jellies and caramels, when temperatures have to be more precise. (The Maverick CT-03, available on Amazon, is our absolute favorite.) They're also more reliable in the long run—analog thermometers' calibration goes off eventually, after a year or two of steady use—but more delicate, and need to be carefully hand-washed to protect the electronic components from moisture.

As far as actually measuring the temperature goes, most analog thermometers have a little metal guard on the bottom that keeps the heat-sensitive tip from touching the pan's surface. This is good; you want to measure the temperature of the liquid, not the temperature of the pan. (And while you're at it, you want to measure the temperature at the *center* of the liquid, not on its surface.) For this reason, analog thermometers are better at measuring temps in shallow sugar syrups. It's a little different with digital; the probe (long skinny metal part) usually measures the temperature either at the very tip or at a dimple ½ inch or so from the tip. Either way, make sure the sensor area is submerged in the liquid but not touching metal.

HEATPROOF MIXING SPATULAS. Sure, you could probably get by with just one heatproof spatula and a couple other plastic or rubber ones; but you can buy the non-fancy kind on the cheap, so why not get a few? Our favorite is a standard red-and-white model made by Vollrath (Rubbermaid makes one that's comparable)—we own about twenty of them—but any spatula made of silicone and/or marked "heatproof" or "high heat" will be just peachy.

(NOTE-ULA: When we refer to "heatproof spatula" in a recipe, this is what we mean. Otherwise we will specify the type.)

RIMMED BAKING SHEETS. We call them rimmed baking sheets in this book, but they're also known as sheet pans, jelly-roll pans, baking trays, or cookie sheets. What we mean when we call for one is a large, flat metal tray with a continuous ¾- to 1-inch-high rim. These are irreplaceable for making candy bars (pages 247–290) and fruit jellies (pages 105–111). We recommend getting two large (half-sheet/13 × 18-inch) size and one small (quarter-sheet/9 × 13-inch) size to start.

STAND MIXER OR ELECTRIC HAND MIXER. Since we're food geeks, we have stand mixers, and they certainly do make life much easier—especially with aerated candies like nougat and marshmallow. However, they can be expensive, so we've made most of these recipes hand-mixer-friendly as well.

KitchenAid is the classic stand mixer, but Viking and Breville make very high-quality mixers, too. For hand mixers, we like Cuisinart and Hamilton Beach—they're economical and reliable. Most of these brands can be found in any large home goods store, or online at Amazon.

JEN SAYS: There are some recipes that just don't work with a hand mixer. European nougat, for example, gets so thick and stiff that it would burn out the motor of a handheld mixer. Or marshmallow—it's really not a great idea to be pouring hot sugar syrup with one hand and using a mixer with the other. We give you cheats when we can, although oftentimes a little elbow grease will end up doing the trick just fine. Any recipes that absolutely require a stand mixer or Popeye-like biceps are marked accordingly with a little or symbol.)

SILICONE MAT/PARCHMENT PAPER. Silicone mats are flexible, nonstick, heatproof mats that consist of a foundation of woven fibers that are completely coated in silicone. They're versatile and reusable, and come in different sizes to accommodate your different baking sheets and pans. They're great for rolling out dough, pouring out hot sugar, setting your dipped chocolates on, and more. They can be expensive, however, and you can't cut on them (they get ruined; we've seen it happen). Parchment paper is relatively inexpensive, can be reused as long as it doesn't get too grimy, cuts to any size you want, is now widely available in supermarkets, and you *can* cut on it—but the cost adds up if you use a lot of it. We use both mats and parchment paper quite often; if you'll be making a lot of candy, it doesn't hurt to have both available. (Wax paper can often be substituted for parchment paper—except in high-temperature applications, like lining a pan that will eventually be filled with hot caramel.)

MIXING BOWLS. For mixing, tempering, and . . . well, holding stuff. Four will get you through most recipes—a couple large, a couple medium. In the home kitchen you really don't need a collection of smaller bowls to keep measured ingredients in (see Mise the Heck Out of That Place, page x)—you can usually get away with using your cereal bowls.

KNIVES. For every recipe in this book, you will really need only two knives: a small (4-inch or so) paring knife, and a large (6- to 8-inch) chef's knife. A serrated knife makes things easier when chopping chocolate, but a non-serrated chef's knife will do for that as well.

COOKING SPRAY/VEGETABLE OIL. We use cooking spray all the time to grease pans, knives, and other utensils so they don't stick to, um, sticky things. You can use a paper towel soaked with a bit of vegetable oil, but spray gets the job done much more quickly and evenly.

STRAINER. Sometimes, you just gotta strain stuff. A standard 4-inch fine-mesh model works well. Bet you a nickel that you already have one of these.

LIZ SAYS: Your handy-dandy strainer has a dual purpose: it also doubles as a sifter. Just set it over a bowl, pour in your already measured confectioners' sugar or flour or what have you, and tap it against the heel of your hand for a clump-free snowfall of powdered whatever.

OVEN MITT(S). Lots of the stuff in this book needs to be cooked to a very high temperature; no matter how well insulated your saucepan handle is, chances are good that it will get very hot. We often use dish towels as pot holders (mostly because that's what tends to be close at hand), but oven mitts are a far safer option, as they cover your whole hand and can help protect you from any rogue splashes. And you know what? They look cool, too.

KITCHEN SCISSORS. You'll want a pair of heavy-duty, dishwasher-safe scissors for cutting marshmallows (page 141) and other various sweets. Wüsthof and KitchenAid make our favorite versions; they're available at some specialty kitchen stores and from Amazon.

Coulds

KITCHEN SCALE. Really, everything turns out better when you can measure by weight, and candy is no exception. You can get a good digital scale for $15 to $20 on Amazon and in most kitchen supply stores (see Resources, page 291); it doesn't need to be at all fancy. A digital scale with a 5-pound capacity and measurements by 1 gram (meaning the smallest unit of measure is 1 gram; you don't need any decimal points) is more than sufficient. For tips on using a scale, see Weight! Weight! Don't Tell Me!, opposite.

CANDY FUNNELS. Candy funnels are large plastic funnels with three main differences between them and your standard household funnel: There's no stem on the bottom, they come with a lollipop-shaped stopper, and the plastic is industrial strength and meltproof. These make depositing soft candy for lollipops (pages 183–192), turtles (page 137), fondant (page 162), and about three thousand other things much, much easier: You just set the funnel and stopper in a mug or measuring cup, pour the liquid candy into the funnel, grasp the funnel with one hand and the stopper with the other, and lift the stopper up and down to portion the candy out (for more tips on using them, see Funnel of Love, page 139). If you're even remotely interested in making hard candy more than once, go ahead and get one. Or two. You'll likely have to order

WEIGHT! WEIGHT! DON'T TELL ME!

Using a digital kitchen scale is fairly straightforward and easy, but a few helpful tips will make it second nature in no time.

TURN ON THE SCALE AND MAKE SURE YOU HAVE THE RIGHT UNITS SET BEFORE YOU DO ANYTHING. On most scales, you can change units mid-measure, but you'll save yourself a lot of confusion by just making sure everything's good to go before you start pouring.

USE THE TARE OPTION. "Tare" just refers to the weight of an empty container. When weighing ingredients, place the empty vessel on the scale and press the Tare button to reset to zero. Now you don't have to worry about mentally subtracting the weight of your bowl.

FEWER MEASURING BOWLS = FEWER TO WASH. You can use the Tare function multiple times. For example, you can just put a bowl on the scale, tare it and measure your first ingredient, tare it and measure your second ingredient, and so on.

KNOW YOUR LIMITS. All scales have a maximum weight that they'll be able to measure. Keep in mind that the tare weight will count as part of that; if you go over the limit you'll get an annoying "error" message and your hard work will be lost. (Luckily you likely won't have to worry about this here; all these recipes are well under many kitchen scales' maximum capacity.)

DON'T GET INTO A STICKY SITUATION. When you're measuring directly into the pan (see Mise the Heck Out of That Place, page x), we like to get the sticky ingredients (honey, corn syrup) out of the way first, so you don't have to gunk up a separate bowl. With other things like butter, you can just place a piece of wax paper directly on the scale; press Tare, measure onto the paper, then just scrape it off the paper once you're ready to use it.

REMEMBER THAT 1 ML = 1 G. Sometimes you don't even need a scale. For liquids, you can use the gram measurement to translate it to your measuring cup. Need 100 g juice? Fill the cup to 100 mL and you're good to go.

LIZ SAYS: Nerd Alert! I know, I know, you're jumping down my throat because of the 1 mL=1 g thing. It's true that different liquids have different densities; but for anything really liquid—water, milk, cream, juice—the difference is nominal. Water has a density of 1 g/mL, so it's a straight trade. Without getting into the finer points of ambient temperature and such, whole milk has a density of about 1.03 g/mL; heavy cream, 0.99 g/mL; orange juice (with pulp), about 1.04. So, say, 300 mL of any of these would give you, respectively, 309 grams whole milk, 297 grams cream, and 312 grams orange juice. All negligible amounts, resulting in a perfectly acceptable (for our purposes) margin of error.

them on the interwebs, at Sugarcraft; but, hey, you can pick up a couple fun candy molds while you're at it (see Resources, page 291).

METAL OFFSET SPATULAS. These are basically really thin butter knives that look like they're bending their elbow to shake hands with you. The bend keeps your knuckles from getting all-up-in whatever it is that you're using the spatula for. They come in very handy when spreading something that you want to lie flat and even: candy bar centers, tempered chocolate, ganache. They're pretty inexpensive and easy to find at specialty kitchen stores or online; we always have a large one (about 9 inches long) and a small one (about 4 inches) on hand.

PIPING BAG(S). These are sold in disposable plastic and reusable fabric versions. The pro of the fabric version is, of course, that it's reusable. However, you need to wash it after each use, and you also need to have piping tips to use with it. The plastic version creates more waste, but it's incredibly easy to use, and you can just cut the tip off to the size you want, instead of having to use a metal tip. If you can't get ahold of any of these, a plastic zip-top bag works; you'll likely want a gallon-size freezer bag, as that is the most versatile size and the sturdiest. For tips on using a piping bag (*tips*?! Get it? Piping bags come with tips?), see Piping Ganache and Other Squishy Stuff (page 43).

SPIDER SKIMMER. No, this doesn't have anything to do with the eight-legged kind. (Silly goose.) This is a long-handled, large-mesh strainer that comes in very handy when you want to dip a lot of small, sturdy things, like Bacon Buttercrunch (page 208) or Honeycomb Candy (page 197). Of course, then you'll want a pair of **big (10-inch) metal tweezers**—also great for placing garnishes on truffles. If you'll be dipping on a regular basis, they're a wise and relatively painless investment—$15 to $20 for both. Check out Resources on page 291.

CHOCOLATE DIPPING FORKS. Delicate little utensils specially made for dipping more fragile items, like truffles. You'll see them in packs of twenty different shapes, but we only ever use three: the two- or three-tined forks (for flat candies) and the little swirly one (for round ones). These are available at most kitchen specialty stores, and online at Amazon.

ZIPLOC STORAGE CONTAINERS. Usually we don't recommend brand names for storage stuff that you can get generic, but Roni-Sue—Liz's mentor, and proprietress of the well-loved chocolate shop Roni-Sue's Chocolates—swears by these as storage containers, and we're inclined to agree with her. The "large rectangle" size (9½-cup capacity) is great for layering bars, truffles, and pretty much anything that's not individually wrapped for storage. They're affordable (about $2 apiece), and if you take care of them, they'll last you a good long time.

IMMERSION BLENDER. Also known as a stick blender, an immersion blender allows you to blend hot liquids right in the pot, eliminating the extra step that cleaning and transferring to another container entails. KitchenAid makes a great, reliable immersion blender that will run you about $30. Once you have one of these, we predict you'll use it for all kinds of other, non-candy stuff too: soup, mayonnaise, pesto, and impromptu smoothies come immediately to mind. (Just don't tell us about it; we're the jealous type.)

BENCH SCRAPER. Also known as a bench knife, pastry scraper, dough scraper, etc., it's a small rectangular sheet of metal with a handle on one end. Bench scrapers are great for folding hot sugar syrup, making even score marks on fudge or buttercrunch—and they're your best bet for getting those obnoxious little drops of hard candy off the counter.

A RELIABLE, EASY-TO-USE TIMER. Not your phone, not your watch, not your clock radio. (Wait. Do they still make those?) You want something sturdy that can hold up to getting splattered with goo and dropped on the floor. Seriously. Don't be a hero.

CHOCOLATE PRIMER

If you've read this far—and we're glad you have—it might seem like there's an awful lot of info coming your way. Well, you're right, there is! Not to fret; we're here to hold your hand through all this homework. We'll start off slow, with everyone's favorite legal drug: chocolate.

How Chocolate Is Made (Hint: It Doesn't Involve Oompa-Loompas)

The first step in the actual chocolate-making process is harvesting cacao. No, that's not just "cocoa" misspelled. Chocolate begins as a seed nestled in a pod that grows on the *Theobroma cacao* tree. These trees are extremely particular: They grow only within 20 degrees north and 20 degrees south of the equator, and only in certain conditions. On top of that, they're notoriously susceptible to pests and disease, and the delicate pods must be harvested by hand just when they're perfectly ripe.

The pods, which resemble autumnal-hued Nerf footballs, are cut down and split open to reveal the seeds inside. Each pod contains twenty to fifty seeds, each of which is encased in a fruity pulp that's called, for some hideous reason, mucilage. The seeds and pulp are placed in bins, covered, and allowed to ferment for several days—up to a week. The real flavor of the final product starts here: fermentation converts the bitter, mouth-drying tannins (think about how your tongue feels after a swig of black tea) inherent in raw cacao into delicate, complex flavor molecules.

Once fermentation is complete, the seeds are spread out to dry in the sun or in special drying tents. After drying for several days, the cacao seeds are cracked into pieces. The husks are winnowed away (apparently they make fantastic garden mulch) and what you're left with is the nib.

Nibs are pure, unadulterated cacao. They have a crunchy texture, like toasted nuts, and a deep, somewhat bitter cacao flavor. They can be eaten on their own, mixed into baked goods, sprinkled on cereal . . . or, hey, even mixed into brittle (see the brittle variation on page 194)! But they're not quite chocolate yet. The nibs are ground into a liquidy paste, known as chocolate liquor. Sometimes the liquor is put in a massive press and squeezed until all the fat—the cocoa butter—is expressed. The cake left over is cocoa powder.

When making chocolate, however, the liquor is mixed with sugar, and often an emulsifier (such as soy lecithin) is added to keep everything uniformly mixed. This becomes dark chocolate; milk chocolate only requires the addition of milk or milk solids along with the sugar, although sometimes vanilla is added as well.

The chocolate-sugar mixture is then put into a machine called a conch, which basically consists of two massive stone wheels that roll in a circle to grind, heat, and aerate the mixture; the longer the chocolate is conched, the finer and smoother it ends up. And once the conching is done, all that's left is tempering the chocolate (see below and page 25), cooling it, and wrapping it.

Temper, Temper

Tempering chocolate is basically a way of tidying it up on a molecular level—it makes the finished product neat and clean: The process gives chocolate a smooth, glossy surface; a nice "snap" when you bite into it; and better resistance to melting and scuffing (i.e., a longer shelf life).

The science behind tempering is complicated but can be explained relatively simply, and has to do with the

WHAT'S UP WITH CHOCOLATE PERCENTAGES

In recent years, it has become very fashionable to put percentages on chocolate bars—the higher, the better. Some labels trumpet "75%!"; others boast "82% EXTRA NOIR." "Oh, hey, Coop. I saw you at the organic chocolate tasting last night. Did you try the 98%? *Unbelievable*." But what the heck does it all mean?

Very simply, the chocolate percentage on the package describes how much chocolate liquor is in the bar. Chocolate liquor is anything that comes from the cocoa bean: cocoa mass (basically cocoa powder—the dark stuff) and cocoa butter. So what makes up the rest? All of the not-chocolate ingredients. Since percentages refer only to the chocolate itself, and not anything mixed into it like fruit or nuts, this means—as one of our pastry school instructors put it—that the remaining percentage is sugar. So, if you have a 65% dark chocolate bar, 35% of it is sugar. Though this doesn't account for trace ingredients like emulsifiers (usually 1% or less) and flavorings like vanilla, it's a good rule of thumb, particularly for dark chocolate, which has negligible amounts of both.

Milk chocolate is a little trickier, since there are milk solids involved, too. So the leftover percentage in milk chocolate is sugar *and* milk solids. Some brands of chocolate that sell to professional chefs note other specifications as well: percentage of cocoa butter for couverture (coating chocolate), or milk solids in milk or white chocolate.

Oh, right—white chocolate. It's not actually chocolate, since it contains no cocoa mass. White chocolate is cocoa butter, milk solids, sugar, and vanilla; that's pretty much it. Before you start hatin', know that white chocolate is great for a number of applications (see the recipes on pages 66, 79, and 81 for examples). And you shouldn't judge people by what their favorite kind of chocolate is anyway, because that's just silly.

Even though white chocolate isn't chocolate.

structure of cocoa butter. We like to think of it in terms of bricks. If you're going to build a structure that is sturdy and even—and likely to stay that way—you want to use bricks that are all the same size, are evenly stacked, and fit tightly together. Right? Right. Well, cocoa butter's structure is crystalline. There are several different shapes and sizes of crystals ("bricks") and you want to make them all the same size. If you just melt chocolate, pour it into a bar, and let it set up, the assorted bricks are scattered all over the place, giving the chocolate a dull, mottled appearance and soft texture. But when you temper, you're making sure the crystals in the cocoa butter are the right kind of crystal: uniform in size and shape, and stacked tightly together.

This is important to know because any chocolate you buy for candymaking will have been tempered beforehand; and when *you* heat it up to bend it to your ~~evil~~ sweet, sweet will, you'll be messing with its structure. Which means you'll need to temper it to get it back into line. *Capiche*?

"Okay, Miss Smarty-Pants," we hear you say, "how exactly *DO* you temper chocolate?" We're so glad you asked! And we'll get to that in a minute. But before you temper chocolate, you gotta melt it . . .

I'll Stop the World and Melt (Chocolate) with You

There are two main ways to melt chocolate, and they both have their pros and cons. We usually use the stove-top method, since it requires no babysitting—we can start it before we begin to measure out the rest of the ingredients for a recipe, and by the time we need it, the chocolate will be melted (or well on its way). But both are totally valid.

STOVE-TOP METHOD

This can also be referred to as the double-boiler or bain-marie method (bain-marie refers to a container, taller and narrower than the average saucepan, that is placed in warm or simmering water to keep its contents warm). You don't actually need to own a double boiler in order to use this method; we usually just place a metal mixing bowl over a saucepan partially filled with simmering water (without the

bowl actually dipping into the water). Although a metal bowl works best, anything heatproof will do; just make sure that the diameter of the bowl is larger than the saucepan, so you have something to grab on to when you want to remove the bowl.

Here's what you do: Fill the saucepan about one-third full with hot water, and place it over medium-low heat. When the water simmers, reduce the heat to low, place the chocolate in the metal bowl, and set it over the simmering water. Allow the chocolate to melt, stirring it occasionally, until it's completely liquid and there are no lumps left, 15 to 20 minutes. Remove the melted chocolate from the heat.

PROS: doesn't require babysitting; very low likelihood of burning the chocolate; can be used for larger amounts of chocolate

CONS: chance of steam burns if you're not careful; increased danger of getting water in the chocolate (see page 28 for why this is a no-no); takes longer than the microwave

MICROWAVE METHOD

This method is fast, easy, and perfect for melting smaller amounts of chocolate (well, really, any amount that will fit into your microwave). All you need is a microwave-proof container and a heatproof spatula.

Put your chocolate in the microwave and zap it on High for 30 seconds. Then stir it well, return it to the microwave, and heat it on High for 10 to 15 seconds at a time, stirring after each interval, until the chocolate is completely melted.

PROS: fast; easy; no danger of getting water in the chocolate

CONS: needs to be attended carefully; higher likelihood of burning the chocolate; amount is limited to the size of the microwave

Tempering for the Masses

Tempering is among the scarier terms that we candymakers throw around, but really it's only because we think it makes us sound tough—like we're working with metal and blowtorches instead of gumdrops and sugar sparkles. But unless you're already a big fan of food-science deities like Harold McGee (and if you are, high-five!), you might be curious about the nuts and bolts of how it works.

Tempering is important in confectionery because it makes several very specific things happen to the chocolate that don't happen when you just melt chocolate and let it set up on its own. When you do that, the chocolate sets up soft and blotchy. We temper chocolate so that:

1. It sets up more quickly, so you don't have to sit around willing it to harden.

2. It develops a nice snap and a high gloss, which is invaluable when making fine chocolates.

3. It contracts slightly as it sets, which is absolutely key when making molded bonbons (otherwise they don't come out of the molds).

4. It keeps all these properties for a longer time. The shelf life for dark tempered chocolate that's stored properly (at cool room temperature, protected from light and humidity) is 2 years; milk and white chocolate, 1 year.

THE BEST-TEMPERED CHOCOLATE YOU EVER MET

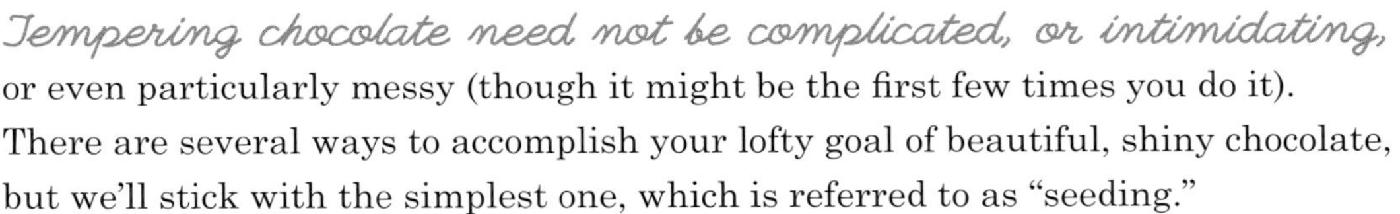

MAKES ABOUT 5 POUNDS TEMPERED CHOCOLATE

Tempering chocolate need not be complicated, or intimidating, or even particularly messy (though it might be the first few times you do it). There are several ways to accomplish your lofty goal of beautiful, shiny chocolate, but we'll stick with the simplest one, which is referred to as "seeding."

Before you jump in, keep in mind that ambient temperature, humidity, and many other factors out of your control can have an adverse effect on how chocolate decides to temper (or not). Hey, why do you think they call it "temper"? So, the first time you attempt to temper chocolate, wait till your kitchen is nice and cool and you have plenty of time. The oven should be off; it shouldn't be pouring buckets outside (humidity is bad, mmkay?), and the ideal ambient temperature is about 60° to 65°F (16° to 18°C). Also, make sure you have 2 to 3 extra cups of chocolate on hand; if you need to start over, it's useful to have some additional seed chocolate ready to go. Practice makes perfect, and once you do get it—which you will—it'll be that much more rewarding.

In this recipe, we're giving you five pounds to start, because it's easier to temper larger amounts of chocolate; and five pounds is the largest amount you'll need for the recipes in this book (it'll be enough for enrobing candy bars, once you get to that). But really, you can temper any amount of chocolate you need—just remember that about one-third of the total weight should be set aside for seeding.

When you're done tempering your chocolate, you can do pretty much anything you want with it! Use it to enrobe some Snacker Bars (page 256), or dip Cherry Cordials (page 85); spread it over some Tropical Toffee (page 211); add shells to your Turtles (page 137); or simply pipe it out into discs for some pretty Nonpareils (page 77).

SPECIAL EQUIPMENT

- Rubber or heatproof spatula
- Tempering thermometer (recommended but optional; see page 14)

INGREDIENTS

About 5 pounds (2.25 kg) high-quality chocolate, such as Ghirardelli, Callebaut, or Valrhona

1. Fill a large (6-quart) saucepan with water to a depth of about 1 inch. Bring it to a boil, uncovered, over high heat.

2. Meanwhile, if using a block of chocolate, chop it with a serrated knife.

3. Once the water has come to a boil, turn off the heat and set a medium-size heatproof bowl on top. Add about two-thirds of the chopped chocolate and allow it to sit for 5 to 10 minutes, stirring only occasionally with a heatproof spatula (you want to make sure the chocolate on the bottom of the bowl doesn't get too hot, but if you stir the whole time, the heat will disperse too much and the chocolate won't melt all the way).

4. Once all the pieces have melted completely, insert the tempering thermometer and check the temperature; for dark chocolate you want it to be around 108°F/42°C; milk, 106°F/41°C; white, 104°F/40°C. If you go a little bit over these temperatures, that's fine; too much under, though, and you won't melt all the "bad" crystals in the cocoa butter (for more science talk, see page 23).

No thermometer? No problem. Dab a bit of the chocolate on your lip instead. At the melted stage, the chocolate should feel distinctly warm—not just lukewarm.

5. Once your chocolate has reached the desired temperature, CAREFULLY lift the bowl off the pot, and place it on top of a folded dish towel. You'll want to wipe the moisture off the bottom and side of the bowl; this will lessen the risk of accidentally getting some in the chocolate, which is *not okay*. (Water will cause the chocolate to "seize," or get lumpy and unworkable, and you'll have to make it into—*quelle horreur!*—chocolate sauce instead.)

6. Now add some of the reserved chocolate, about ¼ cup at a time, stirring constantly until the addition has been incorporated completely and there are no more lumps. You'll want to stir like your life depends on it here, both to agitate the chocolate (the more it is agitated, the nice-n-shinier it'll be) and to reduce its temperature. You want to get it down to about 90°F/32°C for dark; 88°F/31°C for milk; 86°F/30°C for white. (Starting to notice a pattern here? More cocoa solids require working at higher heat.) If you're doing the lip test, you'll want it to feel distinctly cool. Agitating not only encourages the right crystals to form, it also helps cool the chocolate more rapidly. This will take you about 15 minutes.

7. Once the chocolate is close to the desired temperature (a degree or two above is fine), test it: Dip a teaspoon in the chocolate, then stick the dipped spoon on a piece of wax paper and allow it to set up for a few minutes. (If your kitchen is warm, you can put it in the fridge for a bit—2 minutes for dark, more like 5 for milk and white.) If the test sets up completely—a little glossy, not tacky to the touch, not streaky or blotchy (see page 30)—then huzzah and kudos to you! You just tempered chocolate.

SEEDING THE CHOCOLATE

1. Place the bowl of melted chocolate on a dish towel.

2. Add the seed chocolate bit by bit, stirring between each addition.

3. Stir, stir, stir. Also . . . stir. You want to agitate the chocolate and get the temp down.

LIZ SAYS: You can buy bulk chocolate in disks called *pistoles*, which is what we use, or in blocks. If you buy a block, you can use whatever knife you like to chop it, but we especially like serrated knives because they make your life easier (always a plus in our book). The serrated edge basically grates the chocolate while you're chopping it, and the smaller the initial pieces are, the easier they are to melt.

LUMPY CHOCOLATE—WHAT NOW?

We recommend adding the seed chocolate a little at a time for a reason: If you get impatient and just add all the seed chocolate at once, you run the risk of "overseeding." What happens when you overseed is that your chocolate gets over-tempered—super-thick and unworkable—and, since it's too cold to melt any more of the seed chocolate, lumpy. If this happens, you have a couple options. If there's a significant amount of unmelted seed chocolate (enough to make it difficult to dip/enrobe/do whatever it is you were gonna do with it), use a spider skimmer (see page 20) to fish out the big pieces. You can also try what we call "flashing" (put that trenchcoat away, Pervy McGoo!): Bring a pot of water to a lively simmer, and alternate setting the bowl of chocolate over the hot water, and taking it off to stir—5 seconds over the water, and 10 seconds stirring. This will very gently heat the chocolate back to a workable temperature without taking it out of temper. Just make sure to keep checking the temperature on your lip—a degree or two too far, and you'll have to start again from scratch!

JEN SAYS: It may seem silly to test the chocolate on your lip, but lips are very sensitive and well suited to gauging temperatures close to your body's 98.6°F. Thusly and therefore, it'll be easier to judge the relative warmth or coolness of the melted chocolate on your pretty little pout.

TEMPERING TROUBLESHOOTING

If the chocolate you've tested doesn't behave as it should, consider the following questions:

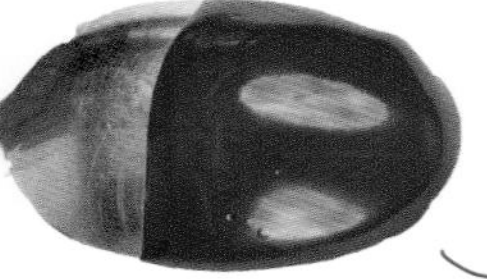

Not tempered yet

Is it wet looking, sticky, or soft to the touch after sitting in the fridge for about 5 minutes?

It's not tempered yet.

Keep stirring! And get that temperature down. Once it's there, test again—you should be fine.

Is it firm and shiny but streaky?

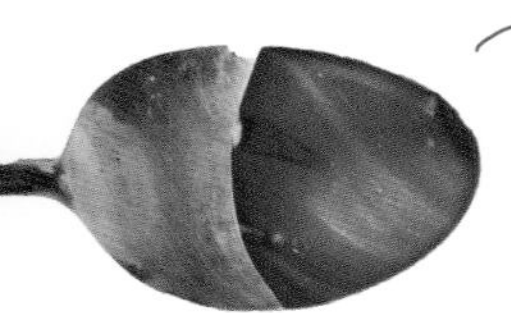

Fat bloom

It's probably in temper—you just need to agitate it more (we promise: you do this enough and you'll have forearms like the Incredible Hulk). When the surface of chocolate is marred by a dull, whitish film, that film is referred to as bloom—and there are two kinds. *This* kind is called *fat bloom,* and it's what happens when the crystals in chocolate's molecular structure aren't aligned quite right. As the chocolate sets up, the fat (cocoa butter) is squeezed out onto the surface, leaving that film behind and altering the texture of the rest of the chocolate beneath. (For the other type of bloom, *sugar bloom,* see below.)

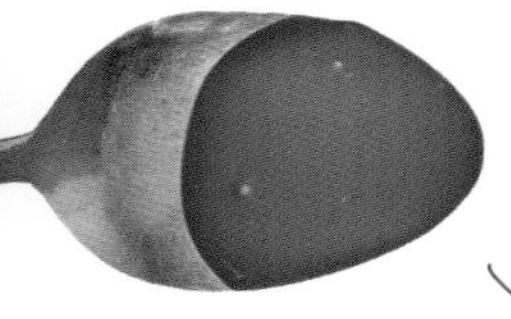

False temper

Will the chocolate not set up even after you've stirred the crap out of it and gotten it down to the correct temperature?

Please don't hurt us, but you should start over. We know; it's unfair. The thing about chocolate is that it's very finicky. Like that guy in high school who ignored you, thereby further inflaming your passion, chocolate will turn up its nose at you for seemingly arbitrary reasons (see the box opposite).

Sugar bloom

Did the chocolate set up perfectly, but later you saw weird splotches on the surface?

This is called *sugar bloom,* and it means the surface of the chocolate was exposed to water at some point while or after it set up. The sugar in the chocolate dissolves into the water, and when the water evaporates, tiny, sandpapery sugar crystals remain on the surface in the same blotchy pattern as the water. Unfortunately there's nothing you can do to fix it. But don't worry—it's purely cosmetic; the candy will still taste as good and last as long.

IT'S NOT YOU, IT'S ME (OR, WHAT YOUR CHOCOLATE'S *REALLY* SAYING)

Does your chocolate refuse to settle down and commit (i.e., temper)? There could be a few reasons at play:

- The chocolate may not have melted enough when you first heated it.
- The seeds may not have been quite in temper to begin with.
- The chocolate may not have cooled quickly enough as it was being tempered.
- The ambient temperature might be too warm.
- The humidity could be preventing it from setting.

Unfortunately, there are no quick fixes to any of these scenarios; in all cases, you must make like Coldplay and go back to the start.* Learn to decipher chocolate's signals and keep at it! You will prevail!

*We hope you enjoy this outdated pop culture reference.

Your Cheatin' Heart

Okay, we'll admit it: Sometimes we just don't feel like tempering chocolate. (You're shocked, aren't you? We can see it on your face. We're so ashamed.) But here's the thing: Sometimes, tempered chocolate is just a pain in the derrière. When it's really hot out (which prevents the chocolate from getting to a low enough temperature), or really humid (which can cause condensation to form on the chocolate so that it "blooms," or turns whitish and not-pretty, see opposite), or you just don't have the time, this coating is a great alternative.

It sets up firm and shiny, it has a bit of a snap to it, and it's less susceptible to melting and deforming in warm weather. There are some people who are very sensitive to the texture of the oil, but for a lot of folks, it's just as good as tempered chocolate (aside from being sturdier and more economical to boot). Really, the only time you *cannot ever* use this is for molded bonbons. (Chocolate has to contract in order to release nicely from the molds; since chocolate has to be properly tempered in order to contract, this stuff just straight-up won't come out of the molds until you've smashed, pried, chipped, scraped, and sandblasted every last atom out of there. No joke—you will want to murder something tiny and adorable because you will be so frustrated.)

CHEATER'S CHOCOLATE COATING

MAKES ABOUT 3½ CUPS (ENOUGH TO DIP ABOUT 40 ONE- BY FOUR-INCH CANDY BARS OR 100 HALF-INCH BUCKEYES)

This is a homemade version of what we in the business call *pâte à glacer* (pronounced paht-ah-glah-SAY). You might know pâte à glacer as the topping for a chocolate éclair, or that stuff that coats those little chocolate donuts you find at the supermarket. It's also known as summer coating or compound coating. The main difference between that stuff and this stuff is that this stuff is much tastier.

INGREDIENTS

3 cups (19 ounces/540 g) chopped milk chocolate or dark chocolate

½ cup (100 g) neutral-flavored vegetable oil, such as sunflower or safflower

1. Melt the chocolate: Place it in a medium-size microwave-safe bowl and heat it in the microwave on High for 20 seconds. Stir the chocolate with a whisk or heatproof spatula, then continue heating it on High in 20-second increments, stirring after each increment, until the chocolate is completely melted.

   Alternatively, fill a small (2-quart) saucepan about one-third full with hot water, and place it over medium-low heat. When the water simmers, place the chocolate in a slightly larger metal bowl and set it over the simmering water (make sure the bowl is large enough for you to easily grasp it for removal). Allow the chocolate to melt, stirring it occasionally, until it's completely liquid and there are no lumps left, 15 to 20 minutes. Remove it from the heat.

❷ Slowly stir the oil into the melted chocolate until it is completely incorporated.

❸ Keep the coating warm by setting the bowl over a saucepan of simmering water until you're almost ready to use it; then remove it from the heat and allow it to cool until it has the consistency of warm fudge sauce, 15 to 20 minutes.

Store the chocolate coating in an airtight container in the fridge for up to 1 month. Reheat it as many times as you need to (see Liz Says, below).

LIZ SAYS: To reheat cooled, solidified coating, simply place the block in the top of a double boiler set over low heat and stir occasionally until melted. Alternatively, you can cut the cooled coating into ½-inch chunks, place them in a microwave-safe container, and microwave on High for 20 seconds. Then microwave the coating in 5- to 10-second intervals, stirring after each, until it's melted.

(You can also impress the heck out of your kids by dipping an ice cream cone or a frozen banana into the coating and adding toppings: homemade—and way tastier—Magic Shell!)

Dippity-Dos (and Don'ts)

Now that you have all this lovely, liquid chocolate, you gotta do something with it. Below are the two main methods you'll be using to cover things in this melted, tempered, cheated awesomeness; and following that, how you'll gussy it up.

FORK DIPPING, the more commonly known method, is great for small, individual candies, Vanilla Marshmallows (page 141), for example, or truffles (page 59). It's fairly self-explanatory: You use a fork to submerge the candy center in chocolate, then you fish it out, gently tap it to get rid of excess chocolate, and place it on a parchment- or wax paper–lined baking sheet (see the step-by-step pics that follow). A dipping fork is the easiest implement to use: The thin wire tines create less friction, making it easier to slide the dipped candy onto a lined baking sheet. However, we've used standard kitchen forks before, and they work just fine; just be prepared to do a little wrasslin' to get the candy off the fork. Don't worry—you'll get the hang of it.

- DO make sure everything is extremely clean and perfectly dry.

• DO wipe off the fork with a clean dish towel or paper towel from time to time, to prevent buildup of set chocolate—whatever you're dipping will want to stick to it.

• DON'T be too overzealous about tapping the fork on the edge of the bowl to get rid of the excess chocolate; the center of the candy will settle onto the tines and refuse to slide off when you want it to.

FORK-DIPPING CANDIES

1. Drop the candy in the chocolate and use the fork to push it under.

2. Fish the candy out with the fork and tap it gently against the side of the bowl to remove any excess chocolate.

3. Carefully transfer the dipped candy to the prepared baking sheet, tipping the fork slightly so the candy slides off.

ENROBING is better suited to larger items, like candy bars. This is covered in greater detail on pages 253–255, but the basic procedure is this: Coat the bottom of the candy slab in about a cup of chocolate (it's easiest to do this before cutting it into individual pieces; see the technique opposite), spread it into a thin layer with an offset spatula, and allow the chocolate to set up somewhat; cut the bars and arrange them on a wire rack set over a parchment- or wax paper–lined baking sheet; pour more liquid chocolate over the bars to cover them; and then quickly run an offset spatula underneath the bars to loosen them from the wire rack before allowing them to set completely on a second lined baking sheet. Things to keep in mind:

• DO have everything set up before you start pouring chocolate. Speed and efficiency are key!

• DO make sure your chocolate or coating is warm enough so that it doesn't set up right after you pour it. If it sets up too quickly, you won't have time to loosen the candy from the rack.

• DON'T place the candies/bars too close together before you coat them—they need enough space so the chocolate can drain through the rack between them, or you'll end up with one giant conjoined candy slab.

ENROBING CANDY BARS

1. Coat the bottom of the candy slab with chocolate.

2. When the chocolate is nearly set, invert the slab onto parchment and cut it into bars.

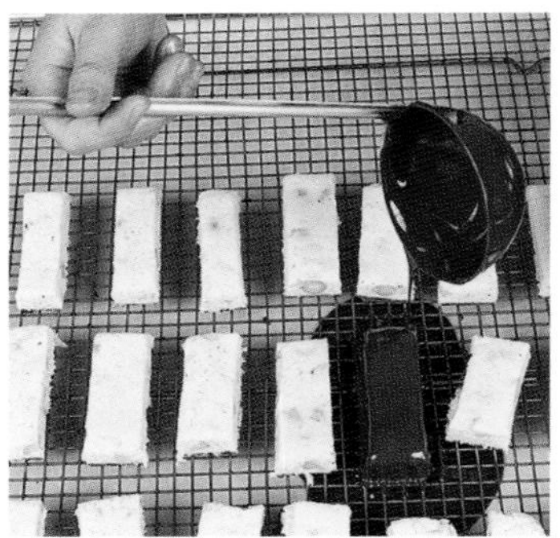

3. Pour the chocolate over the bars.

4. Run a metal spatula underneath the bars to loosen them from the wire rack.

GARNISHING is, quite literally, the cherry on top of the chocolate-covered candy (well, unless the cherry is *in* the candy, like the Cherry Cordials on page 85). You wouldn't show up to a fancy party in your underwear, right? Well, then, why should your candy? Dress it up a little with a garnish that's complementary to the candy itself—for example, a sprinkle of chile powder on top of a Fany's Truffle (page 61)—or that gives a clue as to the contents, like green tea powder on a green tea truffle (page 43). Here are some other DOs and DON'Ts:

• DO play around. Sometimes a couple flakes of sea salt in the middle of a dipped candy is all you need; sometimes it's fun to make a diagonal line with a pinch of spice; and sometimes a rose petal placed at a jaunty angle is just the thing to add that certain je ne sais quoi to a dipped confection. You never know until you try.

• DO give it a minute. If you add a garnish right away, it will sink into the chocolate and not show up against the surface as nicely. Instead, wait until the chocolate is no longer wet-looking, but not completely set, about 5 minutes, and the garnish will settle on the surface just so.

• DON'T overdo it. Remember, it's just a garnish—the main attraction's in the middle.

Ganache with Panache

The term *ganache* refers to a mixture of chocolate and dairy—usually cream, although butter is sometimes used. Ganache is incredibly versatile. Depending on the ratio of chocolate to dairy, it can be a shiny, elegant glaze for a cake, a decadent fudge sauce to pour over ice cream, or a smooth, creamy, melt-in-your-mouth filling for a truffle. It keeps for weeks and weeks in the refrigerator, and can be reheated and reformulated at will. You can flavor it with spices, booze, extracts, and everything in between. And it's a brilliant blank canvas for creative types to play with: You can pipe it, roll it, layer it, or pour it. Really, no matter what you do with it, it's delicious. It's chocolate and cream, for heaven's sake! What on earth could be bad?

CHOCOLATE GANACHE

MAKES ABOUT 3 CUPS

Ganache is an emulsion: a suspension of fat and cocoa solids in liquid. Because chocolate is extremely particular when it comes to dealing with moisture, the balance of moisture to chocolate is very important and must not be overly messed with. The two things you want to keep in mind while making ganache are (1) to be patient while the chocolate melts; and (2) to be gentle when stirring it. Impatience begets lumpy ganache, and overzealous stirring will incorporate tiny bubbles that you don't want at your silky-smooth ganache party.

Ganache is simple to prepare, though it can be a bit finicky. If you follow the steps here, your ganache should turn out smooth and lovely every time. (This recipe makes a lot, but it's easier to work with this amount until you've made ganache a few times.)

Make sure that the bowl you use is large enough to accommodate the chocolate *and* the cream—we don't want you crying over spilled cream! And use caution when heating your cream: You want to heat it just to boiling—and no further! Dairy has a nasty tendency to bubble up like crazy as soon as it comes to a boil, meaning it will get all over your nice clean stove and cost you about half an hour and several coins in the swear jar when you have to clean it up.

INGREDIENTS

17 ounces (480 g) good-quality dark, milk, or white chocolate, chopped into ¼-inch pieces; or 17 ounces (480 g) chocolate chips (about 2½ cups)

¾ cup (175 g) heavy (whipping) cream

1. Place the chopped chocolate or chocolate chips in a medium-size heatproof bowl and set it aside.
2. Pour the cream into a small (2- to 4-quart) saucepan and bring it to a boil over medium heat. Keep a close eye on your cream, keep the heat on medium, and take it off the heat the second you see bubbles forming around the edge.
3. Carefully pour the hot cream over the chocolate, making sure all your nicely chopped pieces are submerged. Now comes the hard part: Wait for 4 minutes. If you rush it, you run the risk of ending up with a lumpy ganache, and that's no fun for anyone. Now, take a rubber spatula (or whisk, but go easy! You're not making whipped cream), and using a gentle hand, stir the two ingredients together. The trick is to keep the stirring action in the center of the bowl; the ganache will start to come together around your chosen utensil as you stir. Again, resist the urge to get aggressive—your patience will be rewarded, grasshoppa!
4. When your ganache looks glossy and smooth and is fully mixed, congratulations! Allow the ganache to cool until it's at a more usable consistency: thick but not set, for piping (about 45 minutes at room temp); or completely set and cool, for scraping and rolling (2 to 3 hours in the fridge, covered).

Store ganache in an airtight container in the fridge, for up to 4 weeks; in the freezer, for 6 months.

MAKING GANACHE

1. Put the chocolate in a bowl.

2. Pour hot cream over the chocolate.

3. Make sure all the chocolate is submerged, then sit tight for a few minutes.

4. Stir gently to incorporate the two ingredients. Keep the stirring in the center of the bowl, and the cream and chocolate will start to come together.

5. When it becomes glossy and smooth, you've got ganache!

GANACHE TROUBLESHOOTING

If your ganache looks separated or curdled, no need to despair. This just means that the fat/water ratio has been thrown off: too much fat in the ganache, and the globules stick together and rise to the top, forming a translucent puddle. If it has separated, gently heat a couple tablespoons of water and add it a tablespoon at a time to the ganache, again stirring gently. It should come back together. If, however, the ganache looks curdled and has physical lumps in it, and adding water makes it worse, it's likely that some water infiltrated your ganache early on and caused the chocolate to seize (see page 28). Curses! Unfortunately, this ganache isn't cosmetically savable—but you can mix a couple spoonfuls of it into scalded milk for a lovely cup of hot chocolate (in which case, store it in a covered container in the fridge; it will keep for up to 8 weeks; or up to 9 months in the freezer).

Uh-oh—separated ganache. (Cue sad trombone.)

FLAVORING GANACHE

The fun part about ganache is that you can make it taste like almost anything you want! Once you have the basic technique down, there's no limit to the varieties you can create.

There are two main methods for flavoring ganache. The first is *infusion*. In this method, you flavor the cream that goes into the ganache by steeping something in

GRAND INFUSION

Get crazy with your cream—you can infuse a whole variety of things into your ganache. You'll want to watch the ratio of "things" to cream, however; below are some general guidelines. (Note that while whole and coarsely crushed spices are included here, finely ground spices are not; they are too fine to strain out, and so are treated as additions—see next page.)

FLAVORING	EXAMPLES	AMOUNT PER QUART (950 g) OF CREAM
Tea	Black tea, green tea, herbal tea	1 to 2 teaspoons, depending on strength
Dried leaf-type spices	Bay leaf, thyme, basil	1 to 2 teaspoons
Fresh herbs	Rosemary, ginger, lemongrass	1 (3-inch) sprig/ piece, bruised or crushed
Whole or coarsely crushed spices	Allspice, star anise, peppercorns	1 teaspoon or 1 to 2 pieces, depending on size
Citrus zest	Orange, lime, grapefruit	2 loosely packed teaspoons

it, such as tea or spices. To do this, simply heat your cream (as directed in step 2 on page 38); remove it from the heat and add your flavoring directly to the pan (for tips on what to add and how much, see Grand Infusion, above). It's best to cover the pan while infusing or you run the risk of losing too much liquid due to evaporation. Let it steep for a while—10 to 20 minutes, depending on how strong you want the flavor to be (keep in mind it will be subtler in the finished ganache)—and then remove the flavoring agent (you'll have to strain the cream if you're using loose tea or coarsely ground spices). Now you're ready to make ganache with your flavored cream.

The second method is *addition*. This means just what it sounds like: adding something to your ganache after it's emulsified—for example, peanut butter. This is a relatively straightforward process, too: Simply incorporate the addition after you've mixed the ganache, stirring it in by hand while the ganache is still warm and fairly liquidy. For basic chocolate ganache (see page 36), start with a tablespoon of any given addition, such as Nutella or jam, and add more to taste; the exception here is finely ground spices—because they pack more of a punch, you'll want to start with ½ teaspoon of those. For liquids—oils, extracts, liqueurs—start with a teaspoon or less (and please keep in mind that adding too much of anything liquid will throw off the delicate fat/water balance of the ganache, thus shortening its shelf life).

Regardless of the method, any flavored ganache benefits from resting overnight, covered, in the fridge; this gives the flavors a chance to meld and mellow, and the ganache will be more stable if it has time (6 to 8 hours) to sit around for a bit.

Now you have all the knowledge you need to start concocting your own wowtastic truffles! We know that having all the choices in the world can be daunting, though; so to give you some inspiration, here are some combos we enjoy:

FOR DARK CHOCOLATE TRUFFLES

VANILLA-ROSE Stir ½ teaspoon pure vanilla extract and ¼ teaspoon rosewater into the finished ganache; add more, drop by drop, to taste.

CINNAMON-CHILE Infuse half a cinnamon stick in the cream, and then strain; add ¼ teaspoon chile powder to the warm finished ganache.

FOR MILK CHOCOLATE TRUFFLES

LAVENDER Infuse a pinch of lavender in the cream, and then strain; add a tablespoon of honey to the warm finished ganache.

AFTER-SCHOOL SPECIAL Stir ½ cup unsweetened peanut butter and ½ cup chopped dried cherries into the warm finished ganache: a twist on a PB&J!

FOR WHITE CHOCOLATE TRUFFLES

LEMON-THYME Infuse ¼ teaspoon dried thyme in the cream, and then strain; stir ¼ teaspoon lemon oil or 1 teaspoon lemon extract into the warm finished ganache.

GREEN TEA-SESAME Infuse 1 teaspoon green tea in the cream, and then strain; stir ½ teaspoon toasted sesame oil into the warm finished ganache.

STORING GANACHE

Have some ganache left over from your truffles/candy bars/cake? You can keep it in an airtight container in the fridge for up to 4 weeks, or very tightly wrapped in the freezer for up to 6 months. Just for the record, it never actually "goes bad," i.e., spoils—it just gets grainy with age and loses its moisture and plush texture. Ganache is great for filling sandwich cookies, spreading on fresh fruit, serving warm over ice cream, or just eating straight out of the container (we won't tell anyone—we do it, too).

LIZ SAYS: Nerd alert! Ganache is often described as an emulsion, but it's really a complex combination of emulsion and suspension. The water from the milk and the sugar from the chocolate form a syrup as the sugar is dissolved into the water; the particles of cocoa butter and cocoa mass are suspended in this syrup, along with the fat and protein molecules from the cream.

PIPING GANACHE (AND OTHER SQUISHY STUFF)

This seems like a fairly self-explanatory procedure: Just open the pastry bag, fill it, and pipe away, right? Yes and no—piping is simple, but there are some tricks that make the process of filling and using the bag easier. Follow these basic rules and you'll pipe cleanly and painlessly, whether it's ganache for molded bonbons (page 62), chocolate for Nonpareils (page 77), or fondant for Mint Patties (page 164).

1. Place the piping bag in a large, vertical container or measuring cup (if the filling will be hot, the container should be heatproof). This acts as a "third hand" for you, while you use your first two hands to pour the candy you'll be piping into the bag.

2. Fold the top edge of the bag over the container, so that any accidental drips end up on the inside of the bag.

3. Pour/scrape the candy you're piping into the bag, making sure not to fill it more than two-thirds full (otherwise you won't be able to close the bag properly).

4. Pull the top edge of the bag back up, and squeeze as much of the candy toward the bottom of the bag as you can, gently shaking the bag to get out any big air bubbles.

5. Twist the top of the bag shut and secure with a piece of tape.

6. Holding the taped part of the bag securely between the thumb and forefinger of one hand, turn it upside down and snip the tip of the bag off with the other hand. (Turning it upside down prevents any delicious liquidy candy from pouring out the second you snip.)

7. Grab the twisted part of the bag with your dominant hand; this will keep the bag's contents from squeezing up through the top. Keeping a good grip on the twist, gently squeeze the bag while using your other hand to help guide the tip. As the bag empties, press any extra contents toward the tip (like a tube of toothpaste) and tighten the twist, moving your squeezin' hand down so that you're gripping the twist right above the bag's contents.

PREPPING A PIPING BAG

1. Place the bag in a container.

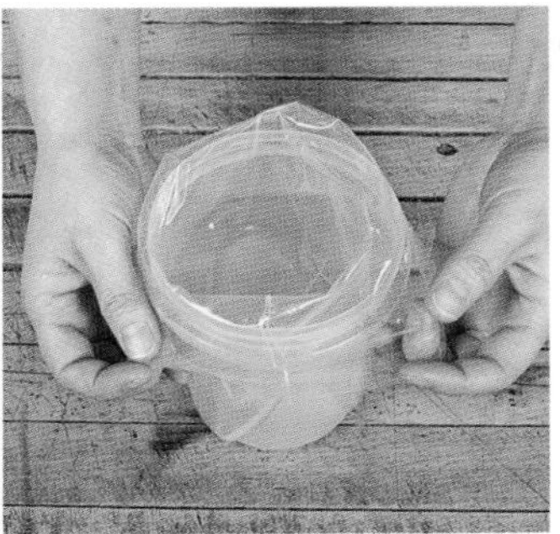

2. Fold the edge of the bag over the top of the container.

3. Pour the candy into the bag.

4. Push the candy toward the tip of the bag.

5. Twist the top and secure it with tape.

6. Upend the bag and snip off the tip (ouch!).

7. Pipe away!

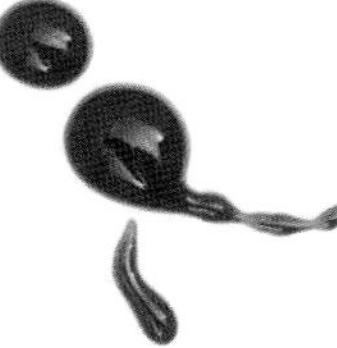

SUGAR IS SWEET—THE JURY'S STILL OUT ON YOU

If you're like most people, when you hear the word "sugar," you probably picture the white granulated stuff. That's sucrose—good old granulated sugar. It's made by pressing sugarcane (or beets) and evaporating the juice into crystals (the less refined version of which is turbinado or "raw" sugar and has a light brown color due to the traces of molasses left behind), then refining the crystals to remove impurities.

Sugar is the building block of all confectionery. As you know from reading the sugar section in Candy: It Is Made of Stuff (you *did* read that section, right?), there are different types of sugar (including the two molecules that compose it: fructose and glucose). But in the most general sense, sugar—sucrose—does a few things in candy: It provides sweetness (duh), adds body, and determines structure.

Different Stages, Different Candies

As you may have noticed, sucrose is crystalline. This means it reacts in very specific ways; most notably, it "wants" to be a crystal. Its default structure is a cube—not a sugar cube that you put in your coffee, but a cube on a molecular level. This is why rock candy forms the way it does, in big square chunks: Undisturbed sugar crystals form large crystalline structures.

Just because this is what sugar *wants* to do doesn't mean it's what it *has* to do; over time, confectioners have learned how to manipulate sugar syrup—by intercepting it at various points (stages) during the cooking process—to change its texture and sometimes also its flavor. This is why fudge, marshmallows, brittles, and gummies are all considered confections, and are all very different from one another.

Following is a brief roundup—a taste, if you will—of the delicious candies that can be made from each stage of sugar:

JELLY CANDY (THREAD STAGE). Thread stage is really just fully dissolved sugar, less a little moisture. On its own, it's not terribly thrilling, but mix it with a thickener like agar or pectin, and it helps give body to chewy, fruity candies like Pâtes de Fruits (page 105).

FUDGE (SOFT BALL STAGE). Fudge is unique in that crystallization of the sugar is encouraged; you just need to make sure the crystals are really, reeeeeeally small—too small to be detected individually by the tongue—so they can give that lovely creamy texture as they melt in your mouth. The sugar needs to be completely dissolved during cooking, so that you have complete control over the final size of the crystals. Start working out that stirrin' arm.

TAFFY AND CARAMEL (FIRM BALL STAGE). Taffy is a sugar syrup containing a very small amount of dairy that's cooked to firm ball stage and then vigorously pulled, aerating it and turning it from a light tan color into a pure satiny white; the pulling also changes taffy's texture from tooth-sticking to light and chewy. Flavoring is generally added after cooking is complete. Caramel is similar to taffy, except the sugar is encouraged to brown. The recipes tend to be mostly different in the levels of fat (very low in taffy, as opposed to high in caramel).

MARSHMALLOWS (HARD BALL STAGE). Marshmallows are a great example of hard ball sugar doing its thing. Sugar cooked to this stage does an excellent job of giving structure to an aerated but unstable mass like whipped egg whites. The hot syrup actually cooks the whites as it's added, stabilizing the proteins and leaving you with a nice, fluffy, flexible end result.

EUROPEAN NOUGAT (SOFT CRACK STAGE). European nougat is a firmer, chewier cousin to the marshmallow and its hard-ball stage kin, Peanut Butter and Snacker nougats (pages 172 and 256). The higher-temperature syrup means firmer and more shelf-stable candy.

LOLLIPOPS (HARD CRACK STAGE). Hard candies like lollies are basically sugar syrup (and usually a little glucose) that have had all the moisture boiled out of them, resulting in sugar that is as hard as its default crystalline structure, but smooth and transparent instead of grainy and opaque. This will change the longer the candy sits and is exposed to moisture; the sugar will re-dissolve and re-form itself into crystals once again. Ever had to nibble that weird, chewy white layer on the outside of your Tootsie Pop? Get yourself a new Tootsie Pop, because that one is old. (Unless you like it, of course—then go ahead and buy a couple extra.)

A NOTE ON TOFFEE. In this book, we refer to the chewy stuff you get on the boardwalk as taffy, and the crunchy Heath Bar-esque treat as toffee. Toffee is more or less a hard candy that has a large quantity of fat (usually butter) added to it. It is usually lightened by constant stirring or by the addition of baking soda after cooking. Toffee combines the nice browned flavors of caramel with the crispness of hard candy.

What's Cookin', Sugar?

Cooking sugar properly doesn't require a PhD, but it does require some basic knowledge and care. The general procedure for sugar syrups, up to a point, is identical: Note that this is the same process we refer to as "wet caramel," which is simply sugar syrup that is cooked to the point where it browns and takes on all those nice caramelly flavors (see What's the Word, Caramel?, page 50).

1. COMBINE. At a minimum, you'll have granulated sugar and water. Sometimes there will also be corn syrup or another type of syrup. You'll want to stir it a little so that all the granulated sugar is at least damp, but don't kill yourself over it.

2. WASH DOWN. The side of the pan, that is. It's almost inevitable that a few (or many) grains of sugar will cling to the side of the pan after you've added the ingredients and stirred a bit. You'll want to take a pastry brush, dunk it in a cup of cold water, and brush the water down the side of the pan so that the extra granules are washed back down into the mix. If you start cooking the syrup and one of these little crystals gets back into the syrup while it's bubbling away, the crystal runs the risk of "seeding" the remaining syrup, causing it to crystallize within a matter of seconds (no joke) and frustrating the crap out of the cook (you). This step greatly reduces the chances of that happening.

3. DON'T TOUCH IT. Unless we specifically tell you otherwise in the recipe, do not stir the syrup while it's cooking! The more you agitate it, the more likely it is to crystallize—so make like Mother Mary and let it be.

4. EASY DOES IT. When you're ready to pour sugar syrup, ALWAYS wear oven mitts; grabbing onto an unexpectedly searing-hot pan is really no fun, especially if the searing-hot pan is full of searing-hot liquid. (Spoiler alert: This one is.)

COOKING SUGAR SYRUP

1. Combine the sugar and water in a saucepan.

2. Wash down the side of the pan with water.

3. Don't touch that cooking sugar!

4. Pour out the cooked syrup onto a heatproof surface. Careful now. (By the by, this syrup has been cooked all the way to caramel stage.)

WHAT'S THE WORD, CARAMEL?

When we hear the word "caramel," we generally think of a finished candy: soft and chewy, light brown, wrapped in wax paper or cellophane. But in traditional French nomenclature, "caramel" simply refers to burnt sugar—which is brittle like glass when it sets, and is used in sugar decorations and to assemble a French specialty, that towering pyramid of cream puffs known as a *croquembouche*.* Our soft, chewy candy is technically known as *caramel moue:* soft caramel.

We don't often use the method for making straight-up caramelized sugar, but it's pretty simple and can be useful—you know, in case you need to assemble a croquembouche in the next five minutes (and *bonne chance* with that).

Once it's done, you can pour it out and let it set up, using shattered pieces as a cake or candy garnish or ice cream topping; or you can stir some cream into the still-liquid caramel (careful—it will sputter!) and make a delightfully simple caramel sauce to spoon over ice cream (we recommend a generous pinch of fine sea salt, too).

DRY CARAMEL TECHNIQUE

1. Place the sugar in a saucepan and set the pan over medium heat and start stirring with a wooden spoon (a heatproof spatula works, too). The sugar will start to melt and clump together.
2. Continue to stir, breaking up any lumps with the spoon, until all the sugar is melted. Once it is, stop stirring *immediately*.
3. Allow the melted sugar to continue cooking over medium heat; it will quickly start to take on a light golden color. While it cooks, fill a bowl with ice water.
4. When the sugar is the color of dark maple syrup, it's done. "Shock" the bottom of the pan by gently lowering it into the bowl of ice water. This halts the cooking process, ensuring that your caramel stays the same color it was when you took it off the heat.

MAKING DRY CARAMEL

1. Stir in the sugar while it heats.

2. Break up any lumps and keep stirring until the sugar melts.

3. Stop stirring immediately and let the sugar cook.

4. When the melted sugar is the color of dark maple syrup, shock the bottom of the pan in ice water.

*Which roughly translates to "crunch-in-the-mouth." Delightful, *non*?

Testing Sugar Syrup

Before you use your cooked sugar syrup in a recipe, you'll want to test it to make sure it's at the proper stage. In pastry school, we had a chef-instructor (Hi, Chef Kir!) who told us there were two ways to check syrup: the regular way and the chicken way. The regular way involves sticking your finger in cold water for a few seconds, dipping it rapidly in the boiling sugar mixture, and quickly returning it to the cold water. Done right, it's a quick and effective way to test how a syrup will set up at any given point in the cooking. Done wrong, it #^&@ing HURTS.

We strongly recommend using the chicken method, which is simply dipping the business end of a heatproof spatula or wooden spoon in the cooking syrup and allowing some of the syrup to drip out into a cup of cold water. The test can then safely be retrieved by your fingers, which you can use to knead and poke the sugar until you get a sense for what the final texture will be. This works for any sugar mixture: caramel, pâte de fruit, agar jellies, what have you. It's good to start practicing testing this way so that you get a feel for how a few degrees can change the end result of a recipe, and eventually learn what a syrup looks and feels like when it's at the temperature you want it to be (for examples, see Behold: the Sugar Stages on page 52).

Tips for Successful Sugar Cooking

Now you know about properly cooking syrup and the different sugar stages—yay for you! You're almost ready to start, but we suggest you read these few guidelines first.

• **READ THROUGH THE RECIPE SEVERAL TIMES.** As we said in the introduction (page x), this is important for every candy recipe—but it's especially so for sugar-syrup–based candies. In a lot of these recipes, you will need to have on hand last-minute additions (flavorings and colorings), prepared surfaces (molds, silicone mats), and/or specific equipment (a candy funnel) the second your sugar syrup is cooked. Not two minutes after; *the moment it's done.* An extra five seconds in a hot saucepan can turn a beautiful, golden caramel into a black, odoriferous mess. So know what you're getting into before you turn on the stove.

BEHOLD: THE SUGAR STAGES

STAGE	TEMPERATURE	BEHAVIOR IN COLD WATER
Thread	220°–235°F/104°–113°C	Forms a thread that dissolves very quickly
Soft ball	235°–240°F/113°–116°C	Forms a squishy, flexible ball that does not hold its shape out of water
Firm ball	245°–250°F/118°–121°C	Forms a firm but pliable ball that holds its shape out of water
Hard ball	250°–265°F/121°–130°C	Forms a hard ball that is only slightly pliable when squeezed
Soft crack	270°–290°F/132°–143°C	Forms threads that bend slightly before breaking
Hard crack	300°–310°F/149°–154°C	Forms hard, brittle threads or drops that harden almost immediately

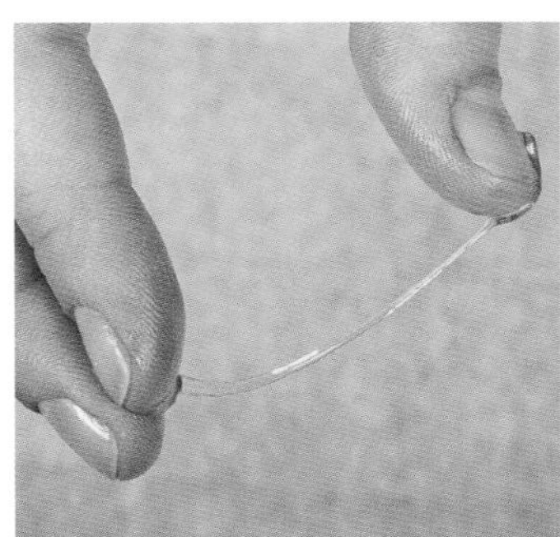
Thread

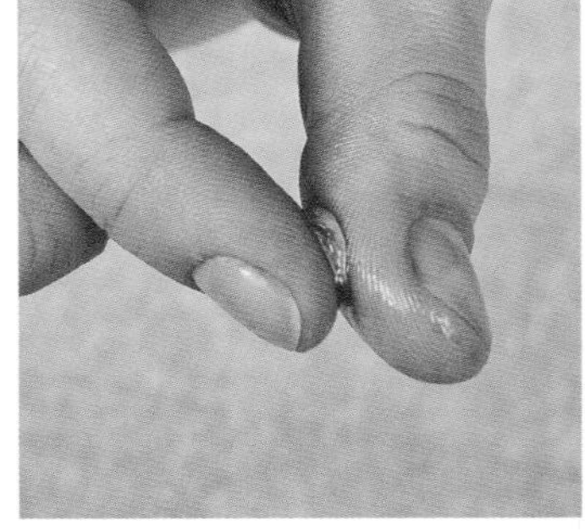
Soft ball

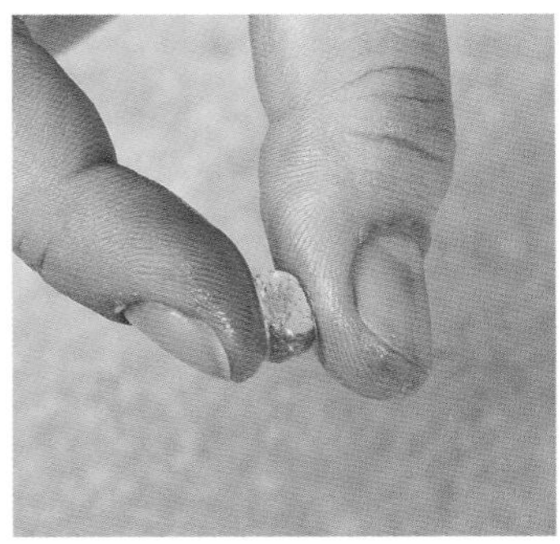
Firm ball

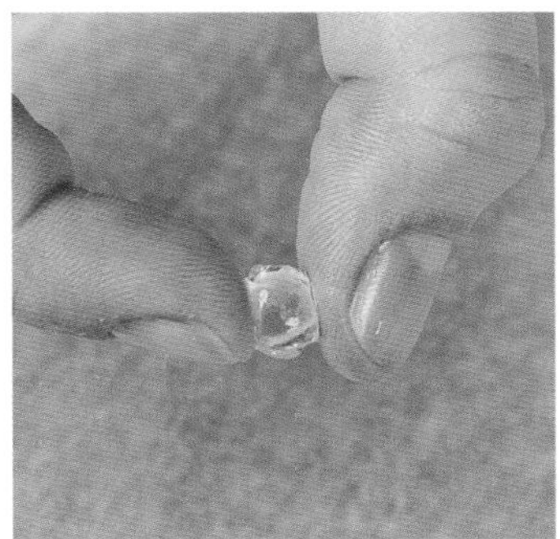
Hard ball

Soft crack

Hard crack

• **MAKE SURE YOUR THERMOMETER IS CORRECTLY CALIBRATED.** Sugar syrups require perfect exactitude on the part of your thermometer—at least when you first start working with sugar. A couple of degrees can make all the difference, so check your thermometer in water that's been brought to a rolling boil. Not at 212°F/100°C? Get yourself a new thermometer.

As we said earlier, our favorite thermometer is the Maverick CT-03; it's a basic white plastic box at the end of a long metal probe, and you can find it online for about $25. The analog thermometers we use are made by Taylor, and they're available at almost any kitchen store and online; they'll run you $10 to $15.

• **YOU CAN NEVER BE TOO CAREFUL.** Sugar syrup is *extremely dangerous.* It can reach temperatures over 300°F—almost half again as hot as boiling water—and if you spill it on yourself, it stays where it is. Sugar burns are unbelievably painful and can cause a lot of damage, so take every possible precaution. Never, ever let small children near hot sugar syrup. Keep pot handles tucked in toward the stove. And, seriously—we recommend pants, oven mitts, and closed-toed shoes when you're dealing with this stuff. Liz has a burn scar on her leg from lollipop syrup that spilled when she was cooking in a skirt. Fair warning! (For more cautionary tips on working with liquid-hot magma, see Boo-urns, page 191.)

COOKED SUGAR TROUBLESHOOTING

We've made it look and sound so easy—how could anything go wrong? You're human, Pinocchio, that's how. It happens to all of us. And there are really only two things that can go awry. Here's what to do if . . .

• **THE SUGAR CRYSTALLIZES.** D'oh! Not to worry—you can start over. If this happens, remove the sugar from the heat and add enough water to cover all the crystals. Add a pinch of cream of tartar (or ⅛ tablespoon fresh lemon juice or distilled white vinegar) per cup of sugar, place it over low heat, and stir frequently with a wooden spoon or heatproof spatula, breaking up the chunks of sugar, until the sugar is redissolved. Wash down the side of the pan again (see page 48), and crank the heat back up to medium. You're good to go!

• **THE SUGAR BURNS.** When you're cooking sugar to any stage beyond hard ball, it can go from A-OK to burnt black in what seems like seconds. Unfortunately, burnt sugar is unsalvageable; the actual sugar molecules have broken down into compounds that are dark and unpleasantly bitter-tasting. Pour the burnt sugar out onto a parchment- or silicone mat–lined baking sheet for later disposal, hum "Taps," and start over.

Crystallized sugar syrup

Cleaning Up Your Mess

When you're working with sugar syrup, start cleaning right away, as in right this minute. Hard-cooked sugar is insanely frustrating to clean off any surface. Here are a few things that help make it easier:

- **SOAK IT.** Once the sugar syrup is poured out of the saucepan, put the pan in the sink and immediately fill it with hot water. It will soak while you finish the recipe, and by the time you get around to cleaning it, much of the sugar will have dissolved.

- **COOK IT.** If you forget to/can't put the pot in the sink right away and have hard sugar coating the inside of your saucepan, just fill it three-quarters full with hot water and place it over medium heat, and let it simmer for 10 minutes or so. The boiling water will clean the inside of the pan, and the hot steam will help loosen any sugar above the waterline.

- **SCRAPE IT.** Use a bench scraper (page 21) to get at any pesky little dribbles and drabbles of sugar; remaining stickiness can be removed by rubbing with a wet dishtowel or scrubby sponge (if the sugar is stubborn, just keep rewetting the cloth; the water will eventually dissolve the sugar).

Okay. So now you know the basic molecular structure of sugar, you know what caramelization is, you've had a rundown of some different types of candy, you know how to cook sugar and clean up after yourself . . . yup, we think you're ready.

LET'S GO MAKE SOME CANDY!

CHOCOLATE MINT
MELTAWAYS
PAGE 82

CHERRY
CORDIALS
PAGE 85

CHOCOLATE
BARK (WOOF!)
PAGE 79

CHOCORRONE
PAGE 89

HIP-TO-BE
SQUARES
PAGE 99

Chapter Two

CHOCOLATE LOVES YOU & WANTS YOU TO BE HAPPY. ☺

Just read the word *chocolate,* and scores of tropes and tired phrases come to mind: Death by Chocolate! Chocolate Makes Everything Better! I'm a Chocoholic! Chocolate Chocolate Chocolate ACK! (Anybody? "Cathy"? *30 Rock*? No? Okay, moving on.)

Aside from all its baggage, mystique, and alleged magical powers, chocolate really is a lovely ingredient—one of our favorite substances to work with, and beloved by almost everybody. Its flavor is impossible to imitate (back away from the carob, please); and its texture, when mixed in the right proportions with the right ingredients, can bring untold amounts of joy. While it can be finicky, it also works wonders as a hermetic seal for delicate ganaches (page 36), fluffy moist nougats (page 145), gooey cherries (page 85) . . . pretty much anything you care to dip in it, really. There's no substitute, and it's totally worth the chocolate stains you'll inevitably get on your dish towels, pant legs, and shirtsleeve elbows. But hey—that's what smocks are for, right?

EASY

SIMPLY PERFECT DARK CHOCOLATE TRUFFLES

MAKES FORTY TO FIFTY 1-INCH ROLLED TRUFFLES

Simply perfect; perfectly simple. This recipe uses a classic 2:1 ratio of chocolate to cream, resulting in a ganache that is pliant and smooth, and ideal for rolled truffles. The corn syrup helps keep it emulsified and helps prevent crystallization, and the sea salt helps temper the sweetness. The ratio leaves room for additions, but the base is delightful on its own (when made with a delicious high-quality dark chocolate, of course—see page 10 for suggestions).

SPECIAL EQUIPMENT

- 2 large (13" x 18") rimmed baking sheets, lined with parchment or wax paper
- Swirly dipping fork (see page 20)

FOR THE GANACHE

16 ounces (455 g) chopped dark chocolate (about 2½ cups)

1 cup (225 g) heavy (whipping) cream

2 tablespoons (45 g) light corn syrup

¼ teaspoon (1 g) fine sea salt

FOR DIPPING

3 cups (19 ounces/540 g) chopped dark chocolate, or 3 cups (19 ounces/540 g) chopped dark chocolate and ½ cup (110 g) mild vegetable oil

1. Make the ganache: Place the chopped chocolate in a medium-size bowl and set it aside.

2. Combine the cream, corn syrup, and salt in a small (1- to 2-quart) saucepan and bring it just to a boil over medium heat (there will be tiny frothy bubbles around the edge and it will begin to steam).

3. Pour the hot cream mixture over the chocolate and use a rubber spatula to push down any pieces that are not submerged. Allow it to sit for 5 minutes.

4. Using the spatula, gently stir in small circles in the center of the bowl until the ganache starts to emulsify, about 5 minutes. Continue to stir gently until

the ganache becomes smooth and glossy, another 3 to 5 minutes.

5 Allow the ganache to cool to room temperature, about 45 minutes. Transfer it to a lidded container and store it in the refrigerator overnight. (Ganache will keep like this for up to 4 weeks; stored airtight in the freezer, it will keep for up to 6 months.)

6 Roll the truffles: Once the ganache has set, scrape along the surface with a metal tablespoon and roll each spoonful between your palms into a 1-inch ball. Place the balls on one of the prepared baking sheets.

7 Dip the truffles: Temper the 3 cups dark chocolate according to the instructions on page 26, or use the 3 cups dark chocolate and ½ cup oil to make Cheater's Chocolate Coating as directed on page 32.

8 Use the swirly dipping fork (or a regular fork) to dip the truffles into the chocolate following the instructions below. Place the dipped truffles on the remaining prepared baking sheet and let them set up, 15 to 20 minutes.

Store the dipped truffles in an airtight container at cool room temperature for up to 3 weeks.

ROLLING AND DIPPING TRUFFLES

1. Scrape the surface of the chilled ganache with a spoon.

2. Pluck the ganache from the spoon when you have enough for a 1-inch ball.

3. Roll the spoonful between your palms to form into a ball.

4. Place the truffles on the baking sheet.

5. Dip the truffles in the chocolate using a swirly dipping fork.

6. Place the truffles on the baking sheet.

Variations

FANY'S TRUFFLES These are named for our good friend and sometime kitchen-mate Fany Gerson, a fantastic pastry chef and author of multiple cookbooks on Mexican specialties. We include cornmeal to mimic the Mexican beverage *atole*, which is a heartier version of hot chocolate and includes masa; if you have masa around, feel free to use it. (Conversely, if you want to keep the consistency perfectly smooth, you can go ahead and omit the cornmeal altogether.) Add 1 tablespoon dark brown sugar with the cream and corn syrup, and proceed as directed. Once the ganache is emulsified in step 4, stir in 2 tablespoons finely ground cornmeal, 1 teaspoon ground cinnamon, ½ teaspoon chile powder, ½ teaspoon Trablit coffee extract (see Note on page 132), and ¼ teaspoon cayenne pepper.

PEPPERMINT TRUFFLES Stir in ½ teaspoon pure peppermint oil or 2 teaspoons pure peppermint extract (see page 84) into the warm finished ganache in step 4.

SMOKED TEA TRUFFLES This ganache is subtly smoky; we use it in our S'mores Bars (page 271) to impart a just-roasted-over-the-bonfire flavor. To make it, simply heat the cream in a small saucepan over medium heat. Add ½ teaspoon loose smoked tea, such as Lapsang Souchong (available at specialty grocery stores/coffee shops and online from Amazon), turn off the heat, and let it steep, covered, for 20 minutes. Strain out the tea leaves and use the cream as directed in step 2.

MODERATE

SIMPLY PERFECT MILK CHOCOLATE OR WHITE CHOCOLATE TRUFFLES

MAKES ABOUT 100 MOLDED ONE-INCH BONBONS, OR ABOUT 75 ONE-INCH ROLLED TRUFFLES

You may notice that the ratio of chocolate to cream in this recipe is different from the one for the dark chocolate truffles; though there is more chocolate and the same amount of cream, it's a slightly softer ganache and thus lends itself well to piped and molded bonbons (which is how we make them here). You can roll the truffles too, if you'd rather—see the directions on page 60; just keep a bowl of cool water handy so you can dunk (and then thoroughly dry) your hands if they get too warm and start melting the ganache as you roll it. You'll also need to allow the rolled ganache centers to cool for at least an hour at room temperature so they'll be firm enough to dip without sticking to the fork.

Milk chocolate is a great medium for playing with salty-sweet combos as well as tart fruit like lime and passion fruit. White chocolate is a great palette for more delicate flavors and for florals like rose or orange blossom.

SPECIAL EQUIPMENT

- 3 or 4 bonbon molds with about 100 one-inch cavities total (see Note, opposite, and Resources, page 291)
- Bench scraper
- Piping bag (see page 20)

INGREDIENTS

FOR THE GANACHE

20 ounces (570 g) chopped milk or white chocolate (about 3¼ cups)

1 cup (225 g) heavy (whipping) cream

2 tablespoons (45 g) light corn syrup

¼ teaspoon (1 g) fine sea salt

FOR THE BONBON SHELLS

4 cups (26 ounces/740 g) chopped dark chocolate

1. Make the ganache: Place the chopped chocolate in a medium-size bowl and set it aside.

2. Combine the cream, corn syrup, and salt in a small (1- to 2-quart) saucepan and bring it just to a boil over medium heat (there will be tiny frothy bubbles around the edge and it will begin to steam).

3. Pour the hot cream mixture over the chocolate, and use the spatula to push down any pieces that are not submerged. Allow it to sit for 5 minutes.

4. Using a rubber spatula, gently stir in small circles in the center of the bowl until the ganache starts to emulsify, about 5 minutes. Continue to stir gently until the ganache is smooth and glossy, another 3 to 5 minutes.

5. Allow the ganache to cool to room temperature—it should be thickened but still pourable, like thick cake batter—about 45 minutes. While waiting for the ganache to cool, go on to step 6.

6. Make the bonbon shells: Temper the 4 cups dark chocolate according to the instructions on page 26.

7. Ladle the tempered chocolate into the molds so that each cavity is filled completely, then use the bench scraper to scrape any excess back into the bowl. Gently tap the edge of the molds against the counter (this will shake loose any small air bubbles, which would end up as little divots in the finished bonbons). Allow the filled molds to set up for 3 minutes.

8. Invert the molds completely, and carefully pour the chocolate from each back into the bowl, gently tapping the underside of the mold to get rid of any excess chocolate in the cavities. Scrape the excess off again, and place the mold (still upside down) on a sheet of parchment; leave them be until the shells are set, about 15 minutes.

9. Fill a piping bag with the ganache and use it to fill the bonbon shells most of the way, leaving about ¼ inch of space at the top.

10. Holding the filled molds over the bowl of tempered chocolate, ladle chocolate over the molds again, tilting the molds as needed to distribute the chocolate evenly over the cavities and making sure they are all sealed.

11. Scrape off the excess chocolate and gently tap the bottom of the molds on the counter a few more times to get rid of any remaining air bubbles. Allow the bonbons to set at cool room temperature until you can see the chocolate pulling away from the underside of the molds, about 15 minutes.

12. Flip over the sheet of parchment and gently invert the bonbon-filled molds onto it, moving aside any bonbons that slide out of their own accord. Tap the far edge of the mold on the counter to release the remaining bonbons.

Store the truffles in an airtight container at cool room temperature for up to 3 weeks.

NOTE: We prefer polycarbonate molds, available from JB Prince (see Resources, page 291), since they're the sturdiest and easiest to use, but really, any rigid plastic or silicone mold will work.

MAKING MOLDED TRUFFLES

1. Ladle tempered chocolate evenly into the mold to fill each cavity.

2. Scrape off any excess chocolate from the mold.

3. Tap the mold gently to get rid of any air bubbles.

4. After the chocolate has set up a bit, pour it back into the bowl.

5. Scrape again!

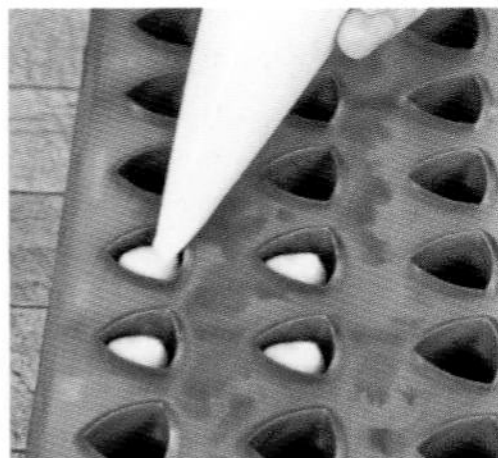

6. Once the shells have set, pipe in the ganache.

7. Ladle more chocolate on top of the ganache.

8. More scraping!

9. When the bonbons have set, flip the mold over onto the prepared counter.

10. The bonbons are released. Run along, bonbons, you're free!

Variations

For Milk Chocolate Truffles

PASSION FRUIT TRUFFLES Adding passion fruit to chocolate results in a pleasantly sweet-rich-tart-silky experience—count on at least several "ooh"s and "ahh"s when your lucky taste-testers first get their chompers around these. Make the ganache as directed. While it is still warm, stir in 5 tablespoons (90 g) passion fruit puree. (The puree is available on Amazon .com. If you can't find it, you can use juice instead: Heat ½ cup passion fruit juice in a small saucepan over medium-high heat, stirring constantly until it is reduced by half. Use the reduced juice plus 1 teaspoon fresh lemon juice in place of the fruit puree.)

SPECULOOS TRUFFLES Speculoos (also known as Speculaas or Biscoff cookies) are delightfully crunchy spiced cookies popular in Belgium and the Netherlands (and on Delta Airlines). They have a lovely, not overwhelmingly sweet cinnamon-and-spice flavor—and Jen also happens to be obsessed with them. Somebody had the unbelievably brilliant idea of turning these cookies into a Nutella-like spread, which you can find online and at a growing number of specialty grocers. When truffle-ized, it magically ends up smack in the middle of the spectrum between cookie and candy: Make the ganache as directed. Warm ¾ cup Speculoos spread for 10 seconds on High in the microwave (or heat it in a bowl set over a pan of simmering water until slightly liquid), and stir it into the warm finished ganache.

For White Chocolate Truffles

APPLE-GINGER TRUFFLES Heat the cream just to boiling and remove it from the heat. Add two 1-inch-thick slices of peeled fresh ginger, cover the pan, and steep for 5 minutes. Remove the ginger and complete the ganache as directed. Stir 3 tablespoons (40 g) apple cider jelly—or regular apple jelly plus 1 teaspoon (5 g) fresh lemon juice—plus 1½ tablespoons (22 g) Calvados or applejack and 1 teaspoon ground ginger into the warm finished ganache.

PAPA GUTMAN'S EGGNOG TRUFFLES Prepare the ganache as directed but increase the chocolate to 24 ounces (680 g). While it is still warm, stir in ¼ cup (60 g) bourbon or brandy. If you like nutmeg, add ¾ teaspoon, too (but know that nutmeg never touches true Gutman-style eggnog).

EASY

SALTED SOFT CHOCOLATES

MAKES ABOUT 50 ONE-INCH PIECES

These are a really unique and delicious chocolaty treat—and vegan-friendly too, if that's your bag. The texture is best described as akin to a Tootsie Roll, though they're so intensely flavored you might need just one to calm your craving. (Okay, maybe two.) They're also incredibly easy to make, so you can get little ones to help stir and knead if you like (as long as you do the actual pouring of the hot syrup). When it comes to the chocolate, go ahead and splurge on the good stuff; it's the only flavoring, so make sure it's top-notch.

SPECIAL EQUIPMENT

- Silicone mat or parchment paper
- Cellophane or wax twisting papers (see Resources, page 291)

INGREDIENTS

17 ounces (480 g) good-quality dark chocolate, chopped into chip-size pieces (about 3 cups)

⅓ cup (75 g) granulated sugar

3 tablespoons (40 g) water

½ cup minus 1 tablespoon (300 g) light corn syrup

1 teaspoon (5 g) coarse sea salt

Mild vegetable oil, for kneading the candy (optional)

1. Put the chopped chocolate in a medium-size bowl and set it aside. Place the silicone mat on a heatproof surface.

2. Place the sugar, water, and corn syrup in a small (2-quart) saucepan and stir with a whisk or heatproof spatula to combine. Bring the mixture to a boil, uncovered, over high heat, then remove it from the heat.

3. Pour the hot sugar syrup over the chocolate, making sure to cover all the pieces, and let it sit until the chocolate is melted, 2 to 3 minutes.

4. With a whisk or heatproof spatula, start to mix in the center of the bowl and continue stirring until the mixture is completely blended. It will take a minute or two to come together; when it's smooth and shiny, you're good to go.

5. Add the salt and stir until incorporated. Pour the mixture onto the center of the silicone mat. If it tries to ooze off the edge of the mat, just keep lifting the corners up until it cools enough to stay put; it should take only 5 minutes or so. Let the mixture sit until it is cool enough to handle but still warm, about 10 minutes.

6. Use the corners of the mat to fold the outer edges of the mixture into the center; this continues the process of cooling it down. Keep folding the mixture over on itself and kneading with your hands (using a little vegetable oil to grease them if things get sticky) until it firms up and kneading becomes difficult, about 10 minutes. Wrap the mixture tightly in plastic wrap and allow it to sit at cool room temperature overnight.

7. The next day, unwrap the mixture and place it back on the silicone mat or on a plastic cutting board. Knead the mixture again with your hands until it is softened and workable. (if it is too firm, you can

pop it in the microwave and warm it on High in 3- to 5-second intervals, kneading between intervals. Alternatively, place it between two pieces of parchment or wax paper and give it 10 to 20 good whacks with a rolling pin, an empty wine bottle, or a sock full of batteries.*)

8. When the mixture is pliable, take about a handful at a time and roll each one out on a clean, flat surface to form a 1-inch-thick log. Use a sharp chef's knife to cut each log into bite-size (1-inch) pieces (don't cut them on the silicone mat!). Wrap the individual pieces in twisting paper.

Store the candies in an airtight container at room temperature for up to 3 weeks.

LIZ SAYS: This recipe makes a LOT of candy (it's hard to work with a smaller amount of sugar syrup than is called for here because it has a tendency to crystallize). If you want to halve the recipe, you can heat the syrup in the microwave—while keeping a very close eye on it—or in a double boiler. If you make the whole amount of candy and don't want to use it all right away, form the remainder into a disk and wrap it tightly in plastic wrap; in this state it will keep in the refrigerator longer than you need it to—at least 2 to 3 months.

*Just kidding. Use a sock full of pennies. **

**Just kidding. Use the rolling pin or wine bottle.

PARTY ON, CANDY!

One of the good news/bad news situations with candy is that one batch usually makes a whole bunch of treats. Great if you live with several dozen sweets-crazy folks; not so great if you're stuck scratching your head about how to ~~get rid of all this sugar~~ share the wealth. Following are a few scenarios you might find yourself in, and candies that work well for each one. (For even more fête-friendly ideas, see chapter 6.)

Potluck/Picnic

CONSIDERATIONS: These tend to be informal gatherings and have short guest lists. It'll be a help-yourself setup, so individually wrapped goodies aren't necessary. If you'll be outdoors, you'll want to stay away from the chocolate.

TOP CONTENDERS: Agar Fruit Jellies (page 109) are eye-catching and dead simple, and hold up well in hot weather; for a thematic twist, make pink lemonade jellies with a 2:1 mixture of lemon juice and water in place of the fruit puree, plus a drop or two of red food coloring. Vanilla Marshmallows (page 141) are heat-stable as well.

LEVEL UP: Make a few different flavors of jellies or marshmallows and present them in a pretty mosaic pattern on a tray.

Friend's Wedding

CONSIDERATIONS: The ideal candy will depend on whether it's indoors or outdoors, but it will have to look extremely pretty. Ease of preparation for large quantities will also be key here.

TOP CONTENDERS: Goody Goody Gumdrops (page 120) or Pâtes de Fruit (page 105) are easy to cut into heart shapes and visually striking (as well as easy to color). Nonpareils (page 77) are a little more elegant, though you can always place whatever you want on top instead of sprinkles—e.g., a piece of the couple's favorite breakfast cereal—if you don't want to go the traditional route.

LEVEL UP: Make bite-size candy bars using their favorite flavors. Take THAT, wedding cake!

Baby Shower

CONSIDERATIONS: Obviously whatever you make will have to be *adorable*. Things that can be taken home as favors are preferable—who doesn't like a favor?

TOP CONTENDERS: Lollipops (pages 183, 187, and 189) are simple, can be poured into any shape of mold imaginable, and can be tied into cute little bouquets. Buttermints (page 177) can be tinted any baby-appropriate pastel color you like and are easily giftable in small cello bags tied with a bow.

LEVEL UP: Get alphabet molds for the lollipops to spell out "boy" or "girl." Swoon!

Surprise Birthday Party

CONSIDERATIONS: You'll either have to one-up the cake or be the substitute for it. Both are tall orders—but it can be done.

TOP CONTENDERS: If no one's bringing a cake, the obvious choice is Birthday Cake Amazeballs (page 232); go crazy with the sprinkles! If that's too on-the-nose for you, Pecan Turtle Caramel Corn (page 230) is a real crowd-pleaser and can easily be portioned out ahead of time into paper drinking cups or tulip-style baking cups.

LEVEL UP: Arrange the cake balls on a tray. Stick a tiny candle in each one, light it, and bring it out in place of an actual cake while singing "Happy Birthday." A thousand points of light. Tears will be shed, people.

Holiday Shindig

CONSIDERATIONS: Anything goes at a holiday party. Autumn/winter is high candy season anyhow, so if you're planning on making candy, bring your A game.

TOP CONTENDERS: Nothing heralds the coming of fall like Caramel Apples (page 223)! For an elegant twist, grab some tiny Lady Apples at your local farmers market and watch everyone ooh and ahh at the two-bite wonders. Hip-to-Be Squares (page 99) will also impress everybody with how impossibly delicious they are, and will take you about half an hour to make.

LEVEL UP: Make molded bonbons and brush them with luster dust (see Resources, page 291). Stand near them during the party and watch people's eyes widen when they gasp, "You MADE these?" Feel smug and/or do a victory dance.

EASY

BUCKEYES

MAKES ABOUT FIFTY 1½-INCH BUCKEYES

We were asked to make these as wedding favors for a friend, and we kind of rolled our eyes. Buckeyes? Really? But they're so . . . boring. Peanut butter filling, rolled into balls and dipped in chocolate to resemble horse chestnuts. Sure, they're a favorite of Ohio natives, where the buckeye is the official state tree; and sure, they're easy enough to make. But where's the challenge? The excitement? Didn't they want something fancier for a wedding?

Yeah, right. Peanut butter and chocolate is a classic combination for a reason, and this recipe gets it all right: rich, peanutty, and smooth, with a little texture from the nut flour, and the richness cut by the bitterness of the dark chocolate. The container of extra buckeyes in the fridge lasted maybe a day. We're not even gonna tell you how many were in there to start with. You wouldn't believe it.

SPECIAL EQUIPMENT

- Stand mixer fitted with paddle attachment, or electric mixer with large bowl
- 2 large (13" x 18") rimmed baking sheets, lined with parchment or wax paper
- Wooden toothpicks

INGREDIENTS

FOR THE CENTERS

¼ cup (60 g) cream cheese, at room temperature

1½ cups (275 g) creamy commercial peanut butter, such as Skippy

10 tablespoons (1¼ sticks/150 g) unsalted butter, at room temperature

2 teaspoons (10 g) fine sea salt

1 cup (85 g) almond or peanut flour (see Note)

3 cups (400 g) confectioners' sugar, sifted

FOR DIPPING AND GARNISH

About 4 cups (26 ounces/740 g) chopped dark chocolate, or 3 cups (19 ounces/540 g) chopped dark chocolate and ½ cup (4 ounces/110 g) mild vegetable oil

Coarse sea salt (optional)

1. Make the centers: Combine all the ingredients in the mixer bowl and beat on medium-high speed until completely incorporated and creamy-looking. Cover and refrigerate the peanut butter mixture until it has firmed up a little (it should be pliable but hold its shape), about 30 minutes.

2. Scoop up a tablespoon of the mixture, roll it into a ball with your hands, and place it on one of the prepared baking sheets; repeat with the remaining mixture. Once all the mixture has been formed, place the balls in the refrigerator until firm, about 30 minutes. (Any leftover peanut butter mixture can be wrapped tightly in plastic wrap and stored in the fridge for up to a week.)

3. Prepare the dipping chocolate: Temper the 4 cups dark chocolate according to the instructions on page 26 or melt it as directed on page 24. Or use the 3 cups dark chocolate and ½ cup oil to make Cheater's Chocolate Coating, following the directions on page 32. Place the coating of your choice in a large bowl.

4. Dip the buckeyes: Stick a toothpick into a peanut butter ball and dip it in the chocolate, but don't submerge it—leave the top quarter undipped. This spot is what makes a buckeye a Buckeye!

Transfer the buckeye to the second prepared baking sheet. Pull out the toothpick, twisting it gently, and either use your thumb to carefully smooth out the hole left behind or cover it with a few grains of coarse sea salt. Repeat with the remaining buckeyes.

5 Allow the buckeyes to set up until the chocolate is firm, 15 to 20 minutes.

Store the buckeyes, layered with wax paper, in an airtight container in the refrigerator for up to 4 weeks.

NOTE: Nut flours are sold at specialty and health food stores. Bob's Red Mill is a widely available brand; they have a great almond flour that works very well in this recipe, adding a delicate nutty flavor and hearty texture that we love. Peanut flour, which you can find online at Amazon, adds an extra-special peanutty kick that you should definitely try at least once.

LIZ SAYS: When we say "commercial" peanut butter, we mean the emulsified, no-oil-on-the-top kind. In the kitchen, we use Peanut Butter & Co's Smooth Operator; it's not quite as industrially shelf-stable as Jif or Skippy (don't hoard it for the zombie apocalypse), but any minor separation that might occur can be ameliorated by placing the peanut butter in a microwave-safe dish and heating it gently in a microwave on High for 5- to 10-second bursts, stirring well between bursts. It should come back together.

EASY

WOLVERINES (VEGAN BUCKEYES)

MAKES ABOUT FORTY-FIVE 1½-INCH CANDIES

Though we're what you might call "omnivores," in that we eat anything that's technically edible, we do understand that some folks eat in a more structured way, and we admire and respect that. While many of the recipes in this book are vegan-friendly (see page xiii), every once in a while we'll go out of our way to adapt a recipe for our vegan friends (and those with particular allergies). This one took a little doing, and the Wolverines do need to stay refrigerated to hold their shape; but we really like the smooth texture and hint of coconut flavor in these dairy-free Bizarro-Buckeyes. Chances are you'll be hiding 'em from the omnivores, too.

These candies are named in honor of Jen's "hippie" sister, Kat, who graduated from the University of Michigan. Since the buckeye is the symbol of Ohio State, we thought we'd include an appropriately named Michigan version.

SPECIAL EQUIPMENT

- Stand mixer fitted with paddle attachment, or electric mixer with large bowl
- 2 large (13" x 18") rimmed baking sheets, lined with parchment or wax paper
- Wooden toothpicks

INGREDIENTS

FOR THE CENTERS

2 cups almond flour (or peanut flour; see Note), sifted

2½ cups confectioners' sugar, sifted

2½ teaspoons kosher salt or fleur de sel

¼ cup (2 ounces) coconut oil

½ cup (4 ounces) solid vegetable shortening

1 cup creamy commercial peanut butter, such as Skippy

FOR DIPPING AND GARNISH

About 4 cups (26 ounces/740 g) chopped dark chocolate, or 3 cups (19 ounces/540 g) chopped dark chocolate and ½ cup (4 ounces/110 g) mild vegetable oil

Coarse sea salt (optional)

1. Make the centers: In the order listed, place all the ingredients in the mixer bowl (it's easier to mix everything when the dry ingredients are on the bottom). Mix on low speed to combine, about 1 minute. Increase the speed to medium-high and beat until completely mixed and creamy, about 5 minutes. Cover and refrigerate the mixture until it's firm enough to scoop and roll, about 30 minutes.

2. Scoop up a tablespoon of the peanut butter mixture, roll it into a ball with your hands, and place it on one of the prepared baking sheets; repeat with the remaining mixture. Once all the mixture has been formed, place the balls in the refrigerator until they're thoroughly chilled and firm, about 1 hour.

3. Prepare the dipping chocolate: Temper the 4 cups dark chocolate according to the instructions on page 26 or melt it as directed on page 24. Or use the 3 cups dark chocolate and ½ cup oil to make Cheater's Chocolate Coating, following the directions on page 32. Place the coating of your choice in a large bowl.

4. Dip the wolverines: Stick a toothpick into the center of a peanut butter ball and dip it in the chocolate, leaving the top quarter undipped; then transfer it to the second prepared baking sheet. Pull out the toothpick, twisting it gently, and either use your thumb to carefully smooth out the hole left behind or cover it with a few grains of coarse sea salt. Repeat with the remaining wolverines.

Store the wolverines, layered with wax paper, in an airtight container in the refrigerator for up to 1 week.

NOTE: You can find nut flours at specialty and health food stores and on Amazon. Bob's Red Mill is a widely available brand, and their almond flour adds a nice delicate flavor and some texture to this recipe.

JEN SAYS: Coconut oil melts at a heat below body temperature, so these candies can get soft and sticky when you're rolling them. Keep a bowl of ice water and a towel handy; if your hands get too warm while you're rolling, soak them in the ice water for a few seconds, shake the excess onto the towel, and keep a-rollin'.

EASY

NONPAREILS

MAKES ABOUT 90 ONE-INCH CANDIES

One can only guess at the origin of the name for these candies—which translates from the French to "without equal"—since they're about as basic as you can get: chocolate and sprinkles. That's it. You might know them as Sno-Caps, which were Liz's movie-candy-of-choice before she graduated to Junior Mints; and though she never looked back, nonpareils hold a special place in her heart. Perhaps they're unparalleled in their simplicity and ability to impart childlike glee?

Nonpareil sprinkles are the tiny, round, crunchy kind—and no, you can't use jimmies (the long, soft kind). They're just not the same. Nonpareil sprinkles are available at almost any grocery store, at specialty kitchen and cake shops, and online from India Tree (see Resources, page 291).

SPECIAL EQUIPMENT

- Piping bag or plastic zip-top bag (see page 20)
- Tape (optional)
- Scissors
- Large (13" x 18") rimmed baking sheet, lined with parchment or wax paper

INGREDIENTS

1 cup (6.5 ounces/180 g) chopped dark chocolate

2 tablespoons nonpareil sprinkles

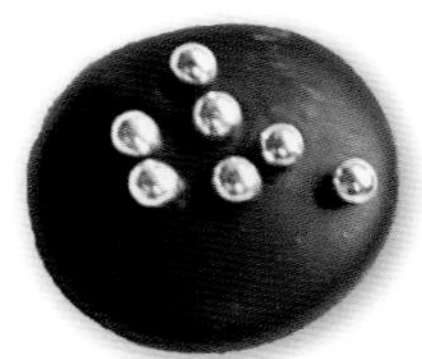

1. Temper the chocolate according to the instructions on page 26.
2. Place the piping bag in a 2-cup measuring cup or coffee mug, and fold the top edge down over the rim of the cup. Pour the tempered chocolate into the piping bag, twist the top, and secure it with a piece of tape as shown on page 45.
3. Cut off the tip of the bag, about ¼ inch from the end, and pipe 1-inch disks onto the prepared baking sheet. Sprinkle the nonpareil sprinkles evenly over the tops of the disks, and allow the disks to set completely, about 15 minutes.

Store the nonpareils in an airtight container at cool room temperature for up to 6 months.

CHOCOLATE BARK

MAKES ABOUT 2 POUNDS; ENOUGH FOR ABOUT 15 PEOPLE

*Woof! Just joshin'. This kind of bark is the classic, easy-to-*make, crowd-pleasing candy that's fun for kids of all ages: a big slab of chocolate topped with goodies and broken into bite-size pieces.

What follows isn't so much a recipe as a guideline; you can use any type of chocolate you like—dark, milk, white (or a combo)—and pretty much any topping. We've included some of our favorite combinations below, but the fun of this is putting your own spin on it.

Instead of straight-up chocolate, you also have the option of using Cheater's Chocolate Coating (page 32), but keep in mind: the simpler the bark, the nicer the chocolate should be. If you're going to the trouble of tempering nice chocolate, you should let it shine, and keep the ingredients spare and complementary to the chocolate (dark chocolate with dried pomegranate seeds, milk chocolate with toffee bits, that sort of thing). With more toppings—or toppings with more assertive flavors—you have a little more leeway, and the textural difference in the chocolate coating will all but disappear under that delicious goodness.

If you need to speed up the set—you're making a last-minute gift, for example, or you just can't wait to get a treat in your face-hole—you can stick the bark in the freezer for 5 to 10 minutes. The chocolate may not set up quite as shiny, but we promise no one will notice. Now git goin'—bark it up!

INGREDIENTS

2 cups (13 ounces/370 g) chopped chocolate, or 2 cups (13 ounces/370 g) chopped chocolate and ⅓ cup (75 g) mild vegetable oil

1½ cups assorted small toppings

SPECIAL EQUIPMENT

- Small (9" x 13") rimmed baking sheet

1. Line the baking sheet with parchment paper, making sure the paper extends over the two long sides of the sheet (this will make it easier for you to lift the finished bark out of the sheet).

2. Temper the 2 cups chocolate according to the instructions on page 26, or use the 2 cups chocolate and ⅓ cup oil to make Cheater's Chocolate Coating as directed on page 32.

3. Pour the chocolate into the lined sheet, and tap it gently on the counter a couple of times to get rid of any bubbles and distribute the chocolate in a uniform layer.

4. Quickly sprinkle the toppings evenly over the chocolate (if the toppings don't want to stick, press down on them gently with another sheet of parchment paper). Let the chocolate set, about 1 hour.

5. Run a paring knife along the unlined edges of the baking sheet to loosen the bark, and then gently lift up on the parchment paper "handles" to remove the bark from the baking sheet. Carefully peel the paper off the underside of the bark, and use your hands to break it into rough 2- to 3-inch pieces.

Store the bark in an airtight container for 2 to 4 weeks (its shelf life will depend on the toppings; for example, nuts, dried fruits, or candies will last longer than stuff like cereal or chips).

Variations

PEPPERMINT SWIRL Dark and white chocolate with peppermint candy topping. Use half dark and half white chocolate for the base: Pour the dark chocolate first, and, when it has cooled somewhat but before it sets completely (after about 5 minutes), pour the white chocolate on top of it. Swirl the chocolates with the tip of a paring knife, and then sprinkle with 1 cup crushed peppermint candy (such as candy canes).

NIBBLES 'N' BITS Crunchy cacao nibs and candied nuts with a touch of sea salt. Use a mixture of 1 part milk chocolate and 2 parts dark chocolate, tempered together. Pour the mixture out and sprinkle it with ½ cup cacao nibs, 1 cup crushed Dragées (page 213) or honey-roasted peanuts, and 1 teaspoon fine sea salt.

COUCH POTATO Milk chocolate and salty snacks. Use milk chocolate as the base. Top it with ½ cup each crushed potato chips, crushed pretzels, and corn nuts.

BREAKFAST TIME Better than Wheaties! Milk chocolate with cereal. Use milk chocolate as the base. Top it with ½ cup each crisped rice cereal, corn flakes, and crumbled Golden Grahams.

CONFETTI CAKE White chocolate with "cake" and sprinkles. Use white chocolate as the base. Top it with 1 cup crushed shortbread cookies or Cap'n Crunch cereal and 1 to 2 tablespoons rainbow jimmies.

EASY

CHOCOLATE MINT MELTAWAYS

MAKES ABOUT 65 ONE-INCH PIECES

Meltaways are that perfect combination of delicious, easy to make, and delicious. Plus—have you heard?—they're delicious. They also impart a lovely cooling sensation as they melt, and the combination of mint and chocolate is a true classic. Need we say more?

SPECIAL EQUIPMENT

- Small (8" x 8") baking pan
- Heatproof spatula

INGREDIENTS

Cooking spray or vegetable oil

2 cups (13 ounces/370 g) chopped dark chocolate

⅓ cup (75 g) coconut oil or solid vegetable shortening (see Notes)

¼ teaspoon (1 g) pure peppermint oil (preferred), or ½ teaspoon (3 g) peppermint extract (see Notes)

½ teaspoon (2 g) fine sea salt

About 1 cup sifted (100 g) confectioners' sugar, for dredging

1. Place a roughly 9 × 9-inch sheet of parchment or wax paper on a cutting board. Set it aside. Lightly grease the baking pan with the cooking spray, and line it with a piece of parchment or wax paper that extends a few inches over two ends of the baking pan (you'll use these ends as handles to lift the candy out after it's set). Set aside.

2. Combine the chocolate and coconut oil in a medium-size heatproof bowl. Place the bowl over a small saucepan of simmering water and stir frequently with the heatproof spatula until melted and completely combined. (Alternatively, place the chocolate and coconut oil in a microwave-safe bowl and heat on High for 30 seconds. Stir, then microwave in 10-second intervals, stirring with the spatula between intervals, until the chocolate and coconut oil are melted and combined.)

3. Add the peppermint oil and salt to the chocolate mixture and stir well with the spatula to combine. Pour the mixture into the lined baking pan, spreading it evenly with the spatula. Allow it to sit until firm to the touch, about 2 hours.

4. Once the meltaways have set, run a sharp chef's knife along the unlined edges of the pan and lift the slab of candy out of the baking sheet. Gently turn it out onto the parchment-lined cutting board and cut it into 1-inch squares (see Jen Says, page 84).

5. Place the confectioners' sugar, in a small bowl and dredge the candy pieces in it (see Dredge Report, page 108) until evenly coated on all sides.

Store the meltaways in an airtight container in the refrigerator for up to 2 weeks.

NOTES: Coconut oil is increasingly available at health food stores, but it's usually in its natural state—meaning it has a mild coconut flavor. Don't worry about off flavors; the peppermint oil will overpower the coconut. You can also experiment with other complementary flavors and spices—replacing the mint oil 1:1 with pure vanilla extract is a good start.

If you're using shortening, we prefer the non-hydrogenated kind; but any solid shortening works just fine.

Peppermint oil is sold in health food stores as a dietary supplement and is really indispensable for that *whoosh* of coolness. Peppermint extract, which is suspended in alcohol instead of water, works, too; you just need to use twice as much.

JEN SAYS: When cutting this candy, it can be helpful to have a tall glass of warm water and a clean dish towel handy. Submerge the knife in the warm water for about a minute to warm it; wipe it dry—*completely* dry!—on the dish towel, and then press down firmly and evenly to cut. Repeat this procedure every two or three cuts to keep the edges of the candy clean.

Variations

LIME TWIST Omit the mint. Wash a fresh lime and grate the zest. Add the zest to the bowl with the solid chocolate and coconut oil. Once the mixture is melted and stirred, cover it and allow it to sit for 10 minutes. Then strain the mixture through a tea strainer or a fine-mesh sieve into the prepared baking pan; discard the zest. Allow the meltaways to set up as directed.

You can also experiment with different types of chocolate and flavored oils! Cinnamon adds a lovely warm flavor, and works especially well with milk chocolate.

For nut-flavored meltaways, stir in ½ cup creamy commercial peanut butter, such as Skippy, or another nut butter (such as almond or cashew), instead of the peppermint oil and increase the salt to ¾ teaspoon.

MODERATE

CHERRY CORDIALS

MAKES ABOUT 80 CORDIALS

*We know, we know—you used to get these in a shrink-*wrapped box from your great-aunt Rosalie and you had to smile politely and thank her and wait until she left to go back home until you could throw them out because you think they're totally gross. The thing is, those were the mass-produced, flat-tasting, overly sweet kind. These are the homemade, kinda-boozy, high-quality, wow-that's-actually-really-tasty kind. See the difference?

No? Well, no worries. You will once you try them. Luckily, they also happen to be stunningly beautiful and make excellent and well-appreciated gifts; they've got that going for 'em, too.

You can often find nice jars of brandied cherries in gourmet or specialty stores. However, when cherries are in season, brandying them (i.e., soaking them in hooch) is a fun way to preserve them for a sweet wintertime project. And if you feel like skipping the chocolate and fondant part of the cordials, straight-up brandied cherries make a great topping for adult sundaes. Note that the homemade brandied cherries need to steep for at least a week, so if you're having a serious cherry cordial jones and need your fix right away, you'll want to take a trip to the store instead.

SPECIAL EQUIPMENT

- 2 large (13″ x 18″) baking sheets, lined with parchment or wax paper

INGREDIENTS

1 batch Brandied Cherries (recipe follows) or high-quality maraschino cherries

2 cups Le Fondant (page 162) or store-bought fondant (see Resources, page 291)

2 cups (13 ounces/370 g) chopped dark chocolate, or 2 cups (13 ounces/370 g) chopped dark chocolate and ⅓ cup (75 g) mild vegetable oil

1. Drain the liquid from the cherries (reserve it if you like; see page 88). Stack 3 or 4 sheets of paper towel on the counter and place the cherries on them in a single layer; gently pat the tops with another paper towel, and allow the cherries to dry for about 10 minutes.

2. Place the fondant in a medium-size heatproof bowl, and heat it in the microwave on High in three 10-second intervals, stirring between intervals. (Alternatively, place the bowl over a pan of simmering water and heat, stirring occasionally, until the fondant is warm and the consistency of pancake batter, 5 to 7 minutes.)

3. Place the cherries in a small bowl, and next to them place the bowl of fondant and then one of the prepared baking sheets.

4. Taking a cherry by the stem, dip it into the fondant so that the fruit is covered completely to the stem. Lift it out of the fondant, hold it for a few seconds to allow any excess fondant to drip off, and then place it on the prepared baking sheet. Repeat until all the cherries are covered. Set the baking sheet aside in a cool place until the fondant is cool, dry, and firm to the touch, 20 to 30 minutes.

5. In a second medium-size bowl, temper the 2 cups chocolate according to the

instructions on page 26, or use the 2 cups chocolate and ⅓ cup oil to make the Cheater's Chocolate Coating as directed on page 32.

6. Grabbing a fondant-coated cherry by the stem, dip it in the chocolate so that all of the fondant is covered; hold it above the bowl for a few seconds to allow any excess chocolate to drip off, and then place it on the second prepared baking sheet. Repeat until all the cherries have been dipped. Allow them to set up until the chocolate is firm, 15 to 20 minutes.

Store the cherries in an airtight container at cool room temperature for up to 6 weeks. The longer you leave them, the nice-n-gooier the insides of the cordials will be.

ASSEMBLING CHERRY CORDIALS

1. Dip the cherries in the fondant.

2. Place them on the baking sheet and let the fondant set.

3. Dip the fondanted cherries in chocolate.

4. Place them on the baking sheet and let them set up.

EASY

BRANDIED CHERRIES

MAKES ABOUT 80 CHERRIES

We like to use a bit of star anise in these for a touch of woodsiness in the final product, but if you're not an anise person (we understand), feel free to leave it out. You can use unpitted cherries if you like—they impart a slight almondy flavor to the mix and work just dandy for cocktail garnishes, too. Just make sure to chomp judiciously.

SPECIAL EQUIPMENT

- Quart-size jars with tight-fitting lids or sturdy Tupperware-type containers

INGREDIENTS

¾ cup granulated sugar

2 teaspoons honey

2 cups brandy

1 stick cinnamon (optional)

1 star anise pod (optional)

1 pound cherries, rinsed and pitted (but not stemmed)

LIZ SAYS: Leftover liquid from the cherries? Mixed with seltzer, it makes a delicious afternoon libation ("No, honey, that's *Mommy's* Shirley Temple").

1. Place the sugar, honey, brandy, cinnamon stick, and/or star anise (if using) in a small (2-quart) saucepan, and bring to a rolling boil over high heat. Turn off the heat, add the cherries, and cover. Allow to sit until the liquid has cooled enough to pour safely, 1 to 2 hours.

2. Remove the star anise pod with a slotted spoon (or leave it in, if you want a stronger anise flavor), and transfer the mixture—including the liquid—to the jars.

3. Close the jars and place them in the fridge. Allow the cherries to steep for at least 1 week before using; they will keep in the fridge for up to 8 weeks.

EASY

CHOCORRONE

MAKES ABOUT 100 ONE-AND-A-HALF-INCH TRIANGLES

This is our tribute to that grand pooh-bah of the duty-free store: the Toblerone. It's a great way to use up any extra Classic European Nougat (page 145) you might have hanging around; if it happens to have gotten stale, so much the better! (The nougat grinds more easily if it's a bit dried out.) If you don't feel like making nougat but are hankering for a hunk of this all the same, you can use whatever nougat you can find at a specialty or gourmet grocery store—just make sure it's nice and stiff before you grind it up.

Though the classic version of this uses milk chocolate, we like the contrast provided by pairing the rich dark chocolate with the sweet nougat. Plus, dark chocolate is good for you. And stuff.

SPECIAL EQUIPMENT

- Food processor; or large heavy-duty zip-top plastic bag and rolling pin or empty wine bottle
- Small (9" x 13") rimmed baking sheet, lined with parchment or wax paper

INGREDIENTS

10 ounces Classic European Nougat (page 145), preferably dried out for a day or two

3 cups (19 ounces/540 g) chopped dark chocolate, or 3 cups (19 ounces/540 g) chopped dark chocolate and ½ cup (110 g) mild vegetable oil

1. Place the nougat in the food processor and pulse until it's ground into coarse crumbs; you'll have about 2 cups. (Alternatively, you can place the nougat in the zip-top bag and pound it with the rolling pin; the pieces will be more coarse, but they'll do in a pinch.)

2. Temper the 3 cups chocolate according to the instructions on page 26, or use the 3 cups chocolate and ½ cup oil to make Cheater's Chocolate Coating as directed on page 32. Place the prepared chocolate in a medium-size bowl.

3. Add the nougat and mix gently but thoroughly with a rubber spatula until completely combined.

4. Pour the mixture onto the prepared baking sheet and spread it into an even layer with the spatula. Allow it to set up until the surface is no longer wet-looking and the chocolate is still somewhat soft to the touch, 5 to 10 minutes.

5. Score the candy into 1½-inch triangles: With a sharp chef's knife, make a crosshatch pattern on the surface of the chocolate (to form diamond shapes); then score a straight line widthwise through the centers of the diamonds to form triangles. Allow the candy to set up completely, 20 to 30 minutes.

6. Remove the candy from the baking sheet, place it on a cutting board, and cut along the score lines, pressing down firmly on the knife with both hands, to make triangular pieces.

Store the candy in an airtight container at cool room temperature for up to 6 months.

MODERATE

PB&J CUPS

MAKES ABOUT 100 BITE-SIZE CANDIES

This is a fancified version of the childhood favorite. While some people might say, "Why put jam in a peanut butter cup?," we say, "Why on earth not?" Liz made a version of these when she first started working at Roni-Sue's Chocolates—a celebrated little chocolate shop on the Lower East Side of Manhattan—and was surprised at how popular they were . . . until our PB&J candy bar was born. (For more retro deliciousness from Roni-Sue, check out the Best Buttercrunch Ever on page 204.) But that's a horse of a different color. For now, these make lovely gifts that are sure to please—and note that the peanut butter is interchangeable with an equal amount of almond butter, or any other nut butter that tickles your fancy.

If you're a visual sort of person (as we are), check out the step-by-step photos on page 94 before you start.

SPECIAL EQUIPMENT

- Heatproof spatula
- 3 plastic piping bags or gallon-size zip-top bags (see page 20)
- Kitchen scissors
- 100 small foil candy cups (see Note)
- 2 large (13" x 18") rimmed baking sheets, lined with parchment or wax paper

INGREDIENTS

FOR THE PEANUT BUTTER FILLING

7½ ounces (225 g) white chocolate, chopped (about 1¼ cups)

¼ cup (60 g) heavy (whipping) cream

1 tablespoon (25 g) light corn syrup

¾ cup (135 g) creamy commercial peanut butter, such as Skippy

1 teaspoon (5 g) kosher salt

FOR THE CHOCOLATE CUPS AND GARNISH

4 cups (26 ounces/740 g) chopped dark chocolate, or 4 cups (26 ounces/740 g) chopped dark chocolate and ⅔ cup (150 g) mild vegetable oil

⅔ cup (175 g) seedless raspberry jam

Maldon sea salt or fleur de sel

1. Make the peanut butter filling: In a medium-size microwave-safe bowl, microwave the white chocolate in 15-second intervals, stirring between each with the heatproof spatuala, until it has softened to the touch (it doesn't need to be melted). (Alternatively, soften it in a bowl set over a saucepan of simmering water.) Set aside.

2. Combine the cream and corn syrup in a small (1-quart) saucepan, and cook over medium heat until the mixture is steaming and bubbles are just starting to form around the edge. Remove the pan from the heat and pour the cream mixture over the white chocolate. Allow it to sit for 1 minute; then stir with the spatula until all the white chocolate is melted and the mixture is smooth.

3. Stir in the peanut butter and kosher salt. Transfer the filling to the piping bag and snip a hole ½ inch from the tip; set it aside in a bowl.

4. Make the chocolate for lining the cups: Temper the 4 cups chocolate according to the instructions on page 26, or use the 4 cups chocolate and ⅔ cup oil to make Cheater's Chocolate Coating as directed on page 32. Transfer the prepared chocolate to a piping bag and snip a hole ¼ inch from the tip; set it aside in a bowl.

5. Set half of the foil cups on one of the prepared baking sheets. Working with 10 cups at a time, pipe the chocolate into the cups, filling them halfway. Then, starting with the first cup, tilt each cup to coat the inside completely, and pour the excess chocolate back into the bowl. Turn the coated cups upside down on the baking sheet and let them stand for 30 seconds. Turn the cups right side up and transfer them to the second baking sheet. Repeat with the remaining foil cups. Allow the coated cups to set until the chocolate is firm, 10 minutes.

6. When the peanut butter filling is no longer warm but still pipes easily, pipe it into each cup to fill it about halfway. (If the peanut butter filling hardens slightly, microwave the bag on High for 3 to 5 seconds and knead it thoroughly. Or place the piping bag in a bowl set over a saucepan of simmering water and gently knead it after 30 seconds. Repeat as needed until the mixture pipes easily.)

7. Fill the remaining piping bag with the jam and snip a hole ½-inch from the tip. Pipe a generous ½ teaspoon of jam over the filling in each cup, being careful to avoid getting jam on the rim (which will prevent the top layer of chocolate from properly adhering to the cup).

8. Pipe the remaining chocolate on top of the jam to fill each cup completely. Tap the bottom of each cup gently against the baking sheet to level the chocolate. Top with a few flakes of Maldon salt. Let the filled cups stand until firm to the touch, about 15 minutes.

Store the PB&J Cups in an airtight container for up to 1 week.

NOTE: We use small, sturdy foil cups that are about an inch across the bottom and three-quarters of an inch high. You can find them online at Candyland Crafts (see Resources, page 291); go for the Gold Foil cups, anywhere between size #3 and size #5.

If you can't find those cups, use 200 small baking cups and double-layer them, which makes them sturdier. Working with five cups at a time, fill each cup about one-quarter full of chocolate. Using a finger or a small pastry brush, coat the sides of the cup with chocolate scooped up from the bottom. Allow the chocolate to set, 5 to 10 minutes, and then proceed from step 6.

Variation

If you want to make straight-up PB cups, you can replace the jam with more of the peanut butter filling (this will yield about 25 fewer candies).

ASSEMBLING THE PB&J CUPS

1. Pipe chocolate into the cup to fill it halfway.

2. Pour the excess chocolate back into the bowl.

3. When the chocolate has set, pipe the peanut butter into each cup to fill it halfway.

4. Pipe the jam over the peanut butter filling.

5. Pipe the remaining chocolate on top of the jam.

LIZ SAYS: This recipe makes a lot of peanut butter filling. If you find you don't want to tackle 100 individual candy cups in one go, you can store it right in the piping bag: Simply squeeze out the filling from the bottom inch of the bag, fold down the tip, tape it shut, and refrigerate the filling. It will keep for up to 1 month like this.

Got leftovers? Make sandwich cookies with the PB filling and the chocolate cookie from The Dorie Bar, page 279.

ROCHERS (CRISPY NUT CLUSTERS*)

MAKES ABOUT TWENTY 1½-INCH CANDIES

Rocher means "rock" in French, which these chocolate-covered little treats certainly resemble—but the similarities end there. A mixture of nuts and dried fruit is a traditional choice, though we like the texture of cereal with the nuts. Feel free to use your favorite, but we particularly enjoy Special K (Chex-type cereal's crunch and light sweetness is nice here, too).

In terms of playing around, you can do the same with the liqueur. We often use an orange-flavored liqueur, like Cointreau, or amaretto, but we've given you some other suggestions in the variations that follow.

*Yeah, we giggled. Because we're twelve years old.

SPECIAL EQUIPMENT

- Large (13" x 18") rimmed baking sheet, lined with silicone mat or parchment paper
- 3 medium-size bowls
- Heatproof spatula

INGREDIENTS

1 cup (110 g) assorted raw nuts, such as slivered almonds, cashews, and peanuts, crushed slightly

1 teaspoon (5 g) liqueur, such as Cointreau or amaretto

2 teaspoons (8 g) granulated sugar

1 teaspoon (4 g) fine sea salt

½ cup (55 g) breakfast cereal, such as Special K

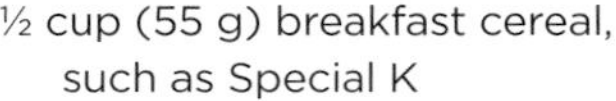

1 cup (6.5 ounces/180 g) chopped dark chocolate, or 1 cup (6.5/ounces, 180 g) chopped dark chocolate and 3 tablespoons (40 g) mild vegetable oil

1. Preheat the oven to 350°F.
2. Toss the nuts, liqueur, sugar, and salt together in the first medium-size bowl until well combined. Spread the mixture in an even layer on the prepared baking sheet and bake, stirring once or twice with the heatproof spatula to ensure that everything is cooking evenly, until lightly browned and toasted, about 15 minutes. Set aside to cool to room temperature.
3. In the second medium-size bowl, toss the nuts with the cereal. When the baking sheet has cooled down to room temp too, flip the silicone mat or parchment (you're going to put the finished rochers on this same sheet).
4. Temper the 1 cup chocolate according to the instructions on page 26, or use the 1 cup chocolate and 3 tablespoons oil to make Cheater's Chocolate Coating as directed on page 32.
5. Gently warm the remaining medium-size bowl by running it under warm water for a few seconds and then drying it *super thoroughly* with paper towels. (Seriously, dry the crap out of it. Water + chocolate = sadface.) Warm two metal tablespoons with your hands.
6. Place about a third of the nut mixture in the warmed bowl, pour 3 tablespoons of the prepared chocolate over it, and stir gently with one of the metal spoons. Working quickly, use the two metal spoons to form about a tablespoon of chocolate-and-nut mixture into a roughly round shape. Place it

on the lined baking sheet, and repeat with the remaining chocolate-and-nut mixture.

7. Once the first batch is shaped, make another one, again using 3 tablespoons of the chocolate and a third of the nut mixture. Proceed this way until all of the chocolate-and-nut mixture has been used up.

8. Allow the rochers to set, at least 15 minutes or up to 1 hour.

Store the rochers in an airtight container in a cool, dry place for up to 2 weeks.

SHAPING THE ROCHERS

1. Pour 3 tablespoons of the chocolate over a third of the nut mixture.

2. Toss, toss, toss (gently, now!).

3. Scoop, shape, and scrape into rochers.

JEN SAYS: You might wonder why this recipe calls for a warmed bowl and spoons. Tempered chocolate (or chocolate coating) will set up on contact with a cold surface, potentially making the shaping and placing of the rochers really difficult. Warming your utensils slightly before you start shaping the candy helps keep it malleable longer, and leaves you with prettier candies. I find my hairdryer to be indispensable for this (strange but true!).

Variations

CRANBERRY STASH Substitute 1 cup raw pistachios for the mixed nuts and use Chartreuse for the liqueur. Toss with ½ cup dried cranberries in step 2.

DATE NIGHT Substitute ½ cup each raw walnuts and raw slivered almonds for the mixed nuts, and use amaretto for the liqueur. Toss with ½ cup chopped dates in step 2.

FIGEDDABOUDIT Substitute 1 cup raw cashews for the mixed nuts, and use triple sec for the liqueur. Toss with ½ cup chopped dried figs in step 2.

MAC ATTACK Substitute 1 cup raw macadamias for the mixed nuts, and substitute white rum for the liqueur. Toss with ¼ cup each chopped dried mango and papaya in step 2.

TAKE ME OUT Substitute 1 cup raw, skinned, unsalted peanuts for the mixed nuts and substitute beer (yup! a brown ale works nicely, though you can use whatever's handy) for the liqueur. Reduce the fine sea salt to ½ teaspoon. Toss with ½ cup Honey Caramel Corn (page 228) in step 2.

MODERATE

HIP-TO-BE SQUARES

MAKES ABOUT 100 ONE-INCH SQUARES

We were going to add a Kit-Kat analog to this book, but between the need for store-bought plain wafers, which are a pain to find, the labor-intensive nature of the candy, and the "rustic"-looking result, we decided against it. Here, instead, is a homestyle riff on the classic French *carré*—which just means "square"—a creamy-crunchy combination of chocolate, hazelnut, and delicately crispy *feuilletine* wafers. The result? Delicious.

You can use either dark or milk chocolate; dark offers a nice counterpoint to the sweet hazelnut flavor of the Nutella, but milk chocolate appeals to our inner child in a way that no high-percentage chocolate ever could. Your move.

The active work time to make the filling is about 3 minutes, so it's a great *Oh-crap-I-have-to-bring-something-to-the-potluck-tomorrow* item. To really speed things up, drizzle the squares with melted chocolate instead of coating them.

SPECIAL EQUIPMENT

- Small (9" x 13") rimmed baking sheet, lined with parchment or wax paper
- Cutting board, covered with parchment or wax paper
- Small offset spatula

INGREDIENTS

3 cups (one 26.5-ounce jar) Nutella or Praline Paste (page 217)

About 1¼ cups (10 ounces/285 g) melted dark or milk chocolate (see page 24)

1½ teaspoons (7 g) fine sea salt

½ cup mild vegetable oil, such as sunflower or safflower

2 cups crushed feuilletine or crushed cornflakes (see Liz Says, opposite)

3 cups (19 ounces/540 g) chopped dark chocolate, or 3 cups (19 ounces/540 g) chopped dark chocolate and ½ cup (110 g) mild vegetable oil, for coating

1. Place the Nutella in a medium-size bowl, add the melted chocolate, and stir well with a rubber spatula until combined.
2. Add the sea salt, oil, and feuilletine, and stir to combine. Pour the mixture onto the prepared baking sheet and spread it in an even layer with the spatula. Cover it with plastic wrap and refrigerate until firm, 60 to 90 minutes.
3. Run the tip of a sharp chef's knife around the edge of the candy to loosen it, if necessary. Gently turn it out onto the prepared cutting board.

4. Temper the 3 cups chocolate according to the instructions on page 26, or use the 3 cups chocolate and ½ cup oil to make Cheater's Chocolate Coating as directed on page 32.

5. Pour ½ cup of the chocolate over the top of the candy and spread it into a thin, even layer with the offset spatula. Allow it to set, about 5 minutes.

6. Place a sheet of parchment paper over the candy and carefully flip it over (the chocolate will be on the bottom). Pour the remaining chocolate over the candy and spread it into an even layer with the offset spatula. Allow it to set up for 2 minutes, then run the tines of a fork through the surface, making a wavy pattern.

7. Score the surface of the chocolate into 1-inch squares using a sharp chef's knife. Allow it to set until the chocolate has firmed up slightly but still has some give, about 5 minutes.

8. Pressing firmly, cut the candy along the score lines. Allow to set completely, 10 minutes.

Store the squares, layered with wax or parchment paper, in an airtight container at cool room temperature for up to 3 weeks.

LIZ SAYS: Feuilletine (FOY-uh-teen) is a French confectionery ingredient that falls somewhere between cornflakes and shards of a paper-thin wafer cookie. Cornflakes are a good substitute, as are crushed unfilled Pirouline-style cookies.

It is available online in 1-pound packages at hauserchocolates.com. Or, if you can find a French cookie called Gavottes Crêpe Dentelle, that's essentially the same thing.

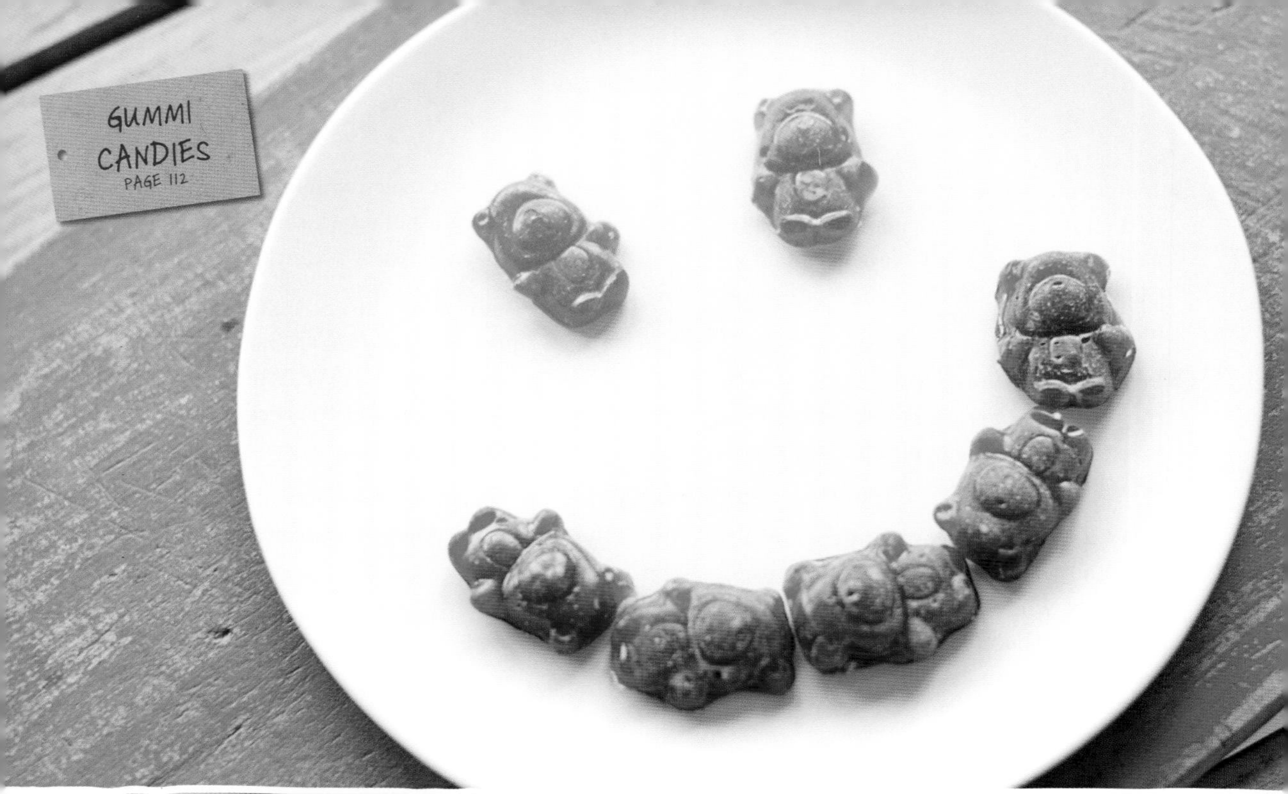
GUMMI CANDIES
PAGE 112

MARISA'S VANILLA BEAN SALTWATER TAFFY
PAGE 149

NON-EVIL TURKISH DELIGHT
PAGE 117

BEER AND PRETZEL CARAMELS
PAGE 133

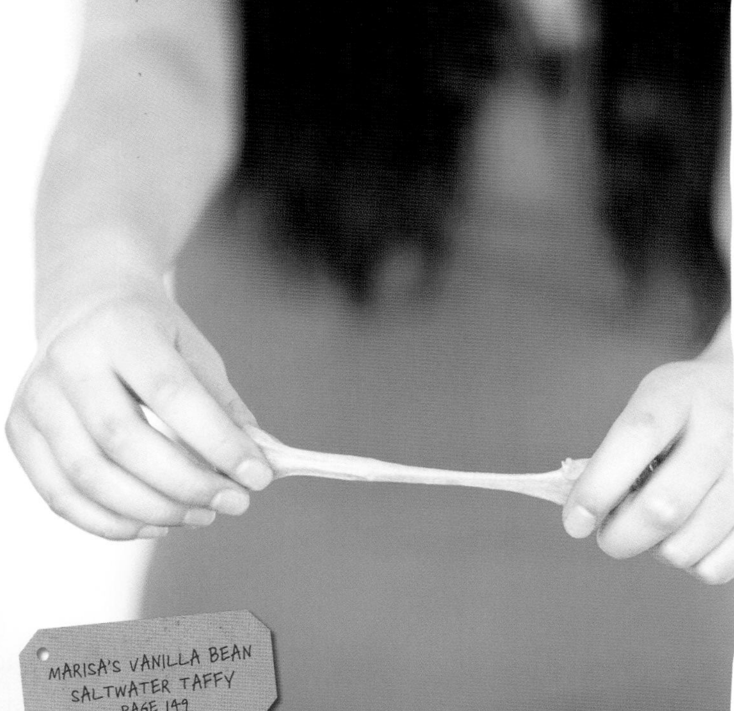

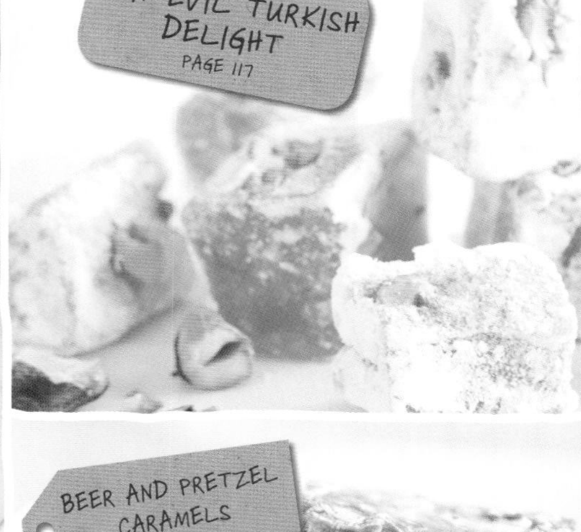

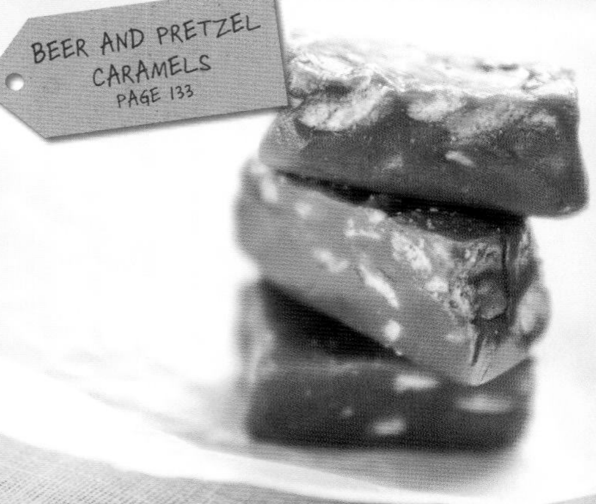

Chapter Three

GUMMI AND GOOEY AND CHEWY, OH MY!

There's something really satisfying about sinking your teeth into a chewy, gooey caramel, or a springy fruit gummi, or a fluffy mallow of marsh. As kids, we loved chewy treats because they always seemed to last longer; now that we have fillings to worry about, we love the soft, yielding texture even more.

Even within this textural category lies a wide spectrum of chewiness. Caramels (pages 123–140) are soft and sticky; if you pull them apart, they make a long string. Taffy (pages 149 and 152) is even more so; a little firmer, a little stickier—the sugar syrup base is what imparts this particular type of chewiness. Gummies (pages 112 and 113) get their bouncety-bounce from gelatin, giving them a gnaw-tastic resilience (same with marshmallow, page 141, which just has air whipped into it). Pâtes de Fruits (page 105) have a jamminess imparted by pectin, which is also used in jams and jellies, while Agar Fruit Jellies (page 109) have a shorter texture and fresher, brighter flavor.

But enough sexy food talk. Before you make anything in this section, we really, strongly urge you to read through the Sugar Is Sweet section on pages 46–55. It really helps to understand sugar theory and the different stages of sugar before you jump in. A quick look at the gelling agents in Candy: It Is Made of Stuff (page 8) wouldn't hurt either. Luckily this book is so amazingly well written and entertaining that it won't seem like a chore!*

*See what we did there?

PÂTES DE FRUITS

MAKES ABOUT 75 ONE-INCH PIECES

The name pâtes de fruits (pronounced paht duh froo-EE) literally means "fruit paste," but doesn't it sound so much nicer in French? These are a very classic confection; almost any traditional candy shop on the Continent is bound to have a version of these, likely arranged in pretty colored mosaics in a clear plastic box.

The fruit really is the star of this recipe, so you'll want to either spring for some professional-grade fruit puree (Perfect Puree and Cap'Fruit are two major brands that are available through Amazon) or make your own with fresh fruit using the recipe that follows.

SPECIAL EQUIPMENT

- Small (9" x 13") rimmed baking sheet
- Candy thermometer
- Cutting board, lined with parchment or wax paper
- Cooling rack (see Nice Rack!, opposite)
- Large (13" x 18") rimmed baking sheet

INGREDIENTS

Cooking spray or vegetable oil

2 cups (450 g) fruit puree, store-bought (see headnote) or homemade (recipe follows)

½ cup (175 g) light corn syrup

3 cups (560 g) granulated sugar, divided in half

1 to 1½ tablespoons (10 to 15 g) powdered pectin (see Note; use the lesser amount if you're making your own fruit puree)

1 tablespoon freshly squeezed lemon juice

About 1½ cups (about 300 g) granulated sugar, preferably superfine, for dredging (see Dredge Report, page 108)

1. Lightly coat the small baking sheet with cooking spray and set it aside.
2. Combine the fruit puree, corn syrup, and 1 cup of the granulated sugar in a medium-size (4-quart) saucepan, and stir with a heatproof spatula or wooden spoon to mix thoroughly. Place the pan over medium-low heat and allow the mixture to warm through, 5 to 7 minutes.
3. In a small bowl, combine the remaining 1 cup sugar and the pectin, and mix with a small whisk until thoroughly combined.
4. When the fruit mixture is warm to the touch, add the sugar mixture and stir until it's dissolved, about 2 minutes. Add the lemon juice, and increase the heat to medium. Insert the candy thermometer and cook, stirring frequently with the spatula until the mixture comes to a boil, 10 minutes. Then stir constantly, scraping the bottom of the pot with the spatula until the temperature reaches 224°F/107°C (thread stage), about 45 to 60 minutes.
5. Pour the mixture into the prepared small baking sheet and allow it to set up at room temperature until it is firm to the touch, at least 6 hours or overnight. If you're worried about anything getting stuck to the surface, cover it loosely with a piece of plastic wrap.

6 Once the candy has set, gently turn it out onto the lined cutting board. Oil a sharp chef's knife lightly with cooking spray, and using quick, firm slicing motions, cut the candy into 1-inch squares.

7 Place the dredging sugar in a small bowl. Set the cooling rack over the large baking sheet. Add the candy, a few pieces at a time, to the bowl of sugar and toss to coat. Arrange the dredged candies in a single layer on the rack and leave them to dry out and form a crispy coating, at least 8 hours or up to 24.

Store the candies, layered with parchment or wax paper, in a loosely covered container at cool room temperature for up to 3 weeks.

NOTE: Powdered pectin is widely available at grocery stores; Sure-Jell and MCP are likely the brands you'll see. Pectin usually comes in 1- to 2-ounce containers, so you'll have to buy a few. Or you can buy bulk pectin online relatively cheaply (see Resources, page 291).

NICE RACK!

A cooling rack—one of those wire doohickeys you put your just-baked cookies on—is necessary when making these (as well as other jelly candies) because they need to dry out; if they're resting on a solid surface, the air can't circulate all the way around them. There really is no substitute for a cooling rack; the best and most versatile kind is also known as an icing screen, and actually has a grid of wire instead of just parallel wires. You'll be fine with a standard cooling rack, though—as long as the wires are close enough together so that whatever is drying on them doesn't fall through. You can find both types of racks at most any kitchen supply shop (see Resources, page 291).

EASY

FRUIT PUREE

MAKES 2½ CUPS

Anything that makes a good jam will make a good pâte de fruit. Just avoid fresh pineapple, kiwi, and papaya—these fruits contain enzymes that prevent gels from forming, so you'll want to either use canned versions (the cooking during the canning process deactivates said enzymes) or choose another fruit. If you are making this for the Agar Fruit Jellies on page 109, omit the apples called for.

SPECIAL EQUIPMENT

- Blender or food processor fitted with steel blade

INGREDIENTS

1 cup water

1 cup fruit (ideally fresh; see headnote), such as hulled berries (halved if large), cut-up pitted stone fruit, or 1-inch pieces of peeled citrus

1 medium-size (3-inch) firm-fleshed apple, such as Granny Smith or Fuji, peeled, cored, and cut into 1-inch pieces

Combine all of the ingredients in the blender, and process on high speed until the mixture is very smooth, 1 to 2 minutes. No need to strain it to remove any pulp: the pulp is what gives the candies body and chew, so just get it as smooth as you can with your blender.

Store the fruit puree in an airtight container for up to 1 day in the fridge; up to 3 months in the freezer.

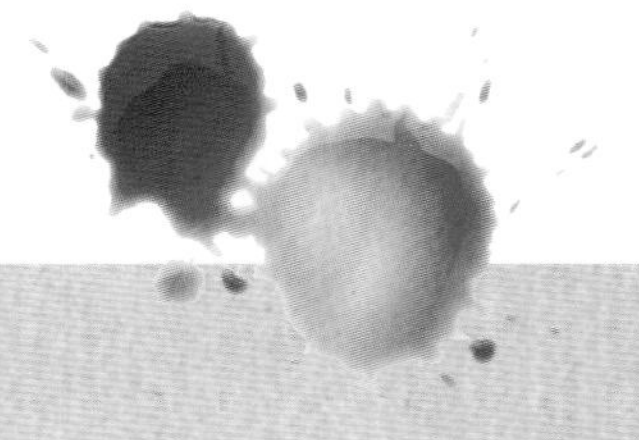

DREDGE REPORT

When we say "dredge the candy in sugar," we just mean "dump it in the bowl of sugar and roll it around to coat it." Coating pâtes de fruits and similar candies in sugar gives them a pretty frosted appearance and actually helps to dehydrate the outer layer, forming a protective (and delightfully crispy) crust that keeps the inside fresh. Superfine sugar (also called caster sugar), if you can find it, is best for this purpose. But if you can't find it, just give the same amount of regular granulated sugar a few quick pulses in a spice grinder or food processor, and you're good to go.

In the process of dredging, some little bits and pieces of candy will dislodge and bury themselves in the sugar. Not to worry: simply pass the sugar through a fine-mesh strainer when you're done, and it's ready for any other use you might have for it.

If it's humid out when you need to dry your candies, you can rig up your (turned-off) oven as a dehydrator of sorts: Place a bowl filled with 2 cups of uncooked rice on the floor of the oven, and set the sheet of dredged candies on a rack. Keep the oven closed (and, again, turned off!) until the candies are sufficiently dry, 8 to 24 hours; then store them as directed. They should keep just fine. (And the rice is perfectly okay to cook and eat afterward.)

EASY

AGAR FRUIT JELLIES

MAKES ABOUT 75 ONE-INCH PIECES

It's hard to describe the texture of agar jellies as opposed to that of pectin jellies (Pâtes de Fruits, page 105). To us, the main difference is that agar jellies have a shorter, less chewy texture. Jen also points out their bright and fresh fruit flavor, which they owe to the addition of juice or puree *after* the syrup is cooked. You can even add—wait for it—booze! Just substitute it, cup for cup, for up to half of the total amount of puree. That is, if you're into that kind of thing. (We're totally into that kind of thing.)

SPECIAL EQUIPMENT

- Small (9" x 13") rimmed baking sheet
- Candy thermometer
- Heatproof spatula
- Cutting board, lined with parchment or wax paper
- 1-inch cookie cutters (optional)
- Cooling rack (see Nice Rack!, page 107)
- Large (13" x 18") rimmed baking sheet

INGREDIENTS

Cooking spray or vegetable oil

¼ cup (25 g) powdered agar agar (see page 9)

1⅓ cups (250 g) granulated sugar

1¾ cups (400 g) water

1 teaspoon (4 g) salt

1⅓ cups (450 g) light corn syrup

1¾ cups (400 g) unsweetened fruit juice or puree (see Fruit Puree, page 107)

1 tablespoon (15 g) freshly squeezed lemon juice

About 1½ cups (300 g) sugar, preferably superfine, for dredging (see Dredge Report, opposite)

1. Lightly coat the small baking sheet with cooking spray, and set it aside.

2. Whisk the agar and granulated sugar together in a small bowl. Set it aside.

3. In a medium-size (4-quart) saucepan, bring the water and salt to a boil over high heat. Whisk in the agar mixture, stirring well for 1 to 2 minutes to ensure that all the agar is dissolved. Insert the candy thermometer.

4. Gently add the corn syrup, being careful not to splatter as you pour it in. Reduce the heat to medium-high and cook, stirring constantly with the spatula (make sure to scrape the bottom of the pan), until the mixture registers 223°F/106°C (thread stage) on the thermometer, about 30 minutes.

5. Remove the pan from the heat, but leave the candy thermometer submerged in the agar mixture. Allow the mixture to cool until the thermometer reads 195°F/90°C (dissolve-to-thread stage), 20 to 30 minutes.

6. Add the fruit juice and lemon juice to the agar mixture, and stir with the spatula until well combined. Pour the mixture into the prepared baking sheet. Let it sit until it's completely cooled and set, at least 1 hour.

7. Gently turn the candy out onto the lined cutting board. Lightly coat the cookie cutters or a sharp chef's knife with cooking spray, and cut the candy into 1-inch pieces (if using a knife, cut it into squares or other shapes).

8. Place the dredging sugar in a small bowl. Set the cooling rack over the large baking sheet. Add the candy, a few pieces at a time, to the bowl of sugar and toss to coat. Arrange the dredged candies in a single layer on the rack and leave them to dry out overnight. (This may take a little longer when using fruit juice or where the climate is very humid; when the candies are ready, a crust of sugar will have formed on the surface.)

Store the jellies in a loosely covered container at room temperature for up to 3 weeks.

LIZ SAYS: Agar agar, unlike gelatin, can be remelted and reset indefinitely—so any scraps you have left over after cutting the jellies can be placed in a saucepan over low heat, melted, poured out again, and cut into additional candies. Just remember: Cooking the fruit juice changes its flavor, so you really don't want to remelt it more than once if you don't have to.

EASY

GUMMI CANDIES

MAKES ABOUT 100 ONE-INCH GUMMIES

Here's the big secret: Gummi candies are basically pumped-up Jell-O. We've tried making naturally flavored gummies at home, from scratch, but—honestly?—the industrial-strength flavors in gelatin dessert mixes are integral to the gummi experience, and there's just nothing you can make at home that will compare. The great thing is that there are so many flavors available, and this recipe is so easy that you can make several batches of different flavors and mix them together for favor bags, or just as a treat to have around the house.

SPECIAL EQUIPMENT

- Candy molds with approximately 100 one-inch cavities, or small (9" x 13") baking sheet
- Cutting board lined with parchment or wax paper (optional)
- Sharp chef's knife, pizza cutter, or 1-inch cookie cutters (optional)

INGREDIENTS

Cooking spray or vegetable oil

2 boxes (6 ounces each) fruit-flavored gelatin dessert mix, such as Jell-O

4 tablespoons unflavored powdered gelatin (1 ounce/30 g total)

⅔ cup (175 g) cold water

About ½ cup cornstarch, sifted (60 g), superfine sugar (100 g), or sour sugar (100 g; see Jen Says, opposite), for dredging (see Dredge Report, page 108)

1. Lightly coat the candy molds or baking sheet with cooking spray, and set it aside.
2. In a small (2-quart) saucepan, stir together the flavored and unflavored gelatins with the cold water; allow the mixture to sit until the gelatin has softened and set slightly, 5 minutes.
3. Place the bloomed gelatin mixture over very low heat and melt it, stirring it constantly (do not allow it to boil—it won't firm up properly), 3 to 5 minutes.
4. Pour the melted gelatin into the prepared molds or baking sheet, and place it in the refrigerator until completely set, about 30 minutes.
5. Turn the gelatin out of the molds. Or if you're using the baking sheet, gently turn the slab out onto the prepared cutting board and cut it into 1-inch pieces with the sharp chef's knife or pizza cutter; or lightly oil cookie cutters and cut the slab into shapes.
6. Place the cornstarch, superfine sugar, or sour sugar in a small bowl. If using cornstarch, dredge the candies in it; if using one of the sugars, roll the candies in it. Place the coated candies in a sieve and toss gently to remove any excess coating.

Store the gummies in an airtight container at cool room temperature, for up to 2 months.

JEN SAYS: Sour sugar is just what it sounds like—sugar that's sweet and also, um, sour. It gives gummies that Sour-Patch-like kick. To make it, stir together ½ cup (95 g) granulated sugar and ¾ teaspoon (3 g) citric acid in a small bowl. (Citric acid also travels incognito as Sour Salt or Lemon Salt in the canning section of some grocery stores, or online at Sugarcraft or Amazon; see Resources, page 291.)

Variation

GUMMI TWO-FERS Halve the recipe, and make the first half one flavor, using one box of Jell-O; pour it into the molds or baking sheet and place it in the fridge to set up slightly. Meanwhile, make the second half a different flavor (and color), and allow it to cool to lukewarm. When the first half has partially set but is still soft (after about 10 minutes), carefully pour the second half on top and allow them to set together completely. Voilà—two-tone gummies!

EASY

CANDIED CITRUS PEEL

MAKES ABOUT 75 PIECES

This is a very traditional confection, one that's been around for a while, like its buddy marzipan (see page 175). It's especially versatile: You can use candied peels as a lovely dessert garnish, dice them and add them to Rochers (page 95) or baked goods, or dip them in dark chocolate for a sophisticated stand-alone sweet. The multiple boilings may seem like a pain, but they're really necessary to remove the bitterness from the peels. Trust us; there's a lot of history backing up this recipe.

SPECIAL EQUIPMENT

- Cooling rack (see Nice Rack!, page 107)
- Large (13" x 18") baking sheet, lined with parchment paper (two of these if dipping peels in chocolate)

INGREDIENTS

FOR CANDYING THE PEELS

5 large (5-inch) oranges or medium-size grapefruits, or 7 medium-size (3-inch) lemons or limes

Cold water

2½ cups (475 g) granulated sugar

1 cup (350 g) light corn syrup

FOR DREDGING AND FINISHING

2 cups (400 g) granulated sugar, preferably superfine, or sour sugar (see Jen Says, page 113), for dredging (see Dredge Report, page 108)

2 cups (13 ounces/370 g) chopped dark chocolate, or 2 cups (13 ounces/375 g) chopped dark chocolate and ⅓ cup (75 g) mild vegetable oil, for dipping (optional)

1. Wash the fruit thoroughly with soap and water to remove any wax. Cut the fruit into quarters with a paring knife, and slice away the pulp from each quarter (see page 116; save it for juice, lemonade, or whatever you like). Remove as much of the spongy white pith as possible without damaging the outer peel. Slice the cleaned peels into ½-inch-wide strips.

2. Place the peels in a medium-size (3- to 4-quart) saucepan and add cold water to cover. Bring it to a boil over high heat. Once the water has come to a rolling boil, pour it off through the strainer, reserving the peels. Refill the saucepan with cold water, add the peels, and repeat the boil-strain procedure two more times.

3. Combine the sugar, corn syrup, and 1 cup of cold water in the same saucepan and bring the mixture to a boil over high heat. Reduce the heat to medium and simmer, uncovered, for 10 minutes.

4. Add the reserved peels to the sugar syrup. Return the heat to high and bring the syrup back to a rolling boil. Then reduce the heat to medium and keep the mixture at a low simmer, uncovered, until the syrup thickens somewhat and the peels look slightly translucent, 1 hour.

5. Remove the saucepan from the heat and allow it to sit until the syrup is lukewarm to cool, 2 to 3 hours. Drain the syrup from the peels (you can reserve it to sweeten tea, cocktails, and other cold drinks). Set the cooling rack over the prepared baking sheet and spread the peels evenly on the

cooling rack, allowing them to drain for 30 to 45 minutes, until they are no longer wet but still sticky.

6. Place the dredging sugar in a small bowl. Dredge the peels in the sugar and return them to the cooling rack. Allow them to sit, uncovered, until they are dry and only very slightly sticky to the touch, 12 to 18 hours. The candied peels are ready to eat!

7. If you want to gussy up the peels with chocolate: Temper the 2 cups chopped dark chocolate according to the instructions on page 26, or use the 2 cups chopped dark chocolate and ⅓ cup oil to make the Cheater's Chocolate Coating as directed on page 32. Grasp the end of a candied peel and dip it about halfway in the chocolate; place the peel on the second prepared baking sheet. Repeat until all the peels are dipped; allow them to set up, 15 to 30 minutes.

Store the candied peels in an airtight container at cool room temperature for up to 1 month.

Variations

Substitute honey for the corn syrup, or add a little ground cayenne pepper to the dredging sugar.

I WANT SECTIONAL PEELING

Cutting the pulp of citrus fruit from the rind can be tricky; here are a couple of tips to help you out:

• Use a sharp knife. This is true for everything you do in your kitchen (a sharp knife is a safe knife!), but especially when you're dealing with juicy/slippery stuff.

• Place the quartered fruit with one flat side on your cutting surface. Make a ½-inch cut with the tip of the knife at the end of the quartered fruit, in the white pith between the pulp and the rind. Often, once you've made this cut, you can just set the knife aside, grab the rind with the fingertips of one hand and the skin surrounding the pulp with the fingertips of the other hand, and gently pull them apart. If that doesn't work, turn the fruit so that the rind side is down and the end with the cut is facing you. Slide the knife in the cut, grab the rind with the fingers of your other hand, and gently slice the knife away from you, toward the other end of the fruit. This should take care of most of the pulp, and you can remove the rest in a couple more passes with the knife.

NON-EVIL TURKISH DELIGHT

MAKES ABOUT 100 ONE-INCH CANDIES

If you're anything like us, the first thing you think of when you hear "Turkish delight" is Edmund, the jerky younger brother from *The Lion, the Witch and the Wardrobe* who's plied with Turkish delight by the evil White Queen. We never really had this candy growing up, and so it has a bit of a magical association. How could something be so good that it would cause you to betray your family?

Well, to be fair, the queen's Turkish delight was actually magical—we can't promise the same for this. But we *can* promise a delightfully soft and chewy sweet that's better than any store-bought version you've encountered. Rosewater is the traditional flavoring, and is available at many specialty and gourmet stores (see Resources, page 291), but feel free to replace it with the same amount of whatever pure extract you like, such as orange or vanilla.

Do note that this recipe requires expert timing (don't worry: that doesn't mean you have to be fast as lightning)—read it through a couple of times before you start! It's not a difficult recipe, but if you don't have a good idea of how everything gets put together before you begin, it's easy to bamboozle yourself in the middle. Be a good Scout and be prepared!

SPECIAL EQUIPMENT

- Small (9″ x 13″) rimmed baking sheet
- Heatproof spatula or wooden spoon
- Candy thermometer
- Large cutting board

Cooking spray or vegetable oil

FOR THE SUGAR SYRUP

3 cups (575 g) granulated sugar

½ cup (175 g) honey

½ cup (120 g) water

Pinch of cream of tartar

FOR THE CORNSTARCH MIXTURE

1 cup (150 g) cornstarch

1 cup (130 g) confectioners' sugar

2½ cups (600 g) water

1 teaspoon (3 g) cream of tartar

FOR THE FLAVORING

2½ teaspoons (12 g) rosewater

2 cups (300 g) shelled roasted unsalted pistachios (if you can only find them raw, check out how to toast them yourself on page 284)

2 or 3 drops red food coloring (optional)

FOR CUTTING AND DREDGING

About ¼ cup confectioners' sugar, for dusting the cutting board

½ cup cornstarch sifted together with 1 cup confectioners' sugar

1. Generously coat the baking sheet with cooking spray, and set it aside.

2. Make the sugar syrup: Combine the sugar, honey, water, and cream of tartar in a medium-size (4-quart) saucepan, and mix with the heatproof spatula to combine. Bring the mixture to a boil over high heat, and insert the candy thermometer. Reduce the heat to medium-high and cook, without stirring, until the temperature reaches 260°F/127°C (hard ball stage), about 15 minutes.

3. Meanwhile (keeping an eye on the sugar syrup), make the cornstarch mixture: In a large (6-quart) saucepan, whisk together the cornstarch, confectioners' sugar, water, and cream of tartar to combine. Once the sugar syrup reaches 250°F/121°C (firm ball stage), place the cornstarch mixture over medium heat and cook, stirring

constantly with the whisk; it will thicken and boil quickly, 2 to 3 minutes. Turn off the heat, but leave the mixture on the hot burner; stir well a few times with a whisk, and set aside.

4. At this point, the sugar syrup should be close to 260°F/127°C (hard ball stage); when it reaches that temperature, remove it from the heat and carefully pour it into the cornstarch mixture. Stir well with the whisk to combine. Bring everything to a low boil over medium heat. Then reduce the heat to low and cook at a low simmer, stirring frequently with the spatula, until the mixture is thick and gluey and a light golden color, 30 to 45 minutes. Don't turn your back on it! You need to make sure to scrape the bottom of the pan with the spatula every few minutes to prevent scorching and lumps.

5. Remove the pan from the heat and add the flavorings: stir in the rosewater, pistachios, and food coloring (if using).

6. Wearing oven mitts, immediately pour the candy into the prepared baking sheet. Place a piece of plastic wrap directly on the surface of the candy to prevent it from forming a skin as it cools. Allow it to cool until it has set and is firm and cool to the touch, 6 to 8 hours.

7. Gently peel off the plastic wrap. Dust the cutting board with the confectioners' sugar. Run the tip of a paring knife between the candy and the sheet, and gently turn the candy out onto the prepared board.

8. Place the cornstarch mixture in a medium-size bowl. Generously coat a sharp chef's knife with cooking spray, and use a gentle slicing motion to cut the candy into 1-inch squares. Dredge the pieces in the cornstarch mixture until well coated.

Store the Turkish delights, layered with wax paper, in an airtight container at cool room temperature for up to 1 month.

WHAT THE WHAT IS CREAM OF TARTAR?

Good question! Well, it doesn't have anything to do with cream, and it won't contribute to any unwanted buildup on your teeth. Cream of tartar is made from tartaric acid, an acid-salt that forms naturally during the winemaking process and is collected and purified. The acidity of cream of tartar is what makes it do what it does—which is inhibit crystal formation (it helps to keep Turkish delight nice and smooth). There really aren't any substitutes for cream of tartar; if you're seriously in a pinch, you can add the same amount of white vinegar or fresh lemon juice, but those both contribute flavor to the candy and aren't as effective. Cream of tartar is cheap, widely available, and effective. Just go get a container, would ya?

MODERATE

GOODY GOODY GUMDROPS

MAKES ABOUT 80 ONE-INCH CANDIES

These won't end up in the classic little domed gumdrop shape (unless you have a bunch of candy molds and more patience than we can muster), but they'll have the same chew, the same bright colors (standard grocery-store food coloring works great), and the same fruit flavors as those old-timey favorites. Except they'll be better.

SPECIAL EQUIPMENT

- Small (9″ x 13″) rimmed baking sheet
- Large (13″ x 18″) rimmed baking sheet, lined with parchment or wax paper
- Sharp chef's knife or small cookie cutters

INGREDIENTS

Cooking spray or vegetable oil

1½ cups (350 g) apple juice

5 tablespoons (1¼ ounces/40 g) unflavored powdered gelatin

4 cups (775 g) granulated sugar

Food coloring (optional)

Natural or artificial fruit flavoring (see Playing Flavorites, opposite)

About 2 cups (375 g) granulated sugar, preferably superfine, for dredging (see Dredge Report, page 108)

1. Coat the small baking sheet with cooking spray, and set it aside.

2. Place the apple juice and gelatin in a small bowl, and allow the mixture to sit until the gelatin is fully hydrated and softened, 5 minutes.

3. Combine the gelatin mixture and the 4 cups sugar in a medium-size (4-quart) saucepan, and bring to a boil over medium heat. Then reduce the heat to medium-low and continue to cook, stirring occasionally, until it forms a syrup, 10 minutes. Remove the syrup from the heat.

4. Add the food coloring, if using, and 1 teaspoon of fruit flavoring, and mix well. Fill a small bowl with cold water and test the flavor of the gelatin mixture: Drop ½ teaspoon or so into the water; when it firms up, taste it. If need be, add more fruit flavoring, a few drops at a time, stir well, and repeat the test until you get the desired taste.

5. Pour the candy onto the prepared small baking sheet, and allow it to set up until it's cool and firm to the touch, about 2 hours.

6. Lightly oil a cutting board and the knife with cooking spray. Run the knife around the edge of the candy to release it from the baking sheet, and gently turn it out onto the cutting board. If using the knife, cut the candy into 1-inch squares with a slicing motion. Alternatively, coat the small cookie cutters with cooking spray and use those to punch out shapes.

7. Place the 2 cups dredging sugar in a small bowl. Dredge the candies in the sugar, place them on the lined large baking sheet, and let them dry, 2 hours.

Store the gumdrops in an airtight container, layered with parchment or wax paper, at cool room temperature for up to 2 weeks.

PLAYING FLAVORITES

Flavorings are often available at specialty grocery stores, but for a wide range of options, you'll want to check online (see Resources, page 291). Amazon carries many brands; LorAnn, Frontier, and Nature's Flavors offer the best variety—cantaloupe, lychee, pumpkin, root beer, and pretty much everything in between. For the purposes of this book, natural and artificial flavorings work equally well. "Natural" simply means the materials to make the flavors have been sourced from natural ingredients (defined as "spice, fruit or fruit juice, vegetable or vegetable juice, edible yeast, herb, bark, bud, root, leaf or similar plant material, meat, seafood, poultry, eggs, dairy products, or fermentation products thereof" in the actual FDA regulations). "Artificial" means the flavors, while often chemically identical, have been synthesized. The choice is completely up to you.

MODERATE

SEA SALT CARAMELS

MAKES ABOUT 120 ONE-INCH PIECES

When we started Liddabit, our foundation was the candy bars. Sure, we had a couple other items—lollipops, things like that—so that people could buy something smaller if they wanted, but we never planned on doing a sea salt caramel. "It's been done," we said. "We don't want to step on anyone's toes," we said. "Boring," we said. Well, one messed-up batch of Snacker caramel (see page 256) sprinkled with salt, and we changed our tune. The Sea Salt Caramel has since become our best seller, and we remain humble and quiet. (Our mouths are too full of this caramel to talk, anyway.)

SPECIAL EQUIPMENT

- Large (13" x 18") rimmed baking sheet
- Candy thermometer
- Heatproof spatula
- Cutting board, lined with parchment or wax paper
- Wax twisting papers (see Resources, page 291)

INGREDIENTS

3½ tablespoons (50 g) unsalted butter, plus about 1 teaspoon for greasing the baking sheet

1¾ cups (350 g) granulated sugar

1½ cups (12 ounces/375 g) evaporated milk

⅔ cup (160 g) heavy (whipping) cream

1 vanilla bean, split open and seeds scraped out, pod reserved; ½ teaspoon vanilla paste (see page 11); or 1 teaspoon pure vanilla extract

¾ cup plus 1 tablespoon (300 g) light corn syrup

1 tablespoon (20 g) coarse sea salt

Cooking spray or vegetable oil

1. Grease the baking sheet with the 1 teaspoon butter, and set it aside on a heatproof surface.

2. Combine the sugar, evaporated milk, heavy cream, and vanilla bean and seeds (if using) in a large (6- to 8-quart) saucepan. Bring to a boil over medium-high heat, uncovered and without stirring.

3. Once the mixture has come to a boil, insert the candy thermometer. Add the light corn syrup, and stir gently with the spatula until everything is mixed well. Reduce the heat to medium-low and cook, stirring often and making sure to scrape the bottom of the pot to keep the mixture from burning, until the mixture reaches 230°F/110°C (thread stage), about 30 minutes.

4. Add the 3½ tablespoons butter and the vanilla paste or extract (if using). If you used a vanilla bean, fish it out with a slotted spoon. Stirring continuously, cook the caramel until it reaches 241°F/116°C (soft-to-firm ball stage), 15 to 20 minutes; it will be a deep tawny color and have slow, rolling bubbles in the center. Remove it from the heat.

5. Stir in the salt and vanilla paste or extract (if using), making sure they're distributed evenly. Put on oven mitts and carefully pour the caramel onto the prepared baking sheet. Allow it to cool completely until it's firm to the touch, at least 3 hours, preferably overnight. (If it's humid, cover the caramel tightly with plastic wrap and store it at cool room temperature until you can cut and wrap it in wax paper.)

6. Lightly oil a sharp chef's knife with cooking spray, and run the tip around the edge of the baking sheet to release the caramel. Gently turn the caramel out onto the lined cutting board, and cut it into 1-inch squares. Wrap the pieces in wax twisting paper (to turn the squares into little logs, fold each piece over on itself, wrap the twisting paper around it and roll the wrapped caramel against the cutting board, then twist the ends of the paper shut).

Store the caramels in an airtight container, at cool room temperature for up to 4 weeks; they'll last for up to 3 months in the refrigerator.

NOTE: We highly recommend a vanilla bean for this recipe. Boiling the scraped bean with the cream gives the vanilla flavor (yes, it is a flavor) a kick in the pants, and the crunchy little flecks add a certain something that you just can't get with extract. Vanilla paste (see Resources, page 291) is a good substitute if you can't get your hands on a bean.

MODERATE

SALTED CHOCOLATE CARAMELS

MAKES ABOUT 120 ONE-INCH PIECES

This is one of those candies we'll forget about for a while, and then when we eat one, we say to ourselves, "Hot dang! That's really good." It can be easy to forget sometimes, in this crazy mixed-up world, how pleasurable a simple combination like caramel, chocolate, and salt can be. If you've never had a real chocolate caramel, we'll spare you the attempt at describing the experience of eating one—just go ahead, make this, and find out for yourself. (Hint: it starts with a D and ends with an Elightful.) When we're feeling extra fancy, we like to reduce butter to 2¼ tablespoons and add 1 teaspoon black truffle oil. Yum!

SPECIAL EQUIPMENT

- Large (13" x 18") rimmed baking sheet
- Candy thermometer
- Heatproof spatula
- Cutting board, lined with parchment or wax paper
- Wax twisting papers (see Resources, page 291)

INGREDIENTS

3½ tablespoons (50 g) unsalted butter, plus about 1 teaspoon for greasing the baking sheet

1¾ cups (350 g) granulated sugar

3½ ounces (100 g) unsweetened dark chocolate, chopped into small pieces (about ½ cup)

1½ cups (12 ounces/375 g) evaporated milk

⅔ cup (160 g) heavy (whipping) cream

¾ cup plus 1 tablespoon (300 g) light corn syrup

1 tablespoon (20 g) coarse sea salt

Cooking spray or vegetable oil

1. Grease the baking sheet with the 1 teaspoon butter, and set it aside on a heatproof surface.

2. Combine the sugar, chocolate, evaporated milk, and heavy cream, in a large (6- to 8-quart) saucepan or stockpot. Bring to a boil over medium-high heat, uncovered and without stirring.

3. Once the mixture has come to a boil, insert the candy thermometer. Add the corn syrup, and stir gently with the heatproof spatula until everything is mixed well. Reduce the heat to medium-low and cook, stirring often and making sure to scrape the bottom of the pot to keep the mixture from burning, until the mixture reaches 230°F/110°C (thread stage), about 30 minutes.

4. Add the 3½ tablespoons butter and, stirring continuously, cook the caramel until it reaches 238°F/115°C (soft ball stage), 15 to 20 minutes. Remove the caramel from the heat.

5. Stir in the salt, making sure to mix well so that it's distributed evenly. Wearing oven mitts, carefully pour the caramel onto the prepared baking sheet. Allow it to cool completely until it's firm to the touch, at least 3 hours, preferably overnight. (If it's humid, cover the caramel with plastic wrap until you can cut it and wrap it in wax paper.)

6. Lightly coat a sharp chef's knife with cooking spray, and run the tip around the edge of the baking sheet to release the caramel. Gently turn the caramel out onto the lined cutting board, and cut it into 1-inch squares. Wrap the pieces in wax twisting paper (to turn the squares into little logs, fold each piece over on itself, wrap the twisting paper around it and roll the wrapped caramel against the cutting board, then twist the ends of the paper shut).

Store the caramels in an airtight container at cool room temperature for up to 4 weeks; they'll last for up to 3 months in the refrigerator.

MODERATE

FIG AND RICOTTA CARAMELS

MAKES ABOUT 120 ONE-INCH PIECES

We debuted this caramel at a wine-tasting event in the spring of 2010, and weren't quite sure what to expect. Sure, we thought replacing some of the dairy in the recipe with ricotta was brilliant; and sure, we love figs and balsamic vinegar. But would anyone else? Turns out they did, and the fig and ricotta is now a fixture on our seasonal menu.

We like these as an after-dinner treat with a sip or two of port wine.

SPECIAL EQUIPMENT

- Large (13" x 18") rimmed baking sheet
- Silicone mat or parchment paper
- Blender, or immersion blender and large bowl
- Candy thermometer
- Heatproof spatula
- Cutting board, lined with parchment or wax paper
- Wax twisting papers (see Resources, page 291)

INGREDIENTS

Cooking spray or vegetable oil

½ cup (100 g) whole-milk ricotta cheese

1⅓ cups (10 ounces/275 g) evaporated milk

1½ cups (315 g) heavy (whipping) cream

2 cups (340 g) granulated sugar

1 teaspoon (6 g) kosher salt

1 cup (300 g) light corn syrup

4 tablespoons (½ stick/60 g) unsalted butter

3 large (75 g) dried figs, finely chopped

2 teaspoons balsamic vinegar reduction (see Note) or Reductiono Balsamico (recipe follows)

1. Lightly coat the inner rim of the baking sheet with cooking spray. Then line the sheet with the silicone mat or parchment, and set it aside on a heatproof surface.

2. Puree the ricotta, evaporated milk, and heavy cream in the blender or place it in a large bowl and have at it with an immersion blender. Pass the ricotta mixture through a strainer to remove any residual clumps.

3. Combine the ricotta mixture, sugar, and salt in a large (6-quart) heavy-bottomed saucepan and bring to a boil over medium-high heat, about 7 minutes.

4. Insert the candy thermometer, stir in the light corn syrup, and continue to cook over medium-high heat. It will want to boil over; stay close by and stir it often with the spatula to avoid making a mess on your stove. (Make sure to scrape the bottom of the pot as you stir, to keep the mixture from burning.) When the mixture comes to 230°F/110°C (thread stage), add the butter, dried figs, and balsamic vinegar reduction and, stirring constantly,

cook it until it reaches 241°F/115°C (soft-to-firm ball stage).

5. Put on your oven mitts, remove the pan from the heat, and carefully pour the caramel onto the prepared baking sheet. Allow it to cool, uncovered, until it is set and cool and firm to the touch, at least 2 hours or overnight. If you're worried about anything sticking to the surface, you can cover it loosely with plastic wrap.

6. Turn the cooled caramel out onto the lined cutting board. Lightly coat a sharp chef's knife with cooking spray, and use it to cut the caramel into 1- by 1½-inch pieces. Wrap each square in wax twisting paper.

Stored in an airtight container at cool room temperature, the caramel will keep for up to 4 weeks; in the fridge, up to 8 weeks.

NOTE: Balsamic vinegar reduction is balsamic vinegar that's been boiled down until it reaches a syruplike consistency. It's available at gourmet food shops and also on Amazon.com; look for *crema de balsamico* or "balsamic cream."

EASY

REDUCTIONO BALSAMICO

MAKES ABOUT ¼ CUP

If you're unable to find balsamic reduction online, you can make it yourself. And if you're feeling sassy, you can make up a fake Italian-ish sounding name for it, like we do. Leftover reduction is amazingly tasty drizzled over salad, cheese, fresh fruit, or vanilla ice cream.

SPECIAL EQUIPMENT

- Heatproof spatula

INGREDIENTS

1 cup balsamic vinegar

1 tablespoon granulated sugar

Combine the vinegar and sugar in a small (1- to 2-quart) saucepan and bring to a boil over medium heat. Reduce the heat to medium-low and cook, stirring constantly with the spatula, until the volume is reduced to ⅓ to ¼ cup and the mixture has a syrupy consistency, 10 to 15 minutes.

Store the reduction in a jar in the fridge for up to 3 weeks.

MODERATE

BROWN SUGAR–COFFEE CARAMELS

MAKES ABOUT 120 ONE-INCH PIECES

One of the things Liz does when she thinks Jen isn't looking is drop a small caramel in her coffee and let it sit for a few minutes. She stirs it up, adds some milk, and drinks this lovely, lightly sweetened drink down to the bottom, where a prize awaits: a gooey, melty lump of coffee-ish caramel. On the other hand, Jen likes her caramel with coffee and cream, via the occasional extra-tall caramel-frapponato with extra whip. We figured this was a good compromise: not too sweet, but with the richness of dark brown sugar to complement the coffee flavor. (That won't stop Liz from plopping it in her morning coffee.)

SPECIAL EQUIPMENT

- Large (13″ x 18″) rimmed baking sheet
- Candy thermometer
- Heatproof spatula
- Cutting board, lined with parchment or wax paper
- Wax twisting papers (see Resources, page 291)

INGREDIENTS

7 tablespoons (100 g) unsalted butter, plus 1 teaspoon for greasing the pan

1¾ cups (350 g) granulated sugar

1½ cups (350 g) packed dark brown sugar

3 cups (24 ounces/750 g) evaporated milk

1⅓ cups (325 g) heavy (whipping) cream

2 teaspoons (12 g) salt

¾ cup plus 2 tablespoons (300 g) light corn syrup

¾ cup plus 2 tablespoons (300 g) dark corn syrup

¼ cup (60 g) Trablit coffee concentrate (see Note)

Cooking spray or vegetable oil

1. Grease the baking sheet with the 1 teaspoon butter, and set it aside on a heatproof surface.

2. Combine the sugars, evaporated milk, heavy cream, and salt in a large (6- to 8-quart) saucepan or stockpot. Bring it to a boil over medium-high heat, uncovered and without stirring.

3. Once the mixture has come to a boil, insert the candy thermometer. Add the light and dark corn syrups, and stir gently with the spatula until everything is well mixed. Reduce the heat to medium-low and cook, stirring often and making sure to scrape the bottom of the pot to keep the mixture from burning, until the mixture reaches 230°F/110°C (thread stage), about 30 minutes.

4. Add the 7 tablespoons butter. Stirring continuously, cook the caramel until it reaches 242°F/117°C (soft-to-firm ball stage), 15 to 20 minutes. Remove it from the heat and stir in the coffee concentrate.

5. Put on your oven mitts, and carefully pour the caramel onto the prepared baking sheet. Allow the caramel to cool until it's firm to the touch, at least 3 hours, preferably overnight. (If it's humid out, cover the cooled caramel with plastic wrap until you're ready to cut and wrap it.)

6. Lightly coat a sharp chef's knife with cooking spray, and run the tip around the edge of the baking sheet to release the caramel. Gently turn the caramel out onto the lined cutting board, and cut it into 1-inch squares. Wrap the pieces in wax twisting paper (to turn the squares into little logs, fold each piece over on itself, wrap the twisting paper around it and roll the wrapped caramel against the cutting board, then twist the ends of the paper shut).

Store the caramels in an airtight container at cool room temperature for up to 4 weeks; in the fridge, up to 3 months.

NOTE: Trablit is a highly concentrated, extra-potent coffee extract, available online through Amazon. If you can't find it or don't want to buy it, you can make your own by dissolving 3 tablespoons instant coffee in just enough hot water to make a paste (about 3 teaspoons).

BEER AND PRETZEL CARAMELS

MAKES ABOUT 75 PIECES

There was a lot of speculation about whether we would include this recipe in the book; the Beer and Pretzel Caramel is one of Liddabit's most popular items, and one of our most unique. We've been making it for years, and it's very close to our hearts. Some said we absolutely had to include it; others said we absolutely had to leave it out.

After much thought and discussion, we realized a few things. We'll be the first to admit: It's kind of a pain in the butt to make these. You have to start a day ahead of time, since the beer reduction alone is a daylong project, and your house will smell like last week's frat party afterward. You gotta crush the pretzels; you gotta babysit the pots; and at the end, these caramels don't last quite as long as our other ones do. So, hey—if you're willing to do the recipe, we're more than happy to give it to you.

Second, we're not worried about exposing any big secrets. Other people in the history of the world may have made beer and pretzel caramels; other people may make beer and pretzel caramels in the future. They will all be different, and we bet they all were or will be delicious. (Though we happen to think these are the best, of course.)

Finally, this recipe so embodies everything about us and why we started Liddabit that we just have to share it. It's a little out-there, it's fun, it's delectable; there's a good hit of salt and a touch of bitterness. We had to do a lot of improvising to come up with the final recipe, and it was very much a labor of love. No one in their right mind would attempt to market and sell something that's so expensive to make. But, lucky for you, we've never been quite in our right minds. Take THAT, haters!

SPECIAL EQUIPMENT

- Small (9" x 13") rimmed baking sheet
- Heatproof spatula
- Candy thermometer
- Cutting board, lined with parchment paper
- Wax twisting papers (see Resources, page 291)

INGREDIENTS

7 tablespoons (100 g) unsalted butter, plus 1 teaspoon for greasing the baking sheet

1 cup (700 g) heavy (whipping) cream

3 cups (600 g) granulated sugar

⅓ cup plus 1 tablespoon (150 g) barley malt syrup (see Notes)

2 teaspoons (10 g) fine sea salt

About ¼ cup (100 g) Beer Reduction (recipe follows)

2½ cups (150 g) crushed and sifted crunchy pretzels (see Notes)

1 teaspoon (5 g) coarse sea salt

1. Grease the bottom and sides of the baking sheet with the 1 teaspoon butter, and set it aside on a heatproof surface.

2. Combine the cream, sugar, malt syrup, fine sea salt, and the 7 tablespoons butter in a large (6- to 8-quart) stockpot. Stir a couple of times with the heatproof spatula just to make sure there aren't any big clumps of dry sugar, and then bring to a boil over high heat.

3. Reduce the heat to medium and insert the candy thermometer. Cook, stirring occasionally, until the mixture reaches 252°F/122°C (hard ball stage), about 20 minutes. (Watch it closely: once it reaches 240°F/115°C (soft ball stage), after about

15 minutes, you'll want to stay nearby and stir it more frequently as it tends to scorch on the bottom of the pot.) Remove the pot from the heat.

4. Stir in the Beer Reduction, then the pretzels and coarse sea salt. Mix thoroughly, scraping the bottom of the pot several times to incorporate everything.

5. Put on your oven mitts and carefully (seriously—please be careful!) pour the caramel onto the prepared baking sheet. Spread it out with the spatula, distributing the pretzel pieces as evenly as possible. Allow it to cool until it's firm to the touch, 1 to 2 hours.

6. Run the tip of a sharp chef's knife around the edges of the baking sheet to loosen the caramel. Turn it out onto the lined cutting board, cut it into 1- by 1½-inch pieces, and wrap them in the wax twisting papers. Store the caramels in an airtight container in the refrigerator for up to 3 weeks (let them come to room temperature before you eat them!).

NOTES: Barley malt syrup, made from sprouted barley grains, is what bridges the gap in this recipe between the innocuous buttery flavor of the base caramel and the sharper zing of the reduced beer. It has a toasty, rich flavor that adds depth but isn't too assertive on its own, perfectly bringing together all the other flavors. You can buy it at any natural foods market, such as Whole Foods.

Snyder's of Hanover is a good, widely available choice for the pretzels; the crushed pieces should be about ½ inch. Sift them before they go into the caramel, otherwise you will end up with a lot of pretzel dust ruining the lovely texture of the candy.

WRAPPER'S DELIGHT

If you're planning on eventually making more than one recipe of chews, caramels, or anything else that needs to be wrapped individually, it's worth investing in a package of wax twisting papers (see Resources, page 291). Wrapping chewy candies individually helps protect them from humidity, thus extending their shelf life (and keeping them from sticking together).

You can cut your own wrappers out of parchment or wax paper—3-inch squares are perfect—but that can get tedious after wrapper number 50 or so. That said, if you have a paper cutter, go ahead and use it!

EASY

BEER REDUCTION

MAKES ABOUT ½ CUP

It helps to open the beer a few hours before you start the reduction. This prevents it from boiling over as the bubbles heat and expand, and therefore it requires less babysitting. However, it's not necessary. This should make just what you need for the caramel recipe; if you end up with extra, just go ahead and toss it in as well.

INGREDIENTS

6 bottles (12 ounces each) beer, preferably a strong dark ale (see Near Beer, below)

1. Pour the contents of 3 of the bottles into a large (6- to 8-quart) pot, and place it over high heat. Stir frequently to dissipate the carbonation and prevent the liquid from boiling over. Once the beer is at a rolling boil, slowly add another bottle and, stirring constantly, bring to a boil again. Repeat until all the beer is in the pot.

2. Cook the beer over high heat, stirring constantly, until all the carbonation has dissipated and it's no longer in danger of boiling over, about 20 minutes.

3. Reduce the heat to medium and continue to cook, stirring occasionally, until the volume of the liquid is dramatically reduced (to about ½ cup) and the reduction has the consistency of real maple syrup (it will thicken to the consistency of fakey pancake syrup as it cools). Remove from the heat and allow it to cool to room temperature.

Store the reduction in an airtight container. It will keep in the fridge for up to 1 month.

NEAR BEER

Believe it or not, it *does* make a difference what kind of beer you use in this recipe. You want a good balance of dark, round flavor and bitter hoppiness. We use a combination of Brooklyn Brewery's East India Pale Ale and Brooklyn Brown Ale and that's worked perfectly for us for years. Any brown ale–pale ale combo should serve you well, though we encourage you to take a field trip and check out some local beers at a nearby bar. Chances are you'll find something awesome that's made around the corner from you.

WORTH IT

TURTLES

MAKES ABOUT 20 THREE-INCH TURTLES

It's been scientifically proven that 97.2 percent of the world's population loves the turtle. There's something for everybody, and yet it's elegant in its simplicity: chocolate, caramel, nuts. It's like a little candy haiku. In fact, here's a turtle haiku for you:

Pretty chocolate shell
Body made of caramel
Nuts for feet; delish.

Turtles also have the distinction of being completely freakin' adorable when you get the proportions right. They totally look like little turtles! Awwwww!

This is one of those recipes that isn't particularly difficult but does require a good game plan. Read it through a couple of times before embarking on it, and you're sure to succeed. (Also check out Funnel of Love, page 139, to learn how to use the candy funnels it calls for.)

SPECIAL EQUIPMENT

- Large (13" x 18") rimmed baking sheet, lined with parchment or wax paper
- Candy thermometer
- Heatproof spatula
- 2 large candy funnels (see Funnel of Love, opposite, and Resources, page 291) or 2-cup or larger heatproof (Pyrex) measuring cup

INGREDIENTS (NO ACTUAL TURTLES!)

¾ cup plus 1 tablespoon (175 g) granulated sugar

¾ cup (6 ounces/185 g) evaporated milk

⅓ cup (80 g) heavy (whipping) cream

½ vanilla bean, split open and seeds scraped out, pod reserved; ¼ teaspoon vanilla paste (see page 11); or ½ teaspoon pure vanilla extract

80 to 100 toasted pecan halves (a generous cup or about 4½ ounces)

½ cup (150 g) light corn syrup

2 tablespoons (25 g) unsalted butter

1½ teaspoons (10 g) coarse sea salt

2 cups (13 ounces/370 g) chopped dark chocolate, or 2 cups (13 ounces/370 g) chopped dark chocolate and ⅓ cup mild vegetable oil

Maldon sea salt, for garnish (optional)

1. Stir together the sugar, evaporated milk, heavy cream, and vanilla bean and seeds (if using) in a large (6- to 8-quart) saucepan. Bring to a boil over medium-high heat, uncovered and without stirring.

2. While the caramel mixture is heating up, arrange the nuts on the prepared baking sheet: place 4 or 5 whole pecans in a star shape for each turtle; about 20 stars in all, leaving at least 1 inch between stars.

3. Once the caramel mixture has come to a boil, insert the candy thermometer. Add the light corn syrup, and stir gently with the heatproof spatula until everything is mixed well. Reduce the heat to medium-low and cook, stirring often and making sure to scrape the bottom of the pot to keep the mixture from burning, until the mixture reaches 230°F/110°C (thread stage), about 30 minutes.

4. Add the butter to the caramel mixture, and fish out the vanilla bean with a slotted spoon. Stirring continuously, cook the caramel until it reaches 241°F/116°C

FUNNEL OF LOVE

At first glance, candy funnels seem like they're not much more helpful than a measuring cup: Why would you need to spend 15 bucks on a stupid piece of plastic just to pour something? (By the by, we prefer the no-frills plastic ones from Sugarcraft (see Resources, page 291); we've been using them for 3 years and counting, and they don't have one of those weird trigger mechanisms that's bound to break down on you.) Well, honestly, it's worth the extra bread to save the headache of trying to get consistent pours of super-hot, finicky candy from a measuring cup. Here's how to get your money's worth right off the bat.

- **PRACTICE.** Before you even start with candy, practice holding the funnel, working the stopper—all that jazz. Getting a feel for it ahead of time helps a heap.
- **SET 'EM UP.** That is, get the funnels set up before you even begin the recipe: Place them in mugs or measuring cups, stoppers and all, so that they're ready to go. (Many are the times we've taken a pot of bubbling sugar off the stove, only to have to scramble to find a clean funnel and a place to put it.)
- **DON'T GET COCKY.** We can't stress this enough: NEVER let your guard down around hot caramel and sugar syrup. Funnels make your life a lot easier when working with this stuff, but your hands are much closer to the searingly hot goo. Always move slowly, and always have a bowl of cool water handy in case of an accident (see Boo-urns, page 191).

(soft-to-firm ball stage), 15 to 20 minutes; it will be a deep tawny color and have slow, rolling bubbles in the center. Remove it from the heat.

5. Stir in the salt and the vanilla paste or extract (if using), making sure to mix well so that they're distributed evenly. Wearing your oven mitts, carefully pour the caramel into the candy funnels. Allow it to cool for about 5 minutes, stirring it a couple of times, until it thickens up a little bit and has the consistency of hot fudge.

6. Pour a couple tablespoons' worth of caramel onto each pecan cluster. Allow them to set up until they are no longer warm, about 20 minutes. (It's helpful to clean and dry one of your candy funnels now, so that you can use it to top the turtles with chocolate later.)

7. Meanwhile, temper the 2 cups chocolate according to the instructions on page 26, or use the 2 cups chocolate and ⅓ cup oil to make Cheater's Chocolate Coating as directed on page 32.

8 Once the caramel has set up, pour some prepared chocolate into the clean funnel (you'll need to refill it as it empties). Top each turtle with about a tablespoon of chocolate. You want enough chocolate so that it covers most of the caramel, but the turtles' heads and tootsies should still be visible. Gently tap the baking sheet on the counter, one end first and then the other, to even out the chocolate. Garnish the center of each turtle with a few flakes of sea salt, if desired—just make sure to do it before the chocolate sets up completely.

Store the turtles, layered with wax or parchment paper, in an airtight container at cool room temperature for up to 1 week.

WHAT IS THE DEAL WITH MILK IN A CAN?*

It's often confusing distinguishing between evaporated and condensed milk. We've picked up the wrong kind at the store many times, only to get home and curse our absentmindedness. But remember—knowledge is power! In order to aid in your transformation from candy novice to sweets superhero, here's a handy-dandy chart to help you tell the difference:

	EVAPORATED MILK	CONDENSED MILK
Usually comes in a . . .	12-ounce can	14-ounce can
Sweetened?	No	Yes
Physical properties	Liquid, thin, and pourable	Thick and sticky, like pancake syrup
Example recipes	Sea Salt Caramels (page 122), Marisa's Vanilla Bean Saltwater Taffy (page 149), Spicy Pralines (page 167)	None (in this book, at least)
Also used for	Cream substitute in savory dishes	Dulce de leche, fudge, Vietnamese iced coffee

*With apologies to Mr. Jerry Seinfeld.

EASY

VANILLA MARSHMALLOWS

MAKES ABOUT 95 ONE-INCH PIECES

The difference between these delicate little beauties and the apocalypse-proof cylinders you get at the supermarket is astounding, and *so* worth the effort. We like this recipe, which we adapted from one generously given to us by our friend Mark of the (literally) mom-and-pop Brooklyn bakery Whimsy & Spice, because it has a perfect marshmallow consistency—fluffy without being too chewy, soft and plush, perfectly light and airy. The flavor depends on the vanilla: the better quality you use, the tastier the marshies will be.

This recipe makes a generous layer of marshmallow, and you can cut it in whatever size or shape you desire—or use cookie cutters to make them extra kiddie-friendly. Feel free to snip up any scraps to throw into a batch of Rocky Road ice cream or Bark (page 79), scatter on top of an ice cream sundae, or toast up for a s'more so good you'll want to cuddle up to it and name it Shnookums.

SPECIAL EQUIPMENT

- Small (9" x 13") rimmed baking sheet
- Stand mixer fitted with whisk attachment
- Heatproof spatula
- Candy thermometer
- Large cutting board, lined with parchment paper

INGREDIENTS

½ cup cornstarch

½ cup confectioners' sugar

Cooking spray

1¼ cups (300 g) cold water, divided into ¾ cup (175 g) and ½ cup (125 g)

4 tablespoons plus 1 teaspoon (about 1 ounce/32 g) unflavored powdered gelatin

2¾ cups (550 g) granulated sugar

¾ cup (255 g) light corn syrup

1 vanilla bean, split open and seeds scraped out, pod reserved; or 2 teaspoons pure vanilla extract

3 large egg whites, at room temperature

1. Sift together the cornstarch and confectioners' sugar into a medium-size bowl.

2. Generously coat the sides and bottom of the baking sheet with cooking spray, and dust it well with about ¼ cup of the cornstarch mixture, tapping out any excess. Set it aside.

3. Place ¾ cup of the cold water in a small bowl, sprinkle the gelatin over it, and stir. Set it aside to soften, at least 5 minutes.

4. Place the remaining ½ cup water, the sugar, corn syrup, and vanilla bean and seeds (if using) in a medium-size (4-quart) saucepan, and stir with the heatproof spatula to combine. Bring the mixture to a boil, without stirring, over medium-high heat. Then insert the candy thermometer and cook, uncovered, until it reaches 240°F/116°C (firm-to-hard ball stage), about 10 minutes.

5. Place the egg whites in the mixer bowl and beat at medium speed until they hold soft peaks, 4 to 6 minutes. Turn the speed down to low; proceed to the next step.

6. Once the syrup reaches 250°F/121°C (firm-to-hard ball stage), remove it from the heat and use a slotted spoon to fish out the vanilla bean. Pour the hot syrup into the bowl containing the egg whites, pouring down the side of the bowl. Add the softened gelatin and turn the speed up to high, beating until the mixture is white, thick, and almost tripled in volume; about 6 minutes for a stand mixer or 10 to 12 minutes with a handheld mixer.

7. If using the vanilla extract, add it, and beat until just combined. Pour the

mixture onto the prepared baking sheet, and sift approximately ¼ cup of the sugar-cornstarch mixture evenly over the top. Let it set up for at least 5 hours, preferably overnight.

8 Run the tip of a paring knife around the edges of the baking sheet and invert it over the lined cutting board. Lift a corner of the pan and loosen the marshmallow slab carefully with your fingers. Once the slab is on the cutting board, generously coat a sharp chef's knife with cooking spray and cut it into 1-inch pieces.

9 Sift the remaining ½ cup of the cornstarch mixture into a medium-size bowl and gently toss each marshmallow in the mixture to coat. Shake off the excess and start eatin'!

Store the marshmallows, layered with wax paper, in an airtight container at cool room temperature for up to 2 weeks.

NOTE: If you prefer shaped marshies, oil the business end of some cookie cutters and go to town.

PETER PIPER PIPED A PACK OF PEEPERS

Want to pipe some marshmallow chicks? Go right on ahead—just make sure to count on some mutants in the first few tries. We also recommend cooking the syrup 5°F (2° to 3°C) *higher* than listed in the recipe, and making sure it's quite cool before you start piping (otherwise the little peepers won't hold their shape). Definitely check out Prepping a Piping Bag on page 45, too. And here are a few more chickalicious* pointers:

- **CHILL; DON'T OVERFILL.** Only fill the piping bag about two-thirds full; you want to make sure you leave yourself enough room to twist off the top. Otherwise marshmallow gets everywhere. And we mean EVERYWHERE.

- **REINFORCEMENTS!** Wrap a piece of duct or packing tape around the end of the bag before you fill and trim it; marshmallow is very stiff and this helps reduce the possibility of seams splitting.

- **REMEMBER THE NUMBER 2.** That's the general shape you're making, though you'll want to do it in two swipes: First, pipe a generous blob of mallow, then draw it toward you to make an inverted teardrop shape. Then pipe another blob on top of that; ease off your pressure on the bag as you draw it up and toward the round end of the teardrop. If the marshmallow is stiff and cool enough, it should resemble a little chick. Or at least resemble a mass-market abstraction of a little chick. Good luck! And don't take it too seriously—it's just marshmallow.

*We mean that in the "chicken" way. Dudes are also encouraged to use these tips.

LIZ SAYS: Don't toss that empty vanilla bean! When you're finished making the marshmallows, rinse it off, let it dry, and tuck it into a jar of sugar to give it a sweet, vanilla-y scent.

Variations

The versatility of this recipe is part of the fun! You can flavor the marshmallows pretty much however you'd like: Simply replace the vanilla bean in step 4 (or the extract in step 7). Some of our favorite variations include chocolate malted (1 tablespoon Dutch-process cocoa powder and 1 tablespoon malted milk powder), passion fruit (2 tablespoons passion fruit pulp/puree; see page 65), and cool mint (2 teaspoons peppermint oil; see the Note on page 84).

JEN SAYS: These are also delicious dipped in chocolate: Temper 8 cups chopped dark chocolate (about 3 pounds/1.35 kg) following the directions on page 26, or use 8 cups chopped dark chocolate (about 3 pounds/1.35 kg) and 1⅓ cups (300 g) mild vegetable oil to make the Cheater's Chocolate Coating on page 32. Dip the marshmallows in the prepared chocolate using the Fork Dipping technique on page 33.

CLASSIC EUROPEAN NOUGAT

MAKES ABOUT 100 ONE-INCH BITES OR 30 ONE- BY THREE-INCH BARS

Also known as torrone, this is a granddaddy confection—well, actually, there should be several "greats" in there, because the oldest known recipe for this kind of treat dates back to the 1500s. It's pretty intensely chewy, but it's well worth the effort on your jaw's part. Light, with big crunchy almonds, hazelnuts, and pistachios, with a lingering flavor of honey . . . once you try it, you'll see how a recipe can stick (ha!) around for over 400 years.

Speaking of stickiness, store-bought torrone often has a somewhat paper-like—but edible—outer layer that keeps the nougat from sticking to, well, everything. It's what's known as wafer paper or rice paper. (And, incidentally, it's what makes putting photos on sheet cakes possible. Technology!) Wafer paper is available from Sugarcraft, and from various sources on Amazon (see Resources, page 291); it is sold in 8 × 11-inch sheets and often in bulk, though you will only need a few. Using it in this recipe is completely optional; as long as you grease the pan very well, you should be able to remove the nougat with no problem. Any excess oil can be gently wiped off with a paper towel, and a little confectioners' sugar should banish any further stickiness.

Although this recipe makes a delectable nutful treat, we also like to mix in some tart dried cranberries or cherries (sub out 1 cup of any of the nuts). But if you're using this for Chocorrone (page 89), skip the fruit.

SPECIAL EQUIPMENT

- Small (9" x 13") rimmed baking sheet
- Heatproof spatula
- Stand mixer fitted with whisk attachment
- Candy thermometer
- Bench scraper (see page 21) or thin metal spatula (optional)
- Parchment paper or wax twisting papers, (see Resources, page 291)

INGREDIENTS

Wafer paper (see headnote), or about 1 teaspoon butter and 1 tablespoon cornstarch, for coating the baking sheet

Cooking spray or vegetable oil

2 large egg whites, at room temperature

¼ teaspoon (1 g) cream of tartar

3 cups (575 g) granulated sugar, divided into ½ cup and 2½ cups

2 cups (675 g) honey

¾ cup (275 g) light corn syrup

¼ cup (60 g) water

½ teaspoon (3 g) salt

2 cups (285 g) toasted whole almonds, preferably Marcona

2 cups (285 g) toasted whole hazelnuts

1 cup (125 g) shelled roasted pistachios

1 vanilla bean, split open and seeds scraped out, pod reserved (see page 11)

About 1 cup (120 g) confectioners' sugar, sifted, for dusting (optional)

1. Prepare the baking sheet: If you're using wafer paper, place a single sheet on the bottom of the pan and trim pieces from another sheet to fill in any gaps. Otherwise, grease the bottom and sides of the baking sheet with the butter and sprinkle the cornstarch over that, tilting and tapping the pan (over the sink or a trash can) to coat all the surfaces evenly. Set it aside. Coat your heatproof spatula generously with cooking spray and set it aside, too.

2. Place the egg whites in the bowl of the stand mixer. Add the cream of tartar and whip on medium speed until the whites are frothy, about 1 minute. Increase the speed to medium-high and slowly stream in the ½ cup sugar. Once it is all mixed in, continue to whip on medium-high speed until soft peaks form (if you lift the whisk out of the whites, they will form a point that flops over onto its side), 3 to 5 minutes. Set this mixture—it's now meringue—aside, but keep it in the mixer bowl, with the mixer ready to go.

3. Combine the remaining 2½ cups sugar with the honey, corn syrup, water, and salt in a medium-size (4-quart) saucepan. Bring to a boil, uncovered and without stirring, over high heat. Reduce the heat to medium-high, insert the candy thermometer, and cook the syrup until it reaches 295°F/146°C (soft-to-hard crack stage), about 15 minutes (see Jen Says on next page—later. For now, stay focused!). Remove it from the heat.

4. Start whipping the meringue on medium speed; then put on your oven mitts and slowly pour the hot syrup in a stream down the inside of the mixer bowl (careful, careful, careful: If you pour the syrup directly on the whisk, it will splatter). Once all the syrup is incorporated, increase the mixer speed to high and whip until the meringue gets very stiff and

sticky, 3 to 5 minutes. When your mixer starts complaining, you'll know it's ready.

5. Remove the bowl from the mixer and immediately and quickly stir in all the nuts and the vanilla seeds with the spatula. Pour the nougat onto the prepared baking sheet and either cover it with a layer of wafer paper or sift a generous amount of confectioners' sugar on top. If you need to spread it out into a more even layer, place a piece of parchment or a silicone mat on top of the wafer- or sugar-covered nougat and gently press down with flat hands until it's even. Allow the nougat to cool to room temperature, about 1 hour.

6. Cover a cutting board with parchment or a generous dusting of confectioners' sugar. Generously coat a sharp chef's knife and a paring knife with cooking spray. Run the paring knife around the edge of the nougat to loosen it, and then gently turn it out onto the cutting board. (If the nougat is being stubborn, oil the bench scraper and use it to help loosen it around the edges.) Using the chef's knife, trim the edges of the nougat and then slice it into bars or little bites.

Store the nougat, layered with parchment or wrapped in wax paper wrappers, in an airtight container at cool room temperature for up to 2 weeks.

JEN SAYS: We recommend cooking the sugar syrup to 295°F/146°C (soft-to-hard-crack stage), but once you've tried this temperature, you can futz with future versions to your liking. If you cook it to 290°F/143°C (soft crack stage), you'll have a soft nougat; to 300°F/150°C (hard crack stage), you'll have a very firm one.

LIZ SAYS: Need to cut something sticky on a cutting board? Cut a piece of parchment paper that is several inches longer than the board. Place the paper on top of the board, flip the board over, tape the edges of the paper to the underside of the board with masking tape, and flip it back over. Nonstick cutting board!

MARISA'S VANILLA BEAN SALTWATER TAFFY

MAKES APPROXIMATELY 120 ONE-AND-A-HALF-INCH PIECES

This recipe comes to us courtesy of the lovely Marisa Wu. An employee of ours for over a year, Marisa struck off on her own to form her saltwater taffy company, Salty Road. Since taffy isn't something we make, we decided to go right to the expert—and her taffy really is outstanding. You'll want to invite a friend (or three) over to help you pull it; but the silky texture and the smooth, ice-creamy flavors are ample reward for the amount of pulling you'll be doing.

INGREDIENTS

Cooking spray or vegetable oil

½ cup (4 ounces/125 g) evaporated milk

1½ cups (275 g) granulated sugar

1⅔ cups (575 g) light corn syrup

½ vanilla bean, split open and seeds scraped out, pod reserved

1 teaspoon (5 g) coarse sea salt

SPECIAL EQUIPMENT

- Small (9″ x 13″) rimmed baking sheet
- Candy thermometer
- Large cutting board, oiled or lined with a silicone mat
- Sturdy kitchen scissors
- Wax twisting papers (see Resources, page 291)

1. Generously coat the baking sheet with cooking spray, and set it aside.
2. Combine the evaporated milk, sugar, corn syrup, and vanilla bean and seeds in a medium-size (4-quart) saucepan. Bring to a boil over high heat, uncovered, and then insert the candy thermometer.
3. Reduce the heat to medium and cook, stirring frequently with a heatproof spatula or wooden spoon to avoid scorching, until the mixture reaches 246°F/119°C (firm ball stage), 10 to 15 minutes. Put on your oven mitts, remove the pan from the heat, and pour the mixture onto the prepared baking sheet.
4. Fish out the vanilla bean with a slotted spoon or tongs, and set it aside (you can rinse it and dry it out to use later, see page 11). Sprinkle the salt evenly over the surface of the taffy mixture, and allow it to cool until it is just warm to the touch, 30 to 45 minutes.
5. Turn the cooled taffy out onto the prepared cutting board. Stretch it out with both hands, fold it over on itself, and stretch it out again. Repeat this continuously until the taffy has turned opaque and white, about 15 minutes. (Elbow grease, indeed.)
6. Generously coat the blades of the kitchen scissors (and your hands) with cooking spray. Pull the taffy apart into 4 equal pieces. Place the first piece on the cutting board and roll it with your hands to form a log approximately 18 inches long. Using the scissors, snip the taffy into 1½-inch pieces, and then immediately roll them in wax twisting paper (otherwise the taffy will not hold its shape). Repeat with the remaining 3 pieces.

Store the taffy in an airtight container at cool room temperature for up to 3 weeks.

MARISA SAYS: Taffy can be a little tricky. The end result is gonna vary, depending on the weather, temperature, your stove, your saucepan, etc. Don't let it bum you out! If it comes out too soft, try cooking the mixture a couple degrees lower next time. Play with it till it comes out the way you like it.

PULLING TAFFY

1. Pull that taffy apart! Keep pulling!

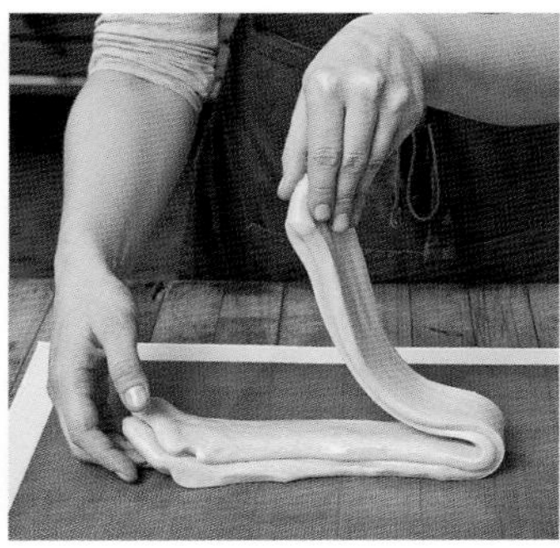

2. Fold the taffy onto itself. Repeat the pulling and folding until . . .

3. The taffy turns opaque and white.

JEN AND LIZ SAY:

★ If you don't want to cut and wrap all the taffy at once, you can store the extra lump in an oiled plastic zip-top bag at room temperature for up to 2 days. Just pull it a couple of times to soften it up before you start cutting and wrapping again.

★ If the taffy is too firm to cut and wrap, heat it in the microwave on High in 10-second intervals until it's just soft enough to pull. Be careful not to overheat it—it will become very soft and sticky!

★ This is one of those candies you really cannot make on a humid day. Sugar syrup sucks moisture right out of the air, and since this gets so much exposure to air during the pulling process, making it on a sticky day is just asking for trouble.

SALTY PEANUT TAFFY

MAKES ABOUT 120 ONE-AND-A-HALF-INCH PIECES

When we first tried this, it made us really proud; we helped teach Marisa! And Marisa invented peanut taffy! And it's REALLY GOOD! This ends up almost like an Abba-Zaba, if anyone even knows what those are anymore—it was one of Liz's favorite candy bars growing up. We give this recipe five thumbs up.

SPECIAL EQUIPMENT

- Small (9" x 13") rimmed baking sheet
- Candy thermometer
- Large cutting board, oiled or lined with silicone mat
- Sturdy kitchen scissors
- Wax twisting papers (see Resources page 291)

INGREDIENTS

Cooking spray

⅔ cup (5½ ounces/170 g) evaporated milk

1 cup (200 g) granulated sugar

1⅓ cups (450 g) light corn syrup

4 teaspoons (30 g) honey

½ teaspoon (3 g) pure vanilla extract

1 cup (170 g) creamy commercial peanut butter, such as Skippy

2 teaspoons (5 g) coarse sea salt

1. Generously coat the baking sheet with cooking spray, and set it aside.
2. Combine the evaporated milk, sugar, corn syrup, and honey in a medium-size (4-quart) saucepan. Bring to a boil over high heat, uncovered, and then insert the candy thermometer.
3. Reduce the heat to medium and cook, stirring frequently with a heatproof spatula or wooden spoon to avoid scorching, until the mixture reaches 246°F/119°C (firm ball stage), 10 to 15 minutes. Remove the pan from the heat.
4. Stir in the vanilla and peanut butter until fully incorporated. Mix in the sea salt. Pour the taffy onto the prepared baking sheet. Allow it to cool until just warm to the touch, 30 to 45 minutes.
5. Turn the cooled taffy out onto the prepared cutting board. Stretch it out with both hands, fold it over on itself, and stretch it out again (see the pics on page 151). Repeat this until the taffy has turned opaque and beige, about 15 minutes.
6. Generously coat the blades of the kitchen scissors (and your hands) with cooking spray. Cut the taffy into 4 equal pieces. Place a piece on the cutting board and roll it with your hands to form a log approximately 18 inches long. Using the scissors, snip the taffy into 1½-inch pieces, and then immediately roll them in wax twisting paper (otherwise the taffy will not hold its shape). Repeat with the remaining 3 pieces.

Store the taffy in an airtight container at cool room temperature for up to 3 weeks.

BUTTERMINTS
PAGE 177

SPICY PRALINES
PAGE 167

PEANUT BUTTER
PINWHEELS PAGE 159

OH, FUDGE!
PAGE 169

Chapter Four

CREAMY DREAMY CANDIES

It's difficult not to swoon at the prospect of a nice, creamy sweet. And why not? We're hardwired to love sweet things for survival (immediate energy!), and a creamy mouthfeel implies fattiness (storable energy!). Interestingly enough, many of these creamy treats don't count on fats for that silky texture; it's still sugar that's doing all the heavy lifting here. When you get the crystals of a sugar syrup small enough, by cooling and then vigorously stirring them, they become so tiny that the tongue doesn't even register them as crystals.

Of course, fat has a big part to play in this chapter, too; it *is* flipping delicious. But now you know that there's more than one side to the story. There's a little something for everyone in this section: here be rich Spicy Pralines (page 167), studded with crunchy pecans; versatile and silky Buttermints (page 177), which don't *have* to be minty, but can be any other flavor-y you like; simple, unique Peanut Butter Pinwheels (with a surprise ingredient—page 159); and everyone's favorite boardwalk staple, Oh, Fudge! (page 169). Some of these candies require a mixer (or some dedicated stirring), but all of them are relatively simple to put together—which makes them all the more appealing.

MAPLE CANDY

MAKES ABOUT 25 ONE-INCH CANDIES

Like the Spicy Pralines on page 167, this is one of those stir-till-your-arm-falls-off recipes, and another one that is totally and utterly worth it (we wouldn't put it in the book if it weren't). It's extremely difficult to go wrong with the flavor combination of maple syrup and butter; and since those are the only two ingredients, we like Grade B maple syrup for its rich, deep flavor. If you can only find Grade A, no problem—go ahead and use it! The candy simply will end up with a more delicate flavor, and there ain't nothin' wrong with that.

When you combine the maple syrup and butter, the mixture will bubble up quite a bit. To avoid an overflowing molten sugar situation, make sure your saucepan has ample headroom. (In other words, it should be deep.)

SPECIAL EQUIPMENT

- Small loaf pan (about 8″ x 4″)
- 1-inch candy molds with about 30 cavities (see Resources, page 291)
- Candy thermometer
- Sharp chef's knife, if you're not using molds

INGREDIENTS

1 tablespoon (14 g) unsalted butter, plus extra for greasing the pan or molds

2 cups maple syrup, preferably Grade B

Hot water, if needed

Cooking spray (optional)

1. Generously butter the loaf pan or candy molds. Set aside.
2. Combine the 1 tablespoon butter and the syrup in a small (2- to 3-quart) saucepan, insert the candy thermometer, and bring the mixture to a boil over high heat stirring once or twice with a wooden spoon, about 5 minutes. Continue to cook over high heat, stirring constantly, until it reaches 240°F/115°C (soft ball stage), about 15 minutes.
3. Remove the pan from the heat, but leave the thermometer in. Allow the mixture to cool, without stirring, to about 175°F/80°C (dissolve stage); then start stirring with the spoon as if your life depends on it. (Yes, it'll hurt . . . but it hurts so good!) Stir vigorously until the mixture starts to lose its gloss and becomes opaque, about 10 minutes.
4. Immediately pour the candy into the prepared pan or molds. Beware—it sets up very quickly! If it sets in the pot before you finish pouring it, stir in hot water, a couple of drops at a time, until the mixture softens up.
5. Allow the poured candy to set until it is cool, about 10 minutes. It should have a dense, fudgy texture and a strong maple flavor.
6. Turn the candy out of the molds or pan onto a cutting board (gently run the knife around the edge of the pan to loosen the candy). If you used the baking pan, lightly coat the chef's knife with cooking spray and cut the candy into 1-inch pieces.

Store the maple candies, layered between parchment or wax paper, in an airtight container at room temperature for up to 4 weeks.

EASY

PEANUT BUTTER PINWHEELS

MAKES 50 TO 60 PIECES

Looking at this recipe, you might notice something weird in the ingredient list: a potato. No one knows the exact provenance of this candy, but we like to think it started with a frugal but savvy woman who wanted to make something delicious with the three ingredients she had on hand: a potato, confectioners' sugar, and peanut butter. The result is a creamy, rich, peanut-buttery confection that'll make your heart race and your teeth ache. With love, of course.

We've tweaked the recipe a bit and added butter and salt (because, well, why not?). Just remember that if you add coconut for some extra toothsomeness, it's best to use unsweetened because the potato dough is extremely sugary. Also note that the exact amount of sugar you use will depend on the kind and age of the potato, the humidity that day, and all sorts of other variables we won't bore you with here.

SPECIAL EQUIPMENT

- Cutting board, lined with parchment or wax paper
- Rolling pin, or empty wine bottle with label removed
- Wax twisting papers (see Resources, page 291)

INGREDIENTS

1 medium-size (4 to 5 ounces/100 to 150 g) potato, baked, cooled, and skinned (Yukon or russet varieties work best; don't use any "waxy" potatoes, like the small red ones—it won't turn out right!)

2 tablespoons (30 g) unsalted butter, at room temperature

4 to 6 cups (525 to 775 g) confectioners' sugar, plus about 1 cup for dusting

1 teaspoon (5 g) pure vanilla extract

Cold milk, for thinning the dough if needed

1 cup (75 g) unsweetened shredded coconut (optional)

1 cup (180 g) creamy commercial peanut butter, such as Skippy

1 teaspoon (4 g) fine sea salt

1. In a medium-size bowl, gently mash the baked potato with a fork, just enough so that there aren't any big lumps. Add the butter, 4 cups of the confectioners' sugar, and the vanilla, and mix well with a rubber spatula until smooth. The dough should be very stiff and sticky, almost like Play-Doh. If it's too thick, add a little cold milk; if it's too thin, keep adding confectioners' sugar, ¼ cup at a time, until it reaches the correct consistency. Add the coconut, if you're using it, and mix to combine.

2. Divide the potato dough in half and form it into 2 balls. Wrap each one tightly in plastic wrap, and allow them to rest in the refrigerator for 1 hour.

3. Remove the balls of dough from the refrigerator. Generously and evenly sprinkle confectioners' sugar over the surface of the prepared cutting board.

4. Roll out one ball of the dough into a rough 12-inch circle that's about ½-inch thick. Use the spatula to spread half of the peanut butter evenly over the surface. Sprinkle ½ teaspoon of the sea salt evenly over the peanut butter, and starting at the edge closest to you, carefully roll up the dough into a log shape. Wrap the log in a piece of plastic wrap, or parchment or wax paper secured by twisting the ends together (this will help the log hold its shape). Chill in the refrigerator for

30 minutes. Meanwhile, assemble the second log.

5 Once the first log is firm enough to cut, use a sharp chef's knife to slice it into ½-inch-thick rounds. Wrap each piece in wax twisting paper. Repeat with the second log.

Store the pinwheels, layered between parchment or wax paper, in an airtight container in the refrigerator for up to 4 weeks.

Variations

Replace the peanut butter with any nut butter you like! And/or, melt about ½ cup of dark chocolate as instructed on page 24—¼ cup for each half of the dough—and spread it over the peanut butter. Allow it to cool until it is somewhat set but still soft, about 10 minutes; then roll it up. Alternatively, you can just sprinkle about ¼ cup mini chocolate chips over the peanut butter before rolling it up.

ASSEMBLING PEANUT BUTTER PINWHEELS

1. Roll out the potato dough. (D'oh!)

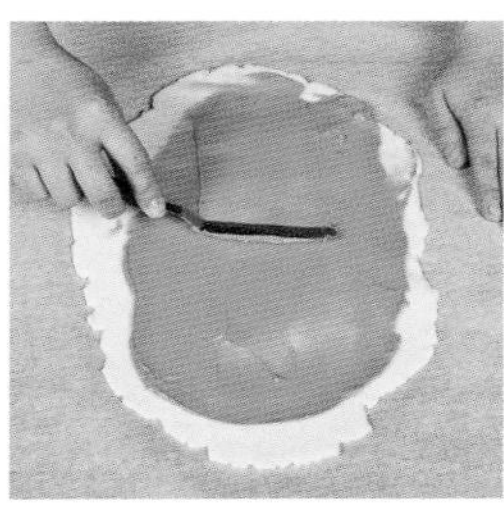

2. Spread the peanut butter into an even layer.

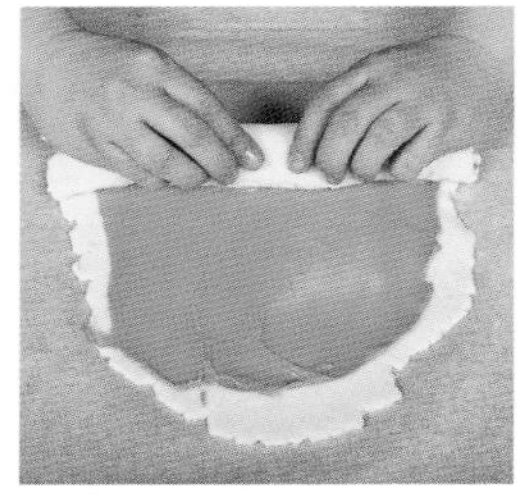

3. Rollin', rollin', rollin'. . .

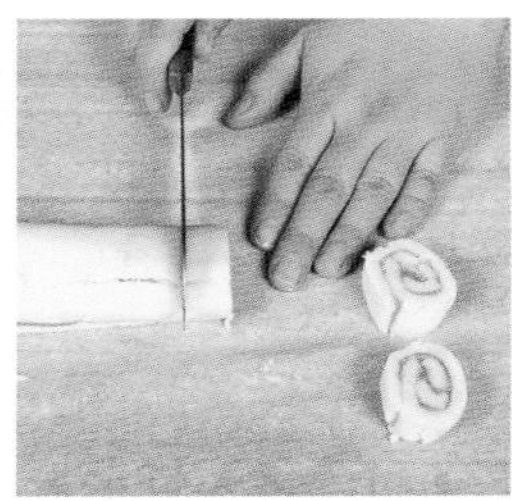

4. Slice the chilled log into rounds.

WORTH IT

LE FONDANT

MAKES ABOUT 2½ CUPS (1 POUND, ENOUGH FOR 2½ BATCHES OF MINT PATTIES OR ABOUT 2 BATCHES OF CHERRY CORDIALS)

Fondant is one of those things that confectioners rarely make themselves anymore. Why would we? It's hard work (though the recipe is simple enough), and cheap, consistent prepared fondant is widely available. That said, this is where you have an advantage being a home cook: Fresh fondant, when used properly (as in the Mint Patties on page 164 and the Cherry Cordials on page 85), is actually quite lovely. Sure, it's pretty much just sugar; but that's where the fun comes in. You can do whatever you want with it—and we'll cop to having an unnatural fixation on Cadbury Crème Eggs. (That stuff in the middle? Pure fondant.) At the very least, making fondant gives you an appreciation for the folks who did it all by hand back in the day. Now *that* was a labor of love. About the hard work thing: This is much easier to make if you have a stand mixer. Otherwise be prepared to flex your muscles. And don't even think about using a handheld mixer unless you're in the market for a new one (the fondant will burn out the motor).

SPECIAL EQUIPMENT

- Candy thermometer
- Stand mixer fitted with paddle attachment (or medium-size heatproof bowl; wooden spoon; silicone mat or cutting board covered with parchment paper; bench scraper; and strong muscles)

INGREDIENTS

2 cups (410 g) granulated sugar

3 tablespoons (50 g) light corn syrup

½ cup (100 g) water, plus 1 tablespoon if needed

1. Combine the sugar, corn syrup, and ½ cup water in a small (2-quart) saucepan and bring to a boil, uncovered and without stirring, over high heat. Insert the candy thermometer, and continue to cook over high heat until the syrup reaches 236°F/113°C (soft ball stage), about 10 minutes.

2. Remove the pan from the heat and pour the syrup into the mixer bowl. Allow the syrup to cool, without stirring, for 20 minutes.

3. *If using a stand mixer:* Start mixing the syrup on low speed until it has thickened considerably and there's no danger of splattering, 4 to 6 minutes. Then increase the speed to medium-low and continue to beat until the fondant turns a dull, opaque white and the texture is creamy and fudgelike, 8 to 10 minutes. If it starts to cake up on the side of the bowl, add 1 tablespoon water, scrape down the side, and mix until it's incorporated.

   If mixing by hand: Stir the syrup vigorously with the wooden spoon until it thickens considerably and begins to hold its shape, 10 to 12 minutes. Pour it onto the silicone mat and begin kneading it with the bench scraper: Scrape underneath the fondant and fold it back over on itself, repeating until the texture is stiff and the mass is an opaque, dull white, about 5 minutes.

Use the fondant immediately, or wrap it tightly in plastic wrap and store it for later use; it lasts for up to a month in the fridge. When using fondant that's been stored for a while, allow it to come to room temperature and knead it with your hands for a few minutes before you use it.

MODERATE

MINT PATTIES

MAKES ABOUT 36 ONE-INCH PATTIES

Classic American candies like this always take us back to sticky-floored multiplexes, and to the torturous decisions that were made down at the concession stand. You could get ONE THING—what was it going to be? Quasi-healthful Raisinets? Something fruity and chewy, like Starburst? Or perhaps a chocolate bar? Jen always wavered between Sour Patch Kids and Milk Duds. For Liz, this was never a question: Junior Mints, every time. (Okay, okay—if you read the Nonpareils recipe on page 77, you may recall that there was a brief period pre–Junior Mints when she favored Sno-Caps. But who's counting?)

This recipe doesn't turn out an exact Junior Mint facsimile, but that's not necessarily a bad thing. The candies end up somewhere between good old JMs and a York Peppermint Pattie—creamy without oozing; nice clean mint flavor. See the note in the Chocolate Mint Meltaways recipe (page 84) about peppermint oil. If you can't find the oil, you can substitute extract; just keep in mind you'll need to use twice as much, as extract isn't quite as potent.

Although a stand mixer makes quicker work of these candies, you can use a hand mixer; if the fondant gets too stiff for the mixer, you can get the mixing done by hand with a wooden spoon—it'll just take you 5 to 10 minutes longer.

When the time comes to pipe the candies, check out the instructions on page 43 for extra guidance.

SPECIAL EQUIPMENT

- Stand mixer fitted with paddle attachment, or electric mixer and medium-size bowl
- Large (13" x 18") baking sheet, lined with a silicone mat or parchment paper
- Rubber spatula
- Piping bag or quart-size zip-top bag
- Two-tined dipping fork (see page 20), optional

INGREDIENTS

1 cup (340 g) Le Fondant (page 162), or store-bought fondant

½ teaspoon (2 g) pure peppermint oil, plus more if needed

½ teaspoon (2 g) minced fresh mint leaves (optional)

3 to 5 teaspoons (15 to 25 g) water

1 teaspoon (3 g) confectioners' sugar, if needed

2 cups (13 ounces/370 g) chopped dark chocolate, or 2 cups (13 ounces/370 g) chopped dark chocolate and ⅓ cup (75 g) mild vegetable oil, for dipping

1. Place the fondant in a small (2-quart) saucepan over medium heat and warm it until liquid, 10 minutes.

2. Combine the fondant, peppermint oil, fresh mint, if using, and 3 teaspoons of the water in the mixer bowl. Mix on low speed to combine. Once the ingredients start to come together, increase the speed to medium-low and beat until smooth and creamy, 1 to 2 minutes. Taste the mixture: If you want a stronger mint flavor, add more peppermint oil, a couple of drops at a time, tasting after each addition.

3. Once the ingredients are combined, check the consistency by dropping a teaspoon of the mixture on the lined baking sheet. It should spread into a disk not much larger than a quarter. If the mixture is too thick,

add a little more water. If it's too thin, add the teaspoon of confectioners' sugar. Just stir it a few times to combine thoroughly and try it again.

4. Use the rubber spatula to scrape the mixture into the pastry bag. Close the bag and cut off about ½ inch from the tip. Pipe 1-inch rounds onto the lined baking sheet, and let them set until firm, 20 to 25 minutes or overnight. (If you want to skip the piping bag altogether, you can drop teaspoons of the mixture individually onto the lined baking sheet.)

5. Meanwhile, temper the 2 cups chocolate according to the instructions on page 26, or use the 2 cups chocolate and ⅓ cup oil to make the Cheater's Chocolate Coating as directed on page 32.

6. When you're ready to dip the patties, loosen them from the baking sheet with a small offset spatula or a butter knife. Using the fork dipping technique illustrated on page 34, dip them individually in the chocolate and place them back on the baking sheet. Allow the dipped patties to set, at least 15 minutes.

Store the patties in an airtight container in a cool, dry place, away from sunlight, for up to 3 weeks.

Variations

LEMON-LIMEADE PATTIES Omit the peppermint oil and fresh mint. Replace the water with freshly squeezed lemon juice and add the grated zest of 1 lime along with it.

ORANGE CREAM PATTIES Replace the peppermint oil with pure vanilla extract. Omit the fresh mint. Replace the water with freshly squeezed orange juice and add 1 teaspoon grated orange zest along with it.

MODERATE

SPICY PRALINES

MAKES ABOUT 35 TWO-INCH PIECES

The perfect praline is an elusive creature: a soft and delicate mound of fudgelike candy, studded with crunchy nuts and sporting a deep, rich, brown-sugar flavor. That's the good news. The bad news is that pralines don't keep very well. However, the other good news is that there's no way you'll need to hang on to them, since they'll be eaten immediately by anyone who comes near them.

Pecans are the classic nut to put in these, but your favorite nut will work, too—and leave out the cayenne if you're not into spicy. We're not here to judge. Whatever you do, act quickly when you're shaping them! The praline mixture will set up very quickly, and though you can thin it a couple times with warm water, the less you have to futz with it, the better.

SPECIAL EQUIPMENT

- Candy thermometer

INGREDIENTS

3 cups (600 g) granulated sugar

3 cups (650 g) firmly packed light brown sugar

1 tablespoon (18 g) fine sea salt

¼ cup (80 g) dark corn syrup

2 cups (16 ounces/450 g) evaporated milk (see page 140)

4 tablespoons (½ stick/110 g) butter

1 teaspoon (5 g) pure vanilla extract

3½ cups (385 g) toasted pecan pieces (or halves crushed slightly with a rolling pin)

½ to 1 teaspoon (1 to 3 g) ground cayenne pepper

Hot water, if needed

1. Place the sugars, salt, corn syrup, evaporated milk, and butter in a medium-size (4- to 6-quart) saucepan and stir with a wooden spoon to combine. Bring the mixture to a boil, uncovered, over high heat.

2. Insert the candy thermometer and lower the heat to medium-high. Cook, without stirring, until the mixture reaches 236°F/113°C (soft-ball stage), about 15 minutes. Immediately remove the pan from the heat and allow the mixture to cool until it thickens slightly, 8 to 10 minutes.

3. Place a large sheet of parchment or wax paper on a work surface.

4. Add the vanilla, pecans, and cayenne to the cooled mixture, and beat with the wooden spoon until it thickens and just starts to lose its gloss, 5 to 7 minutes. (Yes, this will be tiring, but just think of the killer triceps—not to mention candy—you'll have!) Then, working quickly, use two metal tablespoons to shape uniform balls of the mixture and drop them onto the lined work surface. If the mixture hardens too much to work with, add a few drops of hot water and stir with the wooden spoon to soften it. You don't want to have to do this more than once, since continuing to add water will leave the finished candies sticky.

5. Allow the pralines to set up until they are firm to the touch and can easily be loosened from the parchment, 10 to 20 minutes. Then pounce on them and consume immediately!

Store pralines, layered between parchment or wax paper, in an airtight container at room temperature for a day or two, but they're best eaten fresh.

Use leftover evaporated milk to make Sea Salt Caramels (page 123) or Marisa's Vanilla Bean Saltwater Taffy (page 149)!

MODERATE

OH, FUDGE!

MAKES ABOUT 64 ONE-INCH PIECES

Everyone has an opinion about fudge. Most of these opinions are positive; some are ambivalent. Occasionally you'll come across somebody who can't stand fudge, who associates it with stale, crumbly, tasteless little bricks that are only good for grease-spotting paper bags. This recipe is for those folks. If they've never had fresh chocolate fudge, they should try this straight outta the pan. We predict some lives will be changed. (The haters will be equally, if not more, wowed by the yummy variations that follow.)

SPECIAL EQUIPMENT

- Small (8" x 8") baking pan
- Candy thermometer
- Stand mixer fitted with paddle attachment (optional)

INGREDIENTS

1 tablespoon (15 g) unsalted butter, plus about 1 teaspoon for greasing the pan

3¾ cups (750 g) granulated sugar

1½ cups (365 g) whole milk

½ cup (175 g) light corn syrup

2 teaspoons (12 g) fine sea salt

½ cup (4 ounces/110 g) chopped unsweetened chocolate

¼ cup (22 g) unsweetened cocoa powder

1 teaspoon (5 g) pure vanilla extract

1. Grease the sides and bottom of the baking pan with the 1 teaspoon butter, and set it aside.

2. Combine the sugar, milk, corn syrup, salt, chocolate, and cocoa powder in a medium-size (4-quart) saucepan and bring to a boil, uncovered and without stirring, over high heat. Reduce the heat to medium-high, insert the candy thermometer, and cook to 235°F/113°C (soft ball stage), still without stirring, about 1 hour.

3. Remove the pan from the heat, but leave the thermometer in. Add the 1 tablespoon butter and the vanilla, and stir with a wooden spoon until just combined. Allow the mixture to sit until the temperature lowers to 120°F/50°C (dissolve-to-thread stage), about 1 hour.

4. Remove the thermometer and stir the mixture vigorously with the wooden spoon until it turns from glossy to opaque and starts to thicken, about 15 minutes. (Yup, 15 minutes. Start working those dumbbells, or invite a friend over to help!) Alternatively, scrape the mixture into the bowl of a stand mixer and beat on medium speed until the mixture dulls and becomes thick and creamy like cake batter, 7 to 10 minutes.

5. Pour the fudge into the prepared baking pan and spread it out evenly with the wooden spoon. Allow it to set up at room temperature until it is cool and completely firm to the touch, 1½ to 2 hours.

6. Gently turn the fudge out onto a cutting board, and cut it into 1-inch pieces with a sharp chef's knife.

Store the fudge, layered between parchment or wax paper, in an airtight container at cool room temperature for up to 1 week.

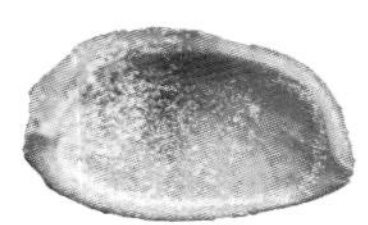

Variations

ORANGE YOU GLAD Right before pouring the fudge into the pan, stir in ½ cup slivered almonds and ¼ cup diced candied orange peel (see page 114).

COFFEE TOFFEE Add 2 tablespoons instant espresso powder to the sugar syrup mixture in step 2; just before pouring the fudge into the pan, stir in ⅓ cup crushed Roni-Sue's Best Buttercrunch Ever (page 204).

MODERATE

FLUFFY PEANUT BUTTER NOUGAT

MAKES ABOUT 100 ONE-INCH PIECES

If you were an eight-year-old girl with a pedigreed pet kitten, this might be what you'd name him. Or if you were an adult with a passion for creamy, fluffy, peanut buttery deliciousness, this might be what you'd name . . . well, anything. We use this frighteningly addictive treat as a component in our King Bars (page 267), but we've also been known to scarf it warm right out of the mixing bowl. (The recipe is adapted from one we used at our alma mater, the French Culinary Institute, and the day we made it in class we made ourselves sick by eating so much of it.)

The salt in this recipe really makes the flavor sparkle, and the crunch component is key—we like to use fleur de sel, but any coarse sea salt or kosher salt works just fine. If you can stand to wait, this nougat is deliciously decadent dipped in dark chocolate as well. Just make sure to keep some well hidden for yourself . . . otherwise we will personally track it down and eat it while you're sleeping. Luckily this recipe makes loads, so there'll be plenty to go around.

SPECIAL EQUIPMENT

- Stand mixer fitted with whisk attachment
- Candy thermometer
- Heatproof spatula
- Small (9" x 13") rimmed baking sheet, lightly coated with cooking spray and lined with parchment paper
- Two-tined dipping fork (see page 20), optional

INGREDIENTS

5 large egg whites (150 g)

3⅔ cups (730 g) granulated sugar

1 cup (250 g) water

2¼ cups (580 g) creamy commercial peanut butter, such as Skippy

1 tablespoon (15 g) coarse sea salt, preferably fleur de sel

About 4 cups (26 ounces/740 g) chopped dark chocolate, or 4 cups (26 ounces/740 g) chopped dark chocolate and ⅔ cup (150 g) mild vegetable oil, for dipping (optional)

1. Place the egg whites in the mixer bowl and set it aside.

2. Combine the sugar and water in a small (2-quart) saucepan, and bring to a boil over high heat while stirring to dissolve the sugar. Once the syrup has come to a boil, insert the candy thermometer. Reduce the heat to medium-high and continue to cook, uncovered and without stirring, while you work on the next step (you will have about 10 minutes).

3. While the syrup is cooking, place the peanut butter in a small bowl and heat it in a microwave in short bursts of 5 to 10 seconds on High, until it is warm and slightly liquidy; you don't need it to be superhot. (Alternatively, gently heat it in a small heatproof bowl set over a saucepan of simmering water.) Set the peanut butter aside.

4. When the syrup reaches 240°F/115°C (soft ball stage), begin whipping the egg whites on medium speed. At the same time, continue to cook the syrup to 255°F/125°C (hard ball stage). This is the trickiest part of the recipe, but it's all in the timing: you want the whites to be around soft peak stage: thick and fluffy but still soft—definitely no further! On medium speed, this should take about 6 minutes. If you need to stop beating the egg whites to let the syrup catch up, that's fine; if you need to turn the heat down on the syrup so you can whip the whites a little more, that's fine, too.

5. When the syrup has reached 255°F/125°C (hard ball stage), remove it from the heat, don your oven mitts, and carefully pour it into the egg whites while they're whipping (pour it down the side of the bowl and not on the beaters themselves; it will splatter). Increase the speed to medium-high. Continue beating until the bowl has cooled so that it is warm to the touch, about 10 minutes.

6. Stop the mixer and remove the bowl. Using the spatula, quickly fold the peanut butter and the salt into the egg whites until just combined—you shouldn't see any more white streaks.

7. Immediately spread the mixture out on the lined baking sheet to a thickness of 1 inch. (You can do this free-form if you like, just on a piece of parchment or a silicone mat.) Allow the nougat to cool, uncovered, at room temperature, until it has set into a firm but yielding texture, 2 to 3 hours or, preferably, overnight. It may form a bit of a crust on top—totally normal and fine! If the idea of this crust bothers you, however, you can place a sheet of parchment on the surface of the nougat as it sets.

8. Cut the nougat into 1-inch pieces with a sharp chef's knife. If you want to coat the pieces in chocolate, temper the 4 cups chocolate according to the instructions on page 26 or use the 4 cups chocolate and ⅔ cup oil to make Cheater's Chocolate Coating on page 32; dip the pieces in the chocolate using the fork-dipping method on page 33.

Store naked nougat layered with wax paper in an airtight container at cool room temperature for up to 1 week. Store dipped nougat in the same manner for up to 3 weeks.

Variations

Peanut aversion? No problem! Virtually any smooth-style nut butter can be used in this recipe, provided it's about the same consistency as peanut butter. And if you like, ½ teaspoon of your favorite spice can be mixed into the nut butter.

LIZ SAYS: To make the top of the nougat smooth, lay a second silicone mat or sheet of parchment on the surface of the spread-out warm nougat, and smooth it out with your hands. Allow the nougat to set for a minute or two; then carefully peel off the parchment. Voilà!

EASY

FIVE-MINUTE MARZIPAN

MAKES ABOUT 2 POUNDS

Marzipan, in some form or another, has been in existence for almost a thousand years—likely even longer. Its history is long and convoluted, but in *One Thousand and One Nights* there is mention of almond paste eaten as a treat, and by the 15th century it was widely documented as a popular indulgence. In fact, according to our hero, food science savant Harold McGee, Leo da Vinci even got into the marzipan-sculpting game (and lamented the philistines who unhesitatingly devoured his little works of art).

These days it's mostly associated with rock-hard models of fruit, but if you've ever tried those and aren't a fan, we urge you to make a batch of your own. Fresh marzipan has a lovely delicate flavor and light texture, and is wonderful dipped in dark chocolate. Of course, if you want to get all arts-n-craftsy on what is basically delicious modeling clay, be our guest. (Leo would approve.)

SPECIAL EQUIPMENT 

- Stand mixer fitted with paddle attachment, or a clean work surface (if using your hands)

INGREDIENTS

3 cups (24 ounces/685 g) almond paste

2½ cups (300 g) confectioners' sugar, plus extra if needed

1 tablespoon (15 g) kirsch or other brandy (see Note), plus extra if needed

1 *If using a stand mixer:* Combine the almond paste, confectioners' sugar, and 1 tablespoon of the brandy in the mixing bowl. Mix on low speed until everything is completely incorporated and the dough is smooth and pliable, about 5 minutes.

If using your hands: Form the almond paste into a flat round on your work surface. Dust half of the confectioners' sugar over the round and begin kneading it into the paste, folding the paste over on itself repeatedly. Drizzle 1 tablespoon of the brandy over the dough and knead it in. Once it's incorporated, dust the remainder of the sugar over the dough and knead until it's completely incorporated.

2 The dough should be uniform and pliable. If it's dry, add a few more drops of flavoring (or warm water) and knead until it's at the desired consistency; if it's sticky, a little more confectioners' sugar.

Store marzipan, wrapped very well in plastic wrap, in the refrigerator for at least 3 months.

NOTE: Kirsch is brandy distilled from cherries. Cherries particularly complement almonds since the two are related, and cherry pits have an almondlike flavor that is imparted to the liquor (which is not so bad ~~swigged~~ sipped on its own, either). If you'd prefer, you can use 1 tablespoon light corn syrup or 1 teaspoon almond extract instead.

MARZIPANTASTIC

The origin of marzipan is somewhat mysterious and widely debated. It's generally agreed upon that it came to Europe either via the Middle East or Spain; that the name means "March Bread" (and may have been adapted from a Moorish word referring to a kind of box the treat was stored in); and that it's probably been around ever since humans have had access to almonds and sweet stuff. Many folks worldwide also agree that it is exceedingly tasty.

EASY

BUTTERMINTS

MAKES 1⅓ POUNDS, ABOUT 300 HALF-INCH PIECES

Remember those little mints by the door at that restaurant you like? No, not *that* restaurant—the nice-but-not-NICE-nice one. This recipe is most closely related to those little post-dinner courtesy mints—but don't think they actually taste alike. These "mints" have a smooth, buttery flavor that's somewhat reminiscent of very thick frosting. And they're not necessarily minty at all: The texture of these little crisp-then-creamy confections lends itself very well to warmer flavors like coffee, chocolate, and cinnamon, too.

Buttermints are great as homemade party favors, since you can get multiple colors out of a single batch and mix and match as you please. Just remember to squirrel away a couple for yourself as a little after-dinner-at-home treat.

SPECIAL EQUIPMENT

- Stand mixer fitted with paddle attachment, or electric mixer and medium-size bowl
- Large (13" x 18") rimmed baking sheet, lined with parchment paper

INGREDIENTS

8 tablespoons (1 stick/115 g) unsalted butter, cold, cut into 1-inch chunks

4 cups (520 g) confectioners' sugar, sifted, plus extra for rolling

¼ teaspoon (1 g) pure peppermint oil (see Note, page 84)

2 tablespoons (30 g) whole milk

Food coloring (optional)

1. Combine the butter and the 4 cups confectioners' sugar in the mixer bowl. Beat on medium-high speed until the mixture is smooth and creamy, 6 to 8 minutes.

2. Add the peppermint oil and milk, and beat on medium speed until combined.

3. Lightly dust some confectioners' sugar onto a cutting board, and turn the dough out onto the board. If you're using food coloring, add 1 to 2 drops (or more for deeper color) and knead it into the dough with your hands until incorporated. If you're making multiple colors, divide the dough into several pieces first (one for each color) and add the food coloring to each piece, starting with 1 drop and kneading, adding 1 drop at a time, until the desired colors are reached. Gather each piece of dough into a ball.

4. Sift more confectioners' sugar over the cutting board. Divide the dough into 4 pieces (if you haven't divided it already), and set 3 of the pieces aside, loosely covered in plastic wrap to prevent them from drying out. Using your hands, and dusting them with confectioners' sugar as needed to reduce any stickiness, gently roll one piece of dough into a log about ½ inch in diameter.

5. Use a sharp chef's knife to cut the log into ½ inch pieces. Lay the pieces in a single layer on the prepared baking sheet to dry. Repeat with the remaining 3 pieces of dough, and allow the candies to dry at room temperature, uncovered, overnight.

Store the buttermints, layered between parchment or wax paper, in an airtight container at room temperature, away from light, for up to 2 weeks.

Variations

COFFEE BUTTERMINTS Replace the peppermint oil with 2 teaspoons coffee extract, 1 tablespoon instant espresso powder dissolved in 1 teaspoon hot water, or 1 tablespoon Trablit (see page 132 and Resources, page 291).

CHOCOLATE BUTTERMINTS Omit the peppermint oil, decrease the milk to 1 tablespoon, and beat 1 tablespoon Dutch-process cocoa powder in with the butter and sugar in step 2. Roll in cocoa powder before drying.

CINNAMON BUTTERMINTS Replace the peppermint oil with ¼ teaspoon pure cinnamon oil.

DRAGÉES
PAGE 213
RONI-SUE'S BEST
BUTTERCRUNCH EVER
PAGE 204

CINNAMON-WALNUT
BRITTLE
PAGE 195

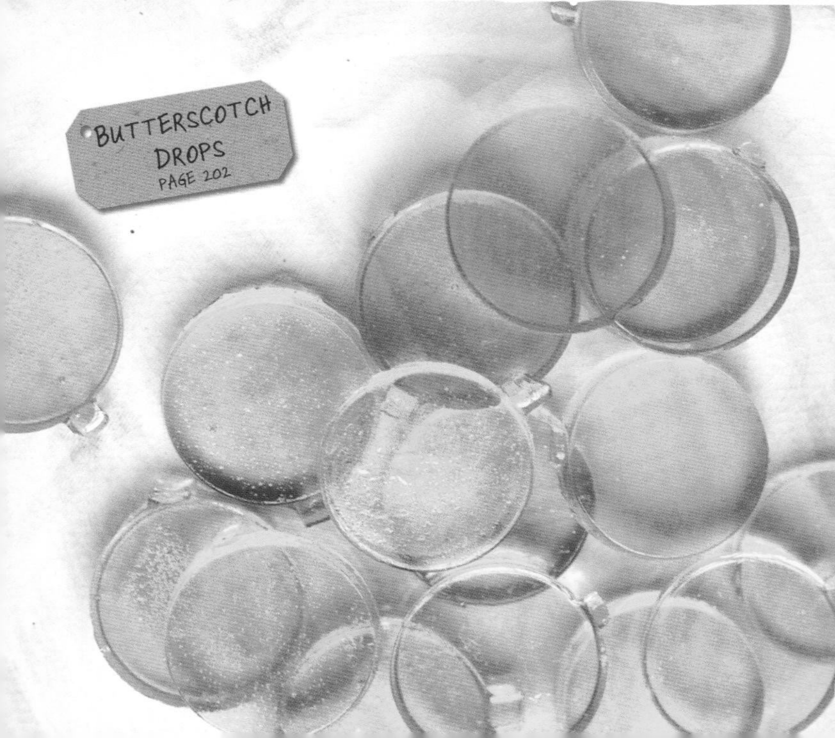
BUTTERSCOTCH
DROPS
PAGE 202

CHOCOLATE-DIPPED
HONEYCOMB CANDY
PAGE 200

Chapter Five

CRISPETY CRUNCHETY, STICKY AND SCRUNCHETY

All the candies in this chapter can be categorized as crunchy—after all, they each involve sugar syrup that's cooked to hard crack stage (300° to 310°F/149° to 154°C), or close enough. Of course, not all the candies in here are meant to be crunched: The simpler, mostly-sugar recipes—Chai Latte Lollipops (page 189), for example—should be savored slowly. Ditto Butterscotch Drops (page 202): Biting right into those can be a really unpleasant wake-up call for your pearlies.

We suppose you could go either way with Cinnamon-Walnut Brittle (page 195); if you're worried about your fillings (as we sometimes are), you could definitely enjoy letting it melt in your mouth. But all brittles have a little butter, a little baking soda, and a bunch of toothsome nuts to help soften the blow, if you will. They're engineered to be light enough that you shouldn't have to be so cautious.

With Roni-Sue's Best Buttercrunch Ever (page 204) or with Tropical Toffee (page 211), you should just take the plunge and sink those chompers in. The larger amount of butter in those treats helps soften the texture of the finished candy, so that with the gentlest of nibbles it easily shatters into tiny, delectable pieces.

Don't forget—ever—that sugar syrup cooked to these levels requires extreme caution and careful planning. So go over your *mise en place* (see page x), get out the oven mitts, and have a bowl of cool water ready—it's time to shine on, you crunchy diamond.

MODERATE

TOOTY FROOTY LOLLIPOPS

MAKES ABOUT 65 ONE-AND-A-HALF-INCH LOLLIPOPS

Making lollipops at home is probably one of the easiest ways to feel like a magical wizard. Lollipops are colorful, fun to eat, and the favorite sweet of almost every little kid we've ever met (hard to go wrong with pure sugar, right?). They're a great party favor, and decorative to boot—try a few nestled in a holiday wreath or as part of a centerpiece, or arranged on a cake in a fanciful lollipop forest.

Though the procedure for making lollies is extremely simple, be warned: Lollipop syrup is *extremely hot* and *extremely dangerous,* and you must exercise caution when handling it. Keep small children out of the kitchen, wear oven mitts, and make sure to have a bowl of cool water handy in the sink so that if you do burn yourself, you can plunge the burn straight in (for more on this, see Boo-urns, page 191).

A note on coloring and flavoring: Any standard liquid food coloring works just fine with this recipe. Just make sure you add it in the saucepan, while the syrup is still hot; that way you have a little extra leeway to adjust the color. For flavoring, you really should seek out special oil-based candy flavors; water-based flavors (usually labeled "extract" and not "oil") are suspended in alcohol, which immediately burns off the moment it touches the hot sugar syrup, as do many of the volatiles that make each flavor unique. While it's possible to use extract in twice the amount of oil-based flavor we call for, we strongly recommend using candy flavors; it just turns out so much better. Nature's Flavors and Frontier Naturals make a wide range of natural flavors, while LorAnn offers variety packs of many different oils for you to play with (see Resources, page 291).

SPECIAL EQUIPMENT

- Lollipop molds (optional, but strongly recommended; see Resources, page 291); or 2 large (13" x 18") baking sheets, lined with parchment paper or silicone mats
- Lollipop sticks (see Resources, page 291)
- Heatproof spatula
- Candy thermometer
- Large heatproof measuring cup or 2 candy funnels (optional, but recommended; see Funnel of Love, page 139, and Resources, page 291)
- Individual cello bags and twist ties (optional; see Resources, page 291)

INGREDIENTS

Cooking spray, if using molds

1 cup (240 g) water

2 cups (400 g) granulated sugar

1 cup (350 g) light corn syrup

Liquid food coloring

¼ to ½ teaspoon oil-based candy flavoring (see above)

1. If you are using molds, lightly coat them with cooking spray and place the sticks in the indentations. (Alternatively, set out the lined baking sheets and sticks.)

2. Place the water, sugar, and corn syrup in a small (2-quart) saucepan, and stir with the heatproof spatula to combine. Bring to a boil over high heat, and insert the candy thermometer. Cook over medium-

high heat until the mixture reaches 300°F/150°C (hard crack stage), 15 to 20 minutes. *Important note:* Once you get past 260°F/128°C (hard ball stage), you'll want to keep a *very* close eye on this mixture; there are mere seconds between "finished" and "burnt beyond repair."

3. Remove the pan from the heat and place it on an adjacent burner or a folded dish towel (this is to help keep in the heat while you futz with the color and flavor). Set out a glass of ice water. Add 3 drops food coloring and ¼ teaspoon flavoring to the candy, and stir well with the spatula to combine. Test the candy by dropping ½ teaspoon of it from the spatula into the ice water; adjust the color and flavor of the syrup as needed and stir once again to combine.

4. Don your oven mitts and very carefully pour the mixture into the large heatproof measuring cup or candy funnels. *If you are using molds,* distribute the mixture evenly among them. *If you are making free-form lollipops on the baking sheets,* let the syrup cool for about 5 minutes; then stir it well and—with oven mitts still on—carefully use a sturdy metal tablespoon to dollop the lollipop syrup into 1½-inch rounds on the prepared sheets. You can add sticks to the lollies as you go, waiting no longer than a minute or two after the lollies have been poured (if the candy sets up completely, you won't be able to add a stick at all, and then the Lollipop Guild will come after you in the night, when you least expect it). It works well to proceed in batches of 10 to 15 free-form lollipops, pouring and then adding sticks.

5. Allow the lollies to set up until they are completely hard to the touch and no longer warm, about 20 minutes.

6. Place the cooled lollies in individual cello bags and secure them with twist ties, or store them in flat layers, separated by parchment or wax paper, in an airtight container.

Stored airtight at room temperature, the lollies will keep for up to 1 month.

MODERATE

BARLEY TEA AND HONEY LOLLIPOPS

MAKES ABOUT 65 ONE-AND-A-HALF-INCH LOLLIPOPS

We basically stole this idea from our friend Rhonda at Roni-Sue's Chocolates, the little Lower East Side treat shop tucked into Essex Market. While we use different flavors, all the credit must go to Rhonda—as must the idea of using bamboo skewers instead of paper sticks. Barley tea is a staple of Korean, Japanese, and Chinese cuisines; it has a lovely nutty flavor that offsets the sweetness of the honey well, and is often consumed as a refreshing cold drink in the hot summer months.

As Rhonda does, we recommend these enjoyed on their own as a natural sore throat soother, or stirred into a cup of hot tea. Make that a hot toddy for us.

SPECIAL EQUIPMENT

- Lollipop molds (optional, but strongly recommended; see Resources, page 291); or 2 large (13" x 18") baking sheets, lined with parchment paper or silicone mats
- Lollipop sticks, or bamboo skewers cut to 4-inch lengths (see Resources, page 291)
- Heatproof spatula
- Candy thermometer
- Large heatproof measuring cup or 2 candy funnels (optional, but recommended; see Resources, page 291)
- Individual cello bags and twist ties (optional; see Resources, page 291)

INGREDIENTS

Cooking spray, if using molds

1¼ cups (300 g) water

3 sachets (3 teaspoons) roasted barley tea (see above)

2 cups (400 g) granulated sugar

½ cup (175 g) honey

½ cup (175 g) light corn syrup

1. If you are using molds, lightly coat them with cooking spray and place the sticks in the indentations. (Alternatively, set out the lined baking sheets and sticks.)

2. Bring the water to a boil in a small (2-quart) saucepan over high heat, or place it in a microwave-safe measuring cup and microwave it on High for 2 to

3 minutes, until it is very hot and steaming. Place the tea bags in the water and allow the tea to steep for 10 minutes.

3. Remove the tea bags, squeezing the excess liquid back into the pan or cup, and discard them. Place paper towels in a double layer over a small bowl, and strain the tea through them. Measure out 1 cup of the filtered tea; drink the rest, or pour it out for all the grandmas who couldn't make it tonight.

4. Place the filtered tea, sugar, honey, and corn syrup in a small (2- to 3-quart) saucepan and stir with the heatproof spatula to combine. Bring to a boil over high heat, and insert the candy thermometer. Reduce the heat to medium-high and cook, stirring a couple of times, until the mixture reaches 300°F/150°C (hard crack stage), 15 to 20 minutes. *Important note:* Once you get past 260°F/128°C (hard ball stage), you'll want to keep a *very* close eye on this mixture; mere seconds separate "done" and "irretrievably ruined."

5. Put on your oven mitts and very carefully pour the mixture into the large heatproof measuring cup or candy funnels. *If you are using molds,* distribute the mixture evenly among them. *If you are making free-form lollipops on the baking sheets,* let the syrup cool for about 5 minutes; then stir it well and—with oven mitts still on—use a sturdy metal tablespoon to dollop the lollipop syrup carefully into 1½-inch rounds on the prepared sheets. Add sticks to the lollies as you go, waiting no longer than a minute or two after the candy has been poured. Work in batches of 10 to 15 free-form lollipops, pouring and then adding sticks.

6. Allow the lollies to set up until they are completely hard to the touch and no longer warm, about 20 minutes.

7. Place the cooled lollies in individual cello bags and secure them with twist ties, or store them in flat layers, separated by parchment, in an airtight container.

Stored airtight at room temperature, the lollies will keep for up to 1 month.

Variation

APPLE-CINNAMON AND MAPLE LOLLIPOPS Use apple-cinnamon tea; replace the honey with pure Grade B maple syrup.

MODERATE

CHAI LATTE LOLLIPOPS

MAKES ABOUT 65 ONE-AND-A-HALF-INCH LOLLIPOPS

This lollipop ended up in limbo, as some great things do, between we-and-about-twenty-five-of-our-customers-are-obsessed-with-these and nobody-else-is-able-to-stay-interested. They were on the menu for a little while; then off; then on; then off for good. People still ask about them, though, so we know they made an impact—we're really proud of this recipe, and so pleased to be able to share it with y'all.

SPECIAL EQUIPMENT

- Lollipop molds (optional, but strongly recommended; see Resources, page 291); or 2 large (13" x 18") baking sheets, lined with parchment paper or silicone mats
- Lollipop sticks, or bamboo skewers cut to 4-inch lengths (see Resources, page 291)
- Heatproof spatula
- Candy thermometer
- Large heatproof measuring cup or 2 candy funnels (optional, but recommended; see Resources, page 291)
- Individual cello bags and twist ties (optional; see Resources, page 291)

INGREDIENTS

Cooking spray, if using molds

1 tablespoon (7 g) powdered milk

½ teaspoon (1 g) ground cinnamon

¾ teaspoon (2 g) ground ginger

¼ teaspoon (1 g) ground nutmeg

Pinch of ground cardamom

1¼ cups (300 g) water

3 sachets (3 teaspoons) chai tea

2 cups (400 g) granulated sugar

1 cup (350 g) light corn syrup

1. If you are using molds, lightly coat them with cooking spray and place the sticks in the indentations. (Alternatively, set out the lined baking sheets and sticks.)

2. Sift together the powdered milk, cinnamon, ginger, nutmeg, and cardamom into a small bowl. Set aside.

3. Bring the water to a boil in a small (2- to 3-quart) saucepan over high heat, or place it in a microwave safe measuring cup and microwave it on High for 2 to 3 minutes, until very hot and steaming. Place the tea bags in the water and allow the tea to steep for 10 minutes.

4. Remove the tea bags, squeezing the excess liquid back into the pan or cup, and discard them. Place paper towels in a double layer over a small bowl, and strain the tea through them. Measure out 1 cup of the filtered tea; drink the rest, or water your plants with it and see what happens (if it's anything interesting, let us know).

5. Place the filtered tea, sugar, and corn syrup in a small (2- to 3-quart) saucepan, and stir with the heatproof spatula to combine. Bring to a boil over high heat, and insert the candy thermometer. Reduce the heat to medium-high, and cook until the mixture reaches 300°F/150°C (hard crack stage), 15 to 20 minutes. *Important note*: Once you get past 260°F/128°C (hard ball stage), keep a very close eye on this mixture—it wants to burn. Once the mixture is cooked, remove it from the heat and stir in the reserved spice mixture.

6. Wearing your oven mitts, very carefully pour the mixture into the large heatproof

measuring cup or candy funnels. *If you are using molds*, distribute the mixture evenly among them. *If you are making free-form lollipops on the baking sheets*, let the syrup cool for about 5 minutes; then stir it well and—keeping those mitts on—use a sturdy metal tablespoon to dollop the lollipop syrup carefully into 1½-inch rounds on the prepared sheets. Add sticks to the lollies as you go, waiting no longer than a minute or two after the candy has been poured. We suggest working in batches of 10 to 15 lollipops, pouring and then adding sticks.

7. Allow the lollies to set up until they are completely hard to the touch and no longer warm, about 20 minutes.

8. Place the cooled lollies in individual cello bags and secure them with twist ties, or store them in flat layers, separated by parchment, in an airtight container.

Stored airtight at room temperature, the lollies will keep for up to 1 month.

BOO-URNS!

Any time you're cooking sugar syrup, keep a bowl of cool water handy in case you burn yourself. It doesn't need to be ice water, and in fact it's better if there's no ice involved at all—putting ice directly on your skin can actually worsen damage from a burn. Kitchen burns will almost always be first- or second-degree burns. (You may notice that third-degree burns are not addressed here. They will only occur if your entire kitchen catches on fire and you are caught in it. *Please* don't let that happen.)

First-degree burns are pink or red, with no blisters; they're painful but will heal in a week or so. A sunburn is a first-degree burn, as are minor steam burns. Second-degree burns cause blisters and more intense pain, and take longer to heal—2 to 3 weeks. This is the burn you're likely to get if sugar syrup or boiling water is spilled on you, or if you accidentally touch a hot pan.

In either case, plunge the burned area into the cool water and keep it submerged—or under cool running water, or with a cool washcloth applied repeatedly—for 15 to 20 minutes. Quicker treatment means less serious damage.

Once you've cooled it off, treat a first-degree burn with aloe gel; a second-degree burn with antibiotic ointment or cream. Oral anti-inflammatories (Advil, Tylenol) help with any pain you can't deal with on your own. Keep the burn covered and change the bandage and ointment a couple times a day, and you should be just fine. (Obviously, if things start to look icky or feel really awful, you should check with your doctor—we know you'll use your best judgment.)

MODERATE

PEANUT BRITTLE

MAKES ABOUT 3 POUNDS, OR ABOUT 16 SERVINGS

This classic treat is pretty straightforward to make—and so much better than anything you can buy in a store. We like this recipe because it produces a light, crispy brittle that's satisfying to snack on and won't pull out your expensive gold fillings. Note before you start that it helps to have an extra set of (steady) hands when making this: one pair to hold the pot and pour, the other to scrape the liquid candy onto the baking sheets. Of course, that means you have to deal with the extra mouth that will want to help you eat all that delicious brittle.

We recommend duct tape.

SPECIAL EQUIPMENT

- 2 large (13" x 18") rimmed baking sheets
- Heatproof spatula
- Candy thermometer

INGREDIENTS

Cooking spray or vegetable oil, for greasing the baking sheets

3 cups (575 g) granulated sugar

1 cup (235 g) water

¾ cup (275 g) light corn syrup

¾ cup (275 g) dark corn syrup

3½ cups (525 g) raw peanuts

2 tablespoons (30 g) unsalted butter

1 tablespoon (15 g) baking soda

1½ teaspoons (7 g) pure vanilla extract

1 tablespoon (15 g) fine sea salt

1. Generously coat the baking sheets with cooking spray and set them aside on a heatproof surface.

2. Combine the sugar, water, and corn syrups in a medium to large (4- to 6-quart) saucepan, and mix well with the heatproof spatula.

3. Bring the mixture to a boil over high heat, and insert the candy thermometer. Cook over high heat, uncovered and without stirring, until it reaches 260°F/125°C (hard ball stage), 20 to 25 minutes.

4. Gently add the peanuts and butter, being careful not to splash (serious ouch potential). Turn the heat down to medium and stir continuously until the mixture registers 300°–305°F/150°–152°C (hard crack stage), 8 to 10 minutes.

5. Remove the pan from the heat. Add the baking soda, vanilla, and salt. The mixture will bubble and increase in volume a little bit; don't panic! Stir well to combine, taking care again not to splash the mixture, and then carefully pour it out, dividing it evenly between the prepared baking sheets. (This is where it's a good idea to have a helper scrape the molten candy out of the pot while you hold it steady.)

6. Using the spatula, spread the mixture as thin as possible. Allow it to cool to room temperature and set up, about 25 minutes.

7. Break the brittle into bite-size pieces and store them immediately. Brittle will become very sticky if left in any kind of humid weather, so wrap this up ASAP!

Store the brittle, layered with parchment or wax paper, in an airtight container at room temperature for up to 1 month.

Variations

We like to change up the additions depending on our mood. Try unroasted cashews or pistachios. And/or adding a little spice with the last few ingredients, like ½ teaspoon ground cardamom or cayenne pepper. You can also go beyond the nut realm and replace the peanuts with whatever you wish—cocoa nibs, corn nuts, even some cooked bacon! Just make sure to add any non-nut ingredients at the very end, along with the baking soda, vanilla, and salt; otherwise they'll burn.

JEN SAYS: If you're like us and don't have any feeling in your fingertips (or just have an excessively high pain threshold), you can try pulling the brittle as it cools. This will aerate the candy and make it even crispier.

MODERATE

CINNAMON-WALNUT BRITTLE

MAKES ABOUT 1½ POUNDS, OR ABOUT 8 SERVINGS

This is light-years (parsecs, even!) from what we ever thought brittle could be. Something about the cinnamon and the walnuts is just so homey and comforting, but deliciously grown-up at the same time. The test version of this brittle disappeared from the kitchen with alarming speed; we can only guess it got up and wandered away on its own, because no one *possibly* could have eaten it all that fast. . . .

As with the Peanut Brittle (page 193), we recommend asking a helper to assist you in scraping the hot candy onto the baking sheet while you hold the pot.

SPECIAL EQUIPMENT

- Large (13" x 18") baking sheet
- Heatproof spatula
- Candy thermometer

INGREDIENTS

2 tablespoons (30 g) unsalted butter, plus extra for greasing the baking sheet

½ teaspoon (2 g) ground cinnamon

1 teaspoon (6 g) fine sea salt

¾ teaspoon (4 g) baking soda

1½ cups (300 g) granulated sugar

¼ cup (85 g) light corn syrup

¼ cup (60 g) water

1 cup (125 g) raw walnuts

½ teaspoon (3 g) pure vanilla extract

1. Generously butter the baking sheet and set it aside on a heatproof surface.
2. Place the cinnamon, salt, and baking soda in a small bowl and stir to combine. Set aside.
3. Put the sugar, corn syrup, and water in a medium-large (4- to 6-quart) saucepan, and stir with the heatproof spatula to combine.
4. Bring the mixture to a rolling boil over high heat, and insert the candy thermometer. Reduce the heat to medium-high and cook, stirring occasionally, until the mixture reaches 260°F/125°C (hard ball stage), 10 to 15 minutes.
5. Add the walnuts, vanilla, and the 2 tablespoons butter, and continue to cook, stirring frequently, until the mixture reaches 300°F/150°C (hard crack stage), 10 to 15 minutes.
6. Remove the pan from the heat and add the cinnamon mixture, stirring vigorously to incorporate (make sure to scrape the bottom of the pan, too). Carefully scrape the brittle onto the prepared baking sheet, and spread it into an even layer with the spatula. Allow the brittle to cool and set completely, about 2 hours.
7. Break the brittle, into roughly 2-inch pieces and store immediately.

Store the brittle, layered with parchment or wax paper, in an airtight container at room temperature for up to 2 weeks.

Variation

HONEY PISTACHIO BRITTLE Omit the cinnamon, replace the corn syrup with honey, and sub unroasted pistachios for the walnuts.

WORTH IT

HONEYCOMB CANDY

MAKES ABOUT 2 POUNDS, OR ABOUT 12 SERVINGS

This is one of our favorite candies to make, and one of the most rewarding. The recipe is adapted from one by genius candymaker, teacher, and author Peter Greweling (seriously, a smart guy—check him out). The confection itself is hard to describe; if you've ever heard of sponge candy, seafoam, ambrosia, fairy food, or hokey-pokey, this is the same thing. If you're familiar with Crunchie or Violet Crumble bars, this is comparable. If you haven't heard of any of these, it's crisp and crunchy but also chewy; light but substantial; honey-flavored and shatter-tastic. It is very much like the physical manifestation of a magical mermaid dream, wrapped in the giggle of a baby bunny rabbit. Or something.

It's very theatrical, too: Watching the syrup expand into an airy golden mass is great fun. Breaking it up into pieces is arguably more so (and a great way to relieve stress). The real tricks to successful honeycomb candy are as follows:

1. Make sure you have everything ready to go before you start (see Mise the Heck Out of That Place, page x). The important parts of the recipe happen one right after the other, so you want to make sure you aren't missing anything essential when it's time to move from one step to the next.

2. In step 4, let the syrup cool just enough, but not too much! You want the bubbles to subside but not completely disappear, and the syrup should still look liquidy when you swirl the pan.

3. Mix carefully, quickly, and very thoroughly: not carefully enough, and you'll splash syrup and burn yourself (or someone else); not quickly enough, and the syrup will cool too much before you pour it out, resulting in flat, dense candy; not thoroughly enough, and you'll end up with slicks of unaerated, tooth-breaking candy on the surface.

There. Now you have all the secrets that it took us years to figure out. (Any secrets we discover from here on out, we're keeping to ourselves.)

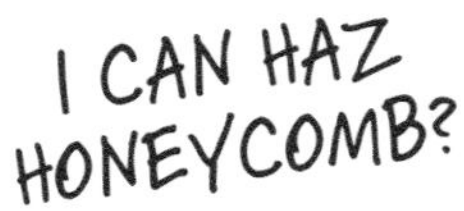

SPECIAL EQUIPMENT

- Disposable aluminum lasagna/casserole pan, about 9″ x 12″ and at least 3″ deep
- Large (13″ x 18″) rimmed baking sheet
- Heatproof spatula
- Candy thermometer
- Very clean chisel or screwdriver, or small hammer (see Breaking Up Is Super-Fun to Do, opposite page)

INGREDIENTS

Unsalted butter or cooking spray, for greasing the pan

Cornstarch or flour, for coating the pan

3½ cups (650 g) granulated sugar

1 cup (350 g) light corn syrup

1 cup (200 g) water

3 teaspoons (20 g) honey

1 teaspoon (5 g) bloomed gelatin (see Note)

4½ teaspoons (20 g) baking soda, sifted

1. Generously butter the bottom and sides of the aluminum pan, and then sift cornstarch over it, making sure to get into the corners. Place the pan on the baking sheet and set both on a heatproof surface.

2. Combine the sugar, corn syrup, and water in a medium-size (4-quart) saucepan, and stir with the heatproof spatula to combine. Bring the mixture to a boil over high heat, uncovered and without stirring, and insert the candy thermometer. Continue to cook over high heat to 285°F/140°C (soft crack stage), about 15 minutes.

3. Add the honey. Reduce the heat to medium-high and continue to cook, uncovered, to 302°F/150°C (hard crack stage), 5 to 7 minutes. The syrup should be significantly thickened and a light golden color.

4. Turn off the heat, but leave the pot on the warm burner. Allow the syrup to cool until most of the large bubbles have dissipated but the syrup is still thin and liquidy when the pan is swirled, 2 to 3 minutes.

5. Add the bloomed gelatin and stir well to combine; the syrup will bubble and steam. Add the baking soda, and stir carefully but vigorously to combine, making sure to scrape the bottom of the pan. The mixture will lighten significantly in color and foam up.

6. Quickly pour the aerated mixture in an even layer into the prepared pan. Don't panic if the candy overflows the pan slightly (that's what the baking sheet is for); *do not touch it* after it's been poured! A) It's incredibly hot and dangerous, and B) you're breaking it into pieces afterward anyway, so it doesn't have to be perfect.

7. Allow the candy to cool without disturbing it (you'll deflate the bubbles) until it is set and completely cool, at least 2 hours.

8. Break the candy into pieces as directed in Breaking Up Is Super-Fun to Do, below.

Store the honeycomb candy in an airtight container at room temperature for up to 3 months.

NOTE: Bloomed gelatin is gelatin that has been mixed with water and allowed to absorb the liquid and soften. Make it as follows: In a small bowl, combine 2 teaspoons (5 g) powdered unflavored gelatin and 1 tablespoon plus 1 teaspoon (20 g) cold water; stir, and let it set, about 5 minutes. Store any extra in an airtight container in the fridge for up to 1 month, for future batches.

Variation

MAPLECOMB Use pure Grade B maple syrup instead of honey for a flavorful, autumn-appropriate treat.

BREAKING UP IS SUPER-FUN TO DO

Breaking up honeycomb candy is, anyway. You'll want a chisel or a screwdriver or a small hammer, available at any local hardware store, for busting the finished candy into pieces. Whatever you choose, be sure to clean it very well first.

A **chisel** with a blade 1 to 1½ inches wide works best. Chisels are great because you get the cleanest breaks and the most control over size. **Flat-head screwdrivers** are the next best. Since they basically punch small holes in the candy, you need to exercise a little more patience, making perforations where you eventually want to break the candy; but they're great for making more uniform pieces, since you have even more control over smaller pieces than with a chisel. A small **hammer** also works just fine. You don't get as much control, and you tend to end up with more dust and crumbs than with the other tools, but a hammer is the best if you have some aggression you need to work out, and there's nothing wrong with honeycomb dust and crumbs.

You'll end up with a fair amount of crumbs no matter what tool you use, and you should never throw them away! Use them as a fantastic and unique ice cream topping, or add them to some Honey Caramel Corn (page 228) or Chocolate Bark (page 79). Honeycomb dust can also be sprinkled over fresh fruit or yogurt for a refreshing change from boring ol' sugar.

MODERATE

CHOCOLATE-DIPPED HONEYCOMB CANDY

MAKES ABOUT 3 POUNDS, OR ABOUT 25 SERVINGS

This is the way we sell Honeycomb Candy at Liddabit, and it's also our favorite way to enjoy it. We're partial to milk chocolate ourselves, but dark chocolate never did honeycomb any harm. Just make sure to store it in a cool place; otherwise the chocolate will lose its temper and ~~beat you about the head and shoulders with a Wiffle bat~~ end up dull instead of shiny.

SPECIAL EQUIPMENT

- 2 large bowls
- Wire or spider skimmer and large (8″ to 10″) tweezers (see Resources, page 291), or regular dinner fork
- 2 large (13″ x 18″) rimmed baking sheets, lined with parchment or wax paper

INGREDIENTS

About 5 cups (32 ounces/900 g) chopped dark or milk chocolate, or 5 cups (32 ounces/900 g) chopped dark or milk chocolate and ¾ cup plus 1 tablespoon (185 g) mild vegetable oil

1 batch Honeycomb Candy (page 197), broken into 1- to 2-inch pieces

1. Temper the 5 cups chocolate according to the instructions on page 26, or use the 5 cups chocolate and ¾ cup plus 1 tablespoon oil to make Cheater's Chocolate Coating as directed on page 32.
2. Place the honeycomb pieces and the tempered chocolate or chocolate coating in two separate bowls. Set up your dipping station, from left to right (or right to left, if you're a lefty), as follows: bowl with honeycomb pieces, bowl with tempered chocolate or chocolate coating, skimmer and tweezers or standard kitchen fork, lined baking sheets.
3. Working with a few pieces at a time, drop the honeycomb into the bowl of chocolate and submerge the pieces with the skimmer. Then use the skimmer to scoop and lift the honeycomb out of the chocolate, tapping the skimmer handle on the rim of the bowl a couple of times to drain off the excess chocolate. Remove the chocolate-covered honeycomb pieces one by one with the tweezers, and place them on the lined baking sheets. (Alternatively, if using a kitchen fork, drop the pieces in the chocolate and push them under with the fork. You just have to fish them out one by one to place them on the baking sheets. For more on this fork-dipping technique, see page 33.)
4. Repeat until all the honeycomb is dipped. Allow the chocolate to set up until it is firm and shiny, 15 to 20 minutes.

Store the dipped honeycomb in an airtight container at cool room temperature for up to 2 months.

JEN SAYS: The leftover dipping chocolate will have a bunch of little honeycomb crumbs in it.. If this doesn't bother you, great! Go make some Chocolate Bark (page 79) with it. If it does, or if you want to use the chocolate for dipping other things in the future, rewarm the chocolate so that it is liquid (it will be out of temper), and pour it through a fine-mesh strainer into a container. Presto! Crumb-free chocolate!

MODERATE

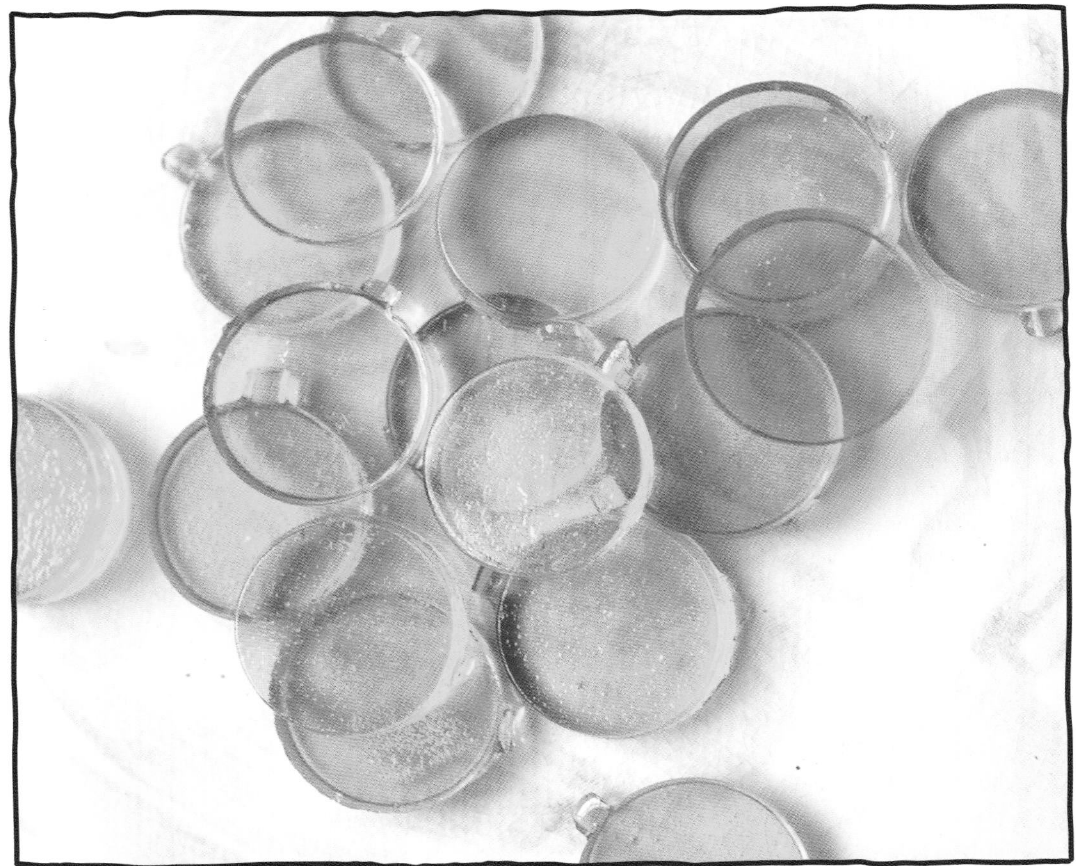

BUTTERSCOTCH DROPS

MAKES ABOUT 75 ONE-INCH DROPS

One of our testers described this as "delicious grandma candy." We couldn't have said it better ourselves! These taste just like you remember them, and the way we see it, we wouldn't want it any other way. Like Liz's grandpa used to say, "If it ain't broke, don't fix it." (He also used to say "Sugar melts, s#!% floats," but that's less applicable in this scenario.)

You can do these free-form, but molds help keep things tidier—we use our plain round lollipop molds, which you can do if you don't feel like buying a bunch of different shapes.

SPECIAL EQUIPMENT

- Small (8″ x 8″) baking pan, or hard candy or lollipop molds with at least 75 one-inch cavities
- Pastry brush
- Candy thermometer
- Heatproof spatula
- 2 candy funnels and heatproof cup (optional; see Funnel of Love, page 139)

INGREDIENTS

Cooking spray or vegetable oil, for greasing the pan

2 cups (450 g) granulated sugar

1 tablespoon (13 g) distilled white vinegar

¼ cup (55 g) water

1 teaspoon (5 g) pure vanilla extract

6 drops yellow food coloring (optional)

1. Lightly coat the baking pan with cooking spray, making sure to get all the corners. Set it aside on a heatproof surface.

2. Combine the sugar, vinegar, and water in a medium-size (4-quart) saucepan. Wet the pastry brush, and use it to wash down the inside of the pan to dissolve any renegade sugar crystals.

3. Bring the sugar mixture to a boil, uncovered and without stirring, over medium-high heat. Insert the candy thermometer and cook until the syrup begins to turn a light gold color and reaches 285°–290°F/141°–143°C (soft crack stage), about 10 minutes.

4. Remove the saucepan from the heat and use the heatproof spatula to gently stir in the vanilla and the food coloring (if using). Stir for a few seconds, until they're completely incorporated.

5. Now you have a couple of options: *Option 1:* Pour the syrup into the prepared baking pan and allow it to cool for about 10 minutes. Generously coat a sharp chef's knife and use it to score 1-inch square marks in the candy, repeating the scores once or twice as it cools, until it's firm enough to hold the score marks. Allow the candy to cool completely, at least 45 minutes. Break the cooled candy along the score lines.

   Option 2: Carefully pour the syrup into the candy funnels, and portion it into the hard candy or lollipop molds. (Unless you have a helper, you'll use first one candy funnel, then the other; use the heatproof cup to hold your funnel-in-waiting.) Let the candy pieces cool completely, at least 20 minutes, before removing them from the molds.

Store the butterscotch drops, layered with wax or parchment paper, in an airtight container at room temperature for up to 3 weeks.

MODERATE

RONI-SUE'S BEST BUTTERCRUNCH EVER

MAKES ABOUT 4 POUNDS, OR ABOUT 16 SERVINGS

We have to give total credit to Liz's former employer, the amazing Rhonda Kave of Roni-Sue's Chocolates, for this recipe. (Thanks, Rhonda!) It's simple, but there's something about the cast-iron skillet, the zenlike focus it takes to sit and stir the mixture while watching it turn from clear liquid and grainy sugar to a thick, bubbly, golden, toasty goo, that makes it magical. This recipe demonstrates the closest thing to alchemy in this book, in our opinion. This is also one of the few sweets that Jen not only enjoys but craves (which is really saying a lot).

Keep in mind: The flavor of the buttercrunch center hinges on the two main ingredients, butter and sugar, so you want the absolute best butter you can find. We like European-style cultured butter, like Plugrá, which is available at most major supermarkets and specialty supermarkets such as Whole Foods. This is the time to splurge on the good stuff.

Bonus: You don't actually need to temper chocolate for this recipe! Straight-up melted chocolate works just fine. Just keep in mind it'll take a little longer to set at room temperature—20 to 25 minutes—so you can put it in the fridge to speed things up. And if you don't have the three baking sheets called for, just wash and reuse what you do have as you go along.

SPECIAL EQUIPMENT

- 3 large (13" x 18") rimmed baking sheets
- Large (12" or so) well-seasoned cast-iron skillet
- Candy thermometer
- Spider skimmer (see page 20) and 10" tweezers, or a regular dinner fork (see Notes)
- Nonpowdered latex or vinyl gloves (optional)

INGREDIENTS

FOR THE BUTTERCRUNCH CENTER

1 pound (4 sticks/450 g) high-quality unsalted butter, cubed, plus about 1 teaspoon for greasing a baking sheet

2 cups (385 g) granulated sugar

½ teaspoon (2 g) kosher salt

FOR THE COATING

About 2½ cups (10 ounces/300 g) chopped walnuts (see Chopping Notes for Nuts, page 207)

1½ teaspoons (5 g) kosher salt

About 4 cups (26 ounces/740 g) chopped milk chocolate, or 4 cups (26 ounces/740 g) chopped milk chocolate and ⅔ cup (150 g) mild vegetable oil (see Notes)

To make the buttercrunch center:

❶ Generously butter one of the baking sheets, making sure to get into the corners. Set it aside on a heatproof surface.

❷ Place the 1 pound butter, the sugar, and the salt in the cast-iron skillet and melt over high heat, stirring once or twice with a whisk to combine.

3. Once the butter is completely melted, reduce the heat to medium-high and cook, stirring frequently with the whisk, until the mixture has thickened slightly and turned a tan color, 15 to 20 minutes.

4. Insert the candy thermometer, holding it with one hand to keep an eye on the temperature. Continue to cook over medium-high heat, stirring constantly with the whisk, until the mixture has reached 305°F/152°C (hard crack stage), 10 to 12 minutes.

5. Wearing oven mitts (the skillet will be extremely hot), immediately remove the skillet from the heat and pour the hot mixture onto the prepared baking sheet. Allow it to cool until it is slightly set but still soft, about 5 minutes.

6. Using a sharp chef's knife or bench scraper, score the buttercrunch into 1-inch squares, marking the scores several times as it cools (the score marks will want to close up when the mixture is still hot).

7. Allow the buttercrunch to cool completely, about 1 hour. (Meanwhile, you can toast the walnuts; see step 8.) When the buttercrunch is completely cooled and set, break it into pieces along the score lines and place the pieces in a medium-size bowl.

To coat the buttercrunch:

8. While the buttercrunch is cooling, toast the walnuts: Preheat your oven to 250°F/120°C. Spread the walnuts in an even layer on a large baking sheet and toast them, stirring occasionally, until they're golden brown and fragrant and the skins are starting to flake, about 20 minutes. Allow them to cool completely on the baking sheet, 20 to 30 minutes. Then place the walnuts in a medium-size bowl, sprinkle the salt over them, and toss well to combine.

9. Melt the 4 cups chocolate as directed on page 24, or use the 4 cups chocolate and ⅔ cup oil to make Cheater's Chocolate Coating following the instructions on page 32. Place the melted chocolate or chocolate coating in a medium-size bowl.

10. Wash and dry the first large baking sheet and line it with wax or parchment paper. Set up your dipping station, from left to right (or right to left, if you're a lefty), as follows: bowl with "naked" buttercrunch pieces; bowl with melted chocolate or chocolate coating; skimmer and tweezers, or fork; bowl of toasted, salted walnuts; lined baking sheet. If you want to use gloves, put them on now (the walnuts will make a sticky, messy layer on your hands).

11. Dip the buttercrunch: Working with a few pieces at a time, drop the naked buttercrunch into the bowl of chocolate and submerge the pieces with the skimmer. Use the skimmer to scoop and lift the candy out of the chocolate, tapping the skimmer handle on the rim of the bowl to drain off the excess chocolate. (Alternatively, if using a fork, drop the pieces in the chocolate and push them under with the fork.)

12. Remove the dipped buttercrunch pieces one by one with the tweezers or fork, and place them, without touching each other,

in the bowl of walnuts. Gently sprinkle the walnuts over the dipped buttercrunch pieces to cover them completely. Carefully remove the pieces from the bowl of walnuts, and lay them on the lined baking sheet. Repeat this procedure until all the pieces are dipped and coated.

13. Let the buttercrunch set completely, about 15 minutes. Enjoy!

Store the buttercrunch, layered with wax paper, in an airtight container at cool room temperature for up to 2 weeks, or in the fridge for up to 1 month. (We dare you to try and hold on to it for that long.)

NOTES: If you don't have a spider skimmer or 10-inch tweezers, you can fake it with a regular dinner fork, but it'll take you about three times as long and the candies won't look quite as nice.

We specify milk chocolate in this recipe, but you can use whatever chocolate you like. Rhonda mixes a roughly 2:1 ratio of milk to dark chocolate, to cut back on the sweetness a bit. If you have the chocolate and the inclination, go for it.

LIZ SAYS: Nerd Alert! More and more, imported and specialty butters are showing up on grocery store shelves. Cultured butter harks back to Ye Olden Dayes before butter-making was mechanized, when cream from several farms and/or several rounds of milking was collected so it could be made into butter all at once. Over the few days it sat around, it would ferment somewhat as good bacteria (think yogurt) munched on the lactose in the cream, converting it to lactic acid and giving the final product a somewhat tangy character. Of course the taste preference is personal; but when butter really has a chance to shine (as in this recipe), I prefer cultured butter for the extra depth of flavor that it imparts.

CHOPPING NOTES FOR NUTS

If you buy your nuts whole, you can pulse them in a food processor in 1-second bursts until they're finely chopped (about ¼-inch pieces); it's not an exact method, and there will be some "dust" along with the chopped pieces, but that's totally okay. Or, you can simply put the nuts in a zip-top plastic bag, press the air out before sealing it, and then give the bag a few good bashes with a rolling pin.

MODERATE

BACON BUTTERCRUNCH

MAKES ABOUT 1½ POUNDS, OR ABOUT 15 SERVINGS

We first encountered Bacon Buttercrunch at Roni-Sue's (see page 204), where it was dunked in chocolate and rolled in spiced pine nuts. Our version is simpler—no chocolate or pine nuts—but we think we nailed the salty-sweet aspect. This is a great gift for the pork-lover in your life, or for any one who enjoys bacon with . . . well, anything. Cook the bacon just before you make the candy, so the rendered fat—which you'll use in the buttercrunch—is still liquid.

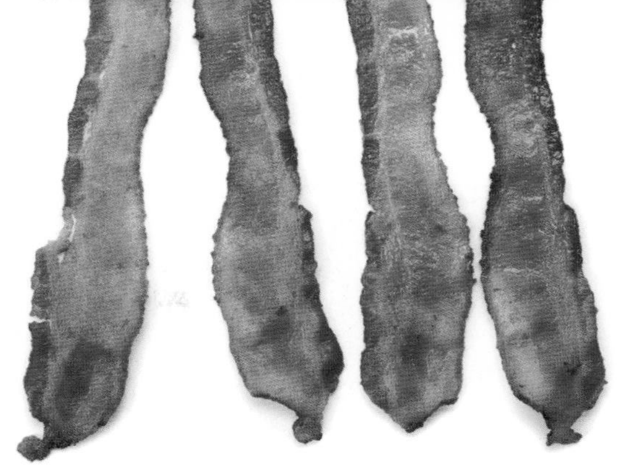

SPECIAL EQUIPMENT

- Large (13" x 18") rimmed baking sheet
- Candy thermometer
- Heatproof spatula

INGREDIENTS

12 ounces (340 g) bacon, cooked very crisp, crumbled (about 1 cup), rendered fat reserved

About 8 tablespoons (1 stick/225 g) unsalted butter, melted, plus extra for greasing the baking sheet

2 cups (385 g) granulated sugar

2 tablespoons (30 g) pure vanilla extract

1½ teaspoons (7 g) fine sea salt

¼ cup (60 g) water

1. Carefully pour the bacon fat into a heatproof measuring cup, and add enough melted butter to make 1½ cups. Set aside.

2. Generously butter the baking sheet and set it aside on a heatproof surface.

3. Combine the bacon fat mixture with the sugar, vanilla, salt, and water in a medium-size (4-quart) saucepan, and bring it to a boil over medium-high heat. Insert the candy thermometer and continue to cook, stirring constantly with a whisk, until it reaches 300°F/150°C (hard crack stage), 18 to 20 minutes.

4. Wearing your oven mitts, remove the pan from the heat and stir in the crumbled bacon. Carefully pour the mixture onto the prepared baking sheet, and use the heatproof spatula to spread it evenly. Allow the buttercrunch to cool completely, at least 1 hour, then break it into bite-size pieces.

Store the bacon buttercrunch, layered with parchment or wax paper, in an airtight container at cool room temperature for up to 1 week.

JEN SAYS: So you're a little type A about your candy and want neat-looking squares? Use a knife or a bench scraper (page 21) to score the buttercrunch, scoring several more times as it cools. Once it's set, the scores will help you break it into pretty little pieces.

EASY

TROPICAL TOFFEE

MAKES ABOUT 3 POUNDS, OR ENOUGH FOR ABOUT 30 HUNGRY FOLKS

Toffee is one of those adaptable treats that lends itself very well to getting dressed up or down. By itself, it's a luscious, comforting, almost-universally loved candy that wallops everyone upside the head with a sock full of nostalgia; with other goodies mixed in, it's just as lip-smacking and gives you an outlet for all those creative impulses you never got to act on before now. Mock your cross-stitched self-portraits, will they? Well, you'll show them—Tropical style! (Hey, in our world, adding rum and macadamia nuts to anything automatically qualifies it as "Tropical." And don't you tell us otherwise.)

SPECIAL EQUIPMENT

- Large (13" x 18") rimmed baking sheet
- Candy thermometer
- Heatproof spatula

INGREDIENTS

1 pound (4 sticks/450 g) unsalted butter, plus extra for greasing the baking sheet

4 cups (775 g) granulated sugar

½ cup (175 g) light corn syrup

½ cup (120 g) light rum

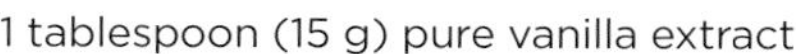

1 tablespoon (15 g) pure vanilla extract

1 teaspoon (5 g) fine sea salt

1 teaspoon (4 g) baking soda

1½ cups (225 g) roasted, salted macadamia nuts, roughly chopped or crushed

1. Generously butter the baking sheet and set it aside on a heatproof surface.

2. Combine the sugar, 1 pound butter, corn syrup, rum, vanilla, and sea salt in a medium-size (4-quart) saucepan and bring to a boil over high heat. Insert the candy thermometer.

3. Reduce the heat to medium-high and cook, stirring constantly with the spatula, until the mixture reaches 300°F/150° (hard crack stage), about 10 minutes.

4. Remove the pan from the heat, and add the baking soda and macadamia nuts, stirring vigorously (but carefully) to incorporate.

5 Pour the mixture out onto the prepared baking sheet, and spread it evenly with the heatproof spatula. Allow the toffee to cool completely, about 2 hours, then break it into bite-size pieces.

Store the toffee, layered with parchment or wax paper, in an airtight container at room temperature for up to 1 week. It will last for 2 to 3 weeks when stored in the refrigerator; just allow it to come to room temperature before serving (the flavor isn't as nice when it's cold).

Variations

Sub out any nut (or combination of nuts) or liquor that you like. Try bourbon whiskey with pecans, or Cointreau with almonds. The corn syrup can also be switched out for honey or pure maple syrup, and using dark corn syrup instead of light it will give the toffee a more caramelized flavor.

LIZ SAYS: Your friends call you Fancy Nancy. You bust out the nice china for an impromptu visit from your neighbor. So what? You enjoy the finer things in life, and so do we! Some might say it's gilding the lily, but sprinkling a generous handful of chocolate chips on top of the warm toffee, spreading them into a thin layer, and then dusting that with toasted unsweetened coconut flakes takes this toffee to the next level.

WORTH IT

DRAGÉES

MAKES ABOUT 1½ POUNDS

Pronounced "druh-ZHAYS," these are a perfect example of a treat exceeding the sum of its parts. Sure, nuts are great. So is caramelized sugar. So is chocolate. But together, they make something really special. And the fresher they are the better, so homemade dragées are a real treasure. Without the chocolate, the caramelized nuts can be used to make Praline Paste (page 217)—or just snacked on by the hardworking chef who made them.

Keep in mind that it's helpful for all the pre-chocolate-dipping ingredients to be warm, or at least not ice cold. This will buy you more time when you're coating the nuts and separating them on the baking sheet (see page 216 for help doing this). Also, it's great to have a friend around when you're coating the nuts in chocolate and dredging them in confectioners' sugar. With one person to do the chocolate and one person to do the sugar, the whole thing is a bit easier.

SPECIAL EQUIPMENT

- Large (13" x 18") rimmed baking sheet
- Candy thermometer
- Nonpowdered latex or vinyl gloves (optional)

INGREDIENTS

Cooking spray or vegetable oil

2 cups (340 g) whole almonds, preferably blanched

1 cup (200 g) granulated sugar

3 tablespoons (45 g) water

Pinch of cream of tartar

1 tablespoon (12 g) mild olive oil

2 cups (13 ounces/370 g) chopped dark chocolate, or 2 cups (13 ounces/370 g) chopped dark chocolate and ⅓ cup (75 g) mild vegetable oil, for coating

About 1 cup sifted confectioners' sugar

1. Toast the almonds: Preheat the oven to 350°F/175°C. Lightly coat the baking sheet with cooking spray, and spread the almonds on it in an even layer. Bake, stirring a couple of times with a heatproof spatula or wooden spoon, until the almonds are golden brown and fragrant, 5 to 10 minutes. Allow the nuts to cool completely on the baking sheet, then transfer them to a medium-size bowl. Line the baking sheet with parchment paper or a silicone mat.

2. Combine the sugar, water, and cream of tartar in a small (2-quart) saucepan, and bring to a boil, uncovered, over high heat. Insert the candy thermometer.

3. Reduce the heat to medium-high and cook, without stirring, until it reaches 280°F/138°C, 8 to 10 minutes. Add the almonds, stir them to coat, and cook, stirring frequently, until the mixture reaches 305°F/152°C (hard crack stage) and is brown and fragrant, another 5 to 7 minutes.

4. Remove the saucepan from the heat. Stir in the olive oil, mix well to combine, and carefully pour the mixture onto the prepared baking sheet, scraping it out and pressing it into an even layer with the spatula.

5. Wait a minute or two for the mixture to cool slightly. Then lay a sheet of parchment paper or a silicone mat on top of it and gently press down to even out the layer of almonds. As the mixture cools, carefully use your fingers to separate the almonds before the sugar sets up and becomes brittle. Allow the caramelized almonds to cool completely, about 30 minutes.

6. In the meantime, temper the 2 cups chopped chocolate according to the instructions on page 26, or use the 2 cups chopped chocolate and ⅓ cup oil to make Cheater's Chocolate Coating as directed on page 32.

7. Transfer the almonds back to their bowl, and line the baking sheet again, this time with parchment or wax paper.

8. Set up your dipping station as follows: Place an empty bowl in front of you; to its left, the bowl of almonds; to its right, the bowl of chocolate and a small bowl with the confectioners' sugar. Set the lined baking sheet nearby. If you don't want to get your hands messy, put on gloves, too.

9. Place a few nuts and a spoonful or two of chocolate in the empty bowl, and gently toss the nuts with your hands until they're coated with chocolate. Drop the chocolate-covered nuts in the confectioners' sugar, and toss to cover. Repeat this procedure until all the nuts are dipped and dredged, fishing the dredged nuts out of the sugar and placing them on the baking sheet every once in a while (this makes more room for the next round of nuts). Allow the dragées to set completely, about 10 minutes.

Store the dragées in an airtight container at room temperature for up to 2 weeks.

COOKING DRAGÉES

1. Cook the sugar syrup until it's brown and toasty.

2. Coat the almonds in the syrup.

3. Scoop those nuts onto a baking sheet.

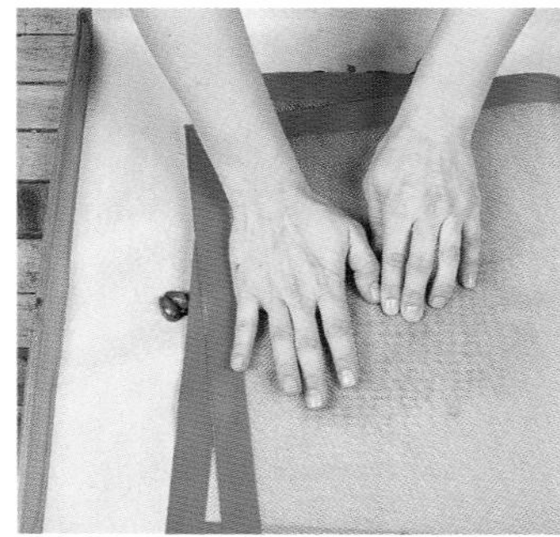
4. Use a silicone mat and press down to even out the almond layer.

5. Carefully separate the almonds by hand so you can break them apart later.

Variation

HACHI MACHI Instead of confectioners' sugar, roll the chocolate-covered nuts in 1 cup unsweetened cocoa powder mixed with ¼ teaspoon ground cayenne pepper or chile powder.

EASY

PRALINE PASTE

MAKES ABOUT 2½ CUPS

Praline paste is fairly simple: caramelized nuts, ground into a paste. The only problem is that it's extremely difficult to stop eating it. You have a little wiggle room to snack if you just want to use the rest to make Hip-to-Be Squares (page 99), but beware: One spoonful quickly turns into two, and then three, and then seven—and then all of a sudden there isn't any left. Don't say we didn't warn you.

SPECIAL EQUIPMENT

- Food processor

INGREDIENTS

1 recipe Dragées (page 213), prepared through step 5 (cooled but without chocolate coating)

1 to 2 tablespoons (15 to 30 g) neutral-flavored vegetable oil, such as safflower or sunflower, if needed

Place the cooled, caramelized nuts in the bowl of the food processor. Grind them in 2-second pulses, scraping down the bowl of the processor once or twice to make sure all the nuts are ground evenly, until the nuts have come together in a fine paste (it should have a peanut-butter-like consistency). If the paste is too dry or sticky, add a little vegetable oil and pulse again. Make sure to pulse just a couple seconds at a time! If you grind the nuts continuously, you run the risk of scorching the delicate nut oils.

Store the paste in an airtight container in the fridge for up to 3 weeks. Let it come to room temperature before using.

EASY

SESAME CANDY

MAKES ABOUT 100 PIECES

The nice thing about making this sesame candy at home is that you have control over the final consistency. Some people love the crisp, brittle snap of hard-cooked candy; others enjoy the firm, chewy texture that results from taking it off the heat a few degrees earlier. (Our preference falls smack in the middle.) However you like the texture, there's no store-bought sesame candy that can compare to this homemade version. You can make this with white sesame seeds, or for a more visually striking variation, mix half black and half white.

SPECIAL EQUIPMENT

- Small (9″ x 9″) baking pan
- Candy thermometer
- Heatproof spatula

INGREDIENTS

Cooking spray

1 cup (340 g) mild honey

1 cup (200 g) granulated sugar

¼ cup (60 g) water

2 cups (300 g) raw sesame seeds

1½ teaspoons (6 g) sesame oil, preferably toasted

2 teaspoons (10 g) fine sea salt

1. Lightly coat the baking pan with cooking spray, and set it aside on a heatproof surface.

2. Combine the honey, sugar, and water in a small (2-quart) saucepan, and bring to boil, uncovered, over high heat.

3. Insert the candy thermometer, reduce the heat to medium-high, and cook until the mixture reaches 270°F/132°C (soft crack stage). Add the sesame seeds and stir gently with the heatproof spatula to combine.

4. Continue cooking the mixture until it reaches 285° to 295°F/140° to 146°C (soft crack stage to low hard crack stage), depending on your taste: at 285°F/140°C,

the candy will be firm but have some chew to it; at 295°F/146°C, it will officially be hard candy.

5. Once the mixture reaches your desired temperature, remove the saucepan from the heat and gently but thoroughly stir in the sesame oil and salt. Pour the mixture into the prepared baking pan, scraping the saucepan with the spatula, and allow it to cool for about 10 minutes.

6. Score the candy into 1-inch squares with a sharp chef's knife, and allow it to cool completely, about 1 hour, then break or cut the candy into pieces along the score lines.

Store the sesame candy in an airtight container, layered with parchment or wax paper, at room temperature for up to 1 month.

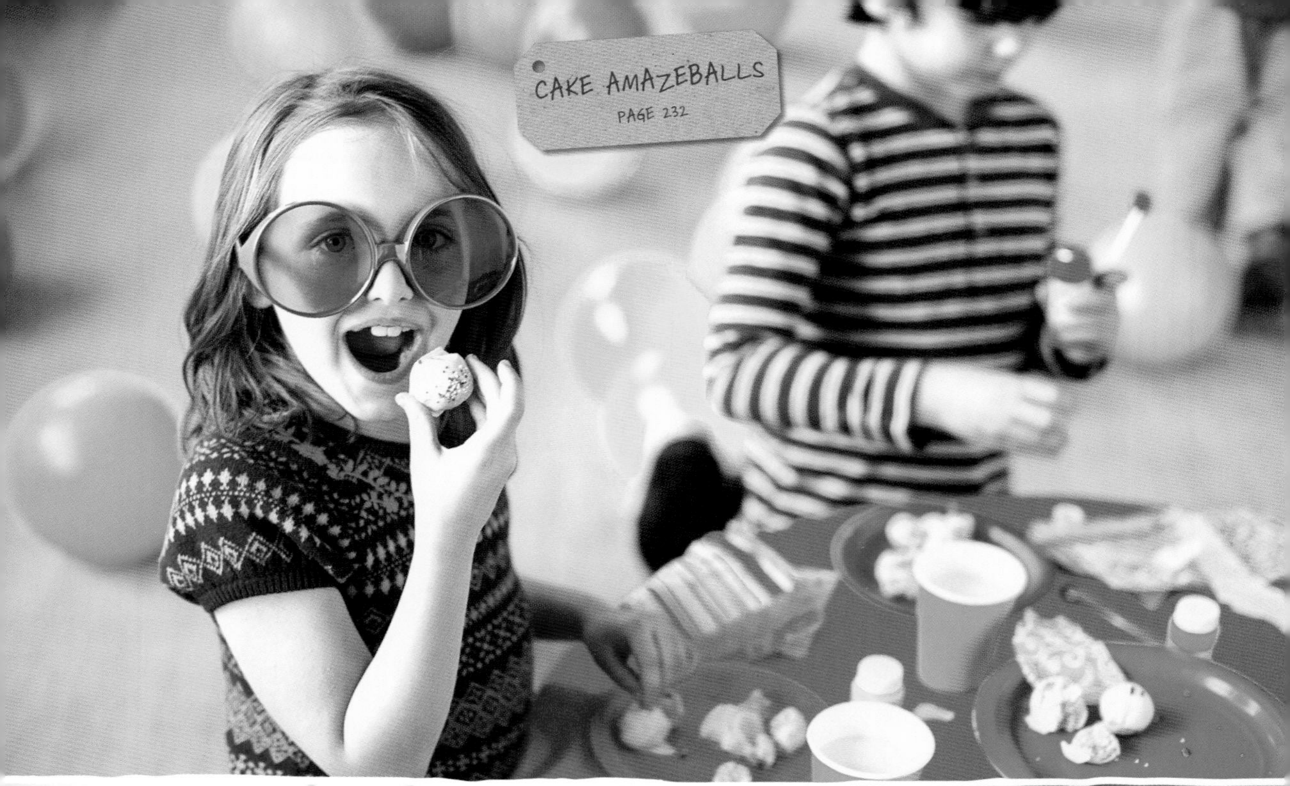
CAKE AMAZEBALLS
PAGE 232

THE BEST HOT FUDGE SAUCE
PAGE 243

HONEY CARAMEL CORN
PAGE 228

CANDY APPLES
PAGE 225

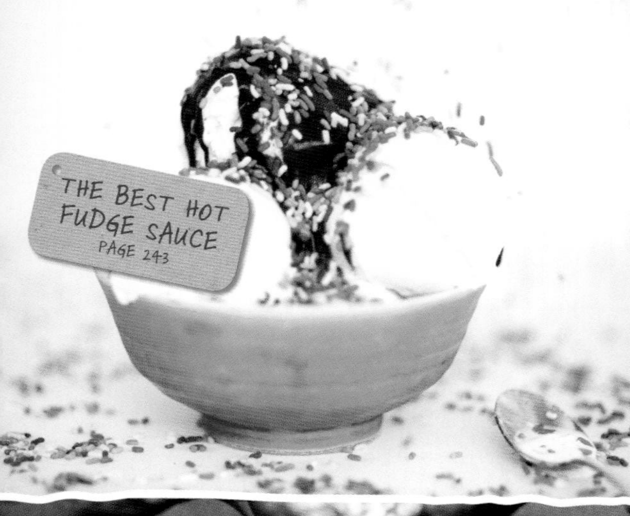

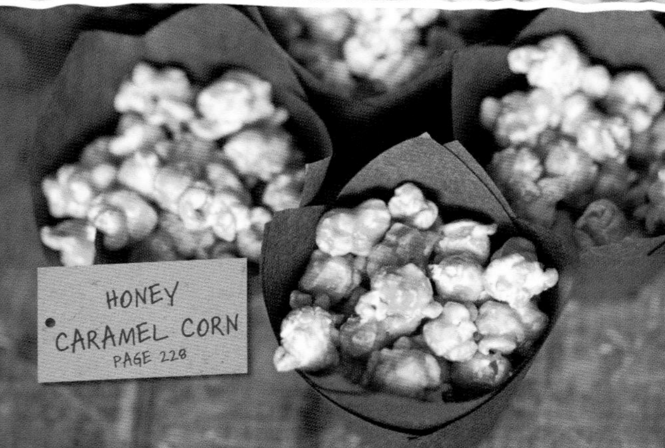

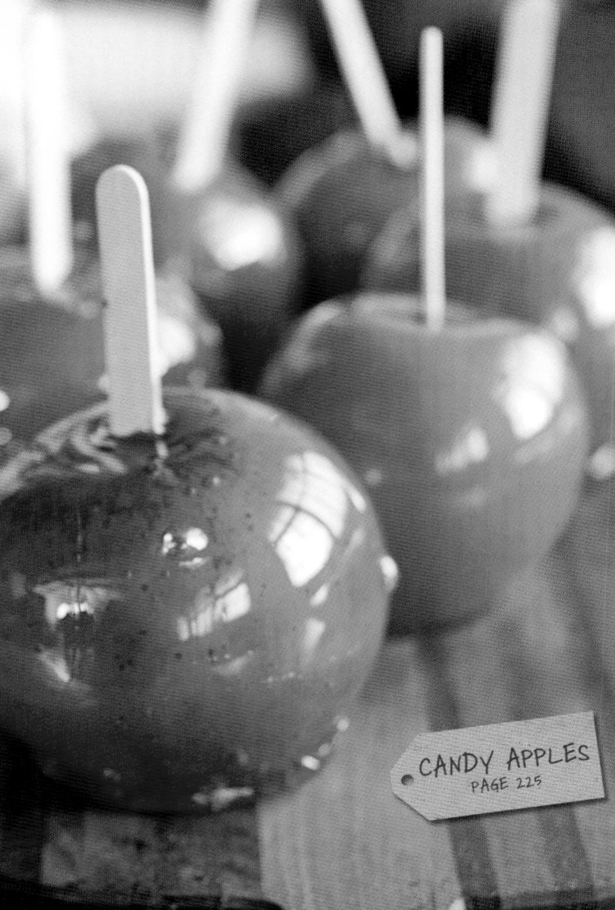

Chapter Six

PARTY TIME IN CANDYLAND

Some recipes just lend themselves to parties. We've heard about many a grandma's taffy-pulling parties back in the day, and who doesn't want to help toss a giant bowl full of caramel corn, or help roll some cake balls? Nobody, that's who.

This section's recipes also, conveniently, happen to be extra-perfect to *take* to parties. Candy Apples (page 225) are especially great when you want something that's really visually stunning; Cake Amazeballs (page 232) can be made in literally* infinite flavor combinations. Hot fudge (page 243) and butterscotch (page 241) sauces are an easy way to please the heck out of a gaggle of kids (ice cream not included).

If you really like to party—and we mean PARTY—you can make everything in this chapter, dump it in a kiddie pool, and go to town. But we can't be held responsible for the consequences of such a party.

*And by "literally," we mean "metaphorically."

MODERATE

CARAMEL APPLES

MAKES 15 CARAMEL APPLES

This is a fun treat to make with slightly older kids—say, age ten and above. Who doesn't love dipping something in goo? Here's another instance where the fresh, homemade version kicks the tar out of the store-bought kind and then steals its lunch money. If you haven't had a fresh caramel apple, you haven't had a caramel apple at all. Another bonus: no leftovers! Run out of caramel? You have apples for the week. Run out of apples? You have some extra caramel to store in the fridge and drizzle over a sundae.

Everybody wins.

SPECIAL EQUIPMENT

- Candy thermometer
- Heatproof spatula
- 15 sturdy wooden skewers, 6 to 8 inches long and roughly ¼ inch in diameter (available at most grocery stores), pointy ends snipped off; or 15 popsicle sticks
- Large (13″ x 18″) rimmed baking sheet, lined with parchment

INGREDIENTS

- 1¾ cups (350 g) granulated sugar
- 1½ cups (12 ounces/375 g) evaporated milk
- ⅔ cup (160 g) heavy (whipping) cream
- 1 vanilla bean, split open and seeds scraped out, pod reserved; ½ teaspoon vanilla paste (see page 11); or 1 teaspoon pure vanilla extract
- ¾ cup plus 1 tablespoon (300 g) light corn syrup
- 3 tablespoons (45 g) unsalted butter
- 1 tablespoon (20 g) coarse sea salt
- 15 medium-size (3-inch) tart apples, such as Granny Smith or Gala, washed well and dried thoroughly, any stems removed

1. Combine the sugar, evaporated milk, heavy cream, and vanilla bean and seeds (if using) in a large (6- to 8-quart) saucepan. Bring to a boil over medium-high heat, uncovered and without stirring. Insert the candy thermometer.

2. Add the light corn syrup, and stir gently with the heatproof spatula until everything is mixed well. Reduce the heat to medium-low and cook, stirring often and scraping the bottom of the pot, until it reaches 230°F/110°C (thread stage), about 30 minutes.

3. Add the butter and vanilla paste or extract (if using), and fish out the vanilla bean with a slotted spoon. Stirring continuously, cook the caramel until it reaches 241°F/116°C (thread-to-soft ball stage), 15 to 20 minutes; it will be a deep tawny color and have slow, rolling bubbles in the middle. Remove the pan from the heat.

4. Stir in the salt, mixing well so that it's distributed evenly. Allow the caramel to sit and thicken up a bit, until it's the consistency of pancake batter, about 10 minutes.

5. Meanwhile, insert a skewer into the stem end of each apple, and push it down as far as you can without breaking through the bottom of the apple; you want at least 3 inches of skewer poking out of the top.

6. Give the caramel a few stirs with the spatula to even out the temperature. Carefully dip an apple in the caramel, holding it horizontally and slowly twirling it as you lift it out (to catch any drips). Place it on the lined baking sheet. When you're handling the apples, remember to keep the skewer horizontal *at all times*! It can be easy to forget how hot this caramel is and hold it up to show off to somebody—and then you have hot caramel all over your hands. Bad News Bears.

7. Repeat with the remaining apples. Allow the caramel coating to set until it is cool and firm but yielding to the touch, about 10 minutes.

Caramel apples are best eaten the day they're made, but you can store them, layered with parchment or wax paper, in an airtight container in the fridge for up to 3 days.

MODERATE

CANDY APPLES

MAKES 8 TO 12 CANDY APPLES

You got your caramel apple people, and you got your candy apple people. Since we've spent the past five years of our lives making caramel, we're partial to caramel apples. But the preference also has to do with the quality of candy apples that are generally available. For most of us, there's one kind of candy apple we remember: the magorgo*, eye-searingly red kind, dipped halfway up its stick and, judging by the thickness of the candy shell, engineered to survive the next few planetary catastrophes (meteorite, dinosaur resurrection, all the volcanoes on earth erupting simultaneously—that sort of thing). This is a different breed of candy apple. Sure, it's bright red (if you use the food coloring), but the candy is delicate and crispy, with a light caramel flavor. Make these for friends in the fall, when the apples are really juicy and delicious, and it's likely to become a tradition.

*Muh-GOR-go: large in size; massive, giant, enormous, humongous. Look it up. (Don't really look it up.)

Speaking of the fall, these are ideal for cool, dry weather; they don't hold up very well to humidity. If it's humid out, hate to say it but you might want to make something else, like the Buttermints on page 177, instead. (And if it's *really* humid out, you shouldn't be making candy at all. Go bake a loaf of bread.)

SPECIAL EQUIPMENT

- 8 to 12 sturdy wooden skewers, 6 to 8 inches long and roughly ¼ inch in diameter (available at most grocery stores), pointy ends snipped off; or 8 to 12 popsicle sticks
- Heatproof spatula
- Pastry brush
- Candy thermometer
- Large (13" x 18") baking sheet, lined with silicone mat or parchment paper

INGREDIENTS

8 large (4") or 12 medium-size (3") apples (any type will work, but the best are firm and tart or sweet-tart, like Granny Smith, Jonathan, or Gala), washed well and dried thoroughly, any stems removed

3 cups (575 g) granulated sugar

1 cup (350 g) light corn syrup

½ cup (120 g) water

2 teaspoons (10 g) red food coloring (optional)

1. Insert a skewer into the stem end of each apple, and push it down as far as you can without breaking through the bottom of the apple; you want at least 3 inches of skewer poking out of the top.

2. Combine the sugar, corn syrup, and water in a small (2-quart) saucepan, and stir with the heatproof spatula to combine. Dampen the pastry brush with water, and use it to wash down the inside of the saucepan to remove any renegade sugar crystals that may have stuck there (see page 48 for more on this).

3. Bring the mixture to a boil, uncovered and without stirring, over high heat. When it has come to a boil, insert the candy thermometer and continue to cook, without disturbing, to 300°F/150°C (hard crack stage).

4. Remove the pan from the heat and let the syrup cool, undisturbed, until the bubbles have mostly subsided and the mixture

has thickened slightly—it should have the consistency of pancake syrup when the pan is swirled gently—5 to 7 minutes. If you're using food coloring, add it now and stir gently but thoroughly to combine, until the syrup is no longer streaky.

5. Carefully dip an apple in the candy, holding it horizontally and slowly twirling it as you lift it out (to catch any drips). Remember to keep the skewer horizontal at all times—*never* hold the candy apple with the stick down until it is *completely* cool! Gently place the apple on the lined baking sheet.

6. Repeat with the remaining apples. Allow the candy coating to cool completely until it is hard to the touch, about 10 minutes.

You really should eat these within a few hours of making them, but if made ahead of time, they will last, tightly wrapped in plastic wrap or a zip-top bag and stored in a cool, dry place, for up to 3 days.

Variation

Try replacing ¼ cup of the corn syrup with pure maple syrup for a hint of maple flavor. Or sprinkle some sea salt on the candy coating as it cools.

MODERATE

HONEY CARAMEL CORN

MAKES ABOUT 20 CUPS, 8 TO 10 SERVINGS

Homemade caramel corn is a really easy way to impress your friends. Even people who don't like caramel corn like homemade caramel corn; it's crunchy, buttery, salty, sweet—all those things that make a treat inherently munchable. It also lends itself to endless variation (we've given you a couple ideas to start with); see how many different things you can add before sinking into a sugar coma!

INGREDIENTS

Cooking spray or vegetable oil

18 cups popped popcorn (about ⅔ cup/65 g unpopped kernels)

8 tablespoons (1 stick/110 g) unsalted butter

1½ cups (300 g) granulated sugar

¼ cup (85 g) honey

¼ cup (85 g) light corn syrup

1 teaspoon (6 g) baking soda

2 teaspoons (10 g) kosher salt

SPECIAL EQUIPMENT

- Extra-large (6- to 8-quart) bowl (with enough room to toss popcorn)
- 2 heatproof spatulas and/or wooden spoons
- Candy thermometer

1. Lightly coat the bowl and the heatproof spatulas with cooking spray. Place the popped popcorn in the bowl and set it all aside.

2. Melt the butter in a medium-size (4-quart) saucepan over medium-high heat. Add the sugar, honey, and corn syrup, and using one of the oiled spatulas, stir to combine. Bring to a boil, and insert the candy thermometer. Stirring often and scraping the bottom of the pot to prevent scorching, cook the mixture to 300°F/150°C (hard crack stage), 5 to 8 minutes.

3. Remove the caramel mixture from the heat, add the baking soda, and stir thoroughly. Careful: This will cause the mixture to foam slightly.

4. Pour the caramel carefully and evenly over the popcorn and, using both spatulas, toss it constantly—like tossing a salad—until all the popcorn is coated with caramel, 8 to 10 minutes. (The more you toss, the less the popcorn will clump and the more even the coating will be.)

5. When the popcorn is coated but still warm, sprinkle the salt evenly over it and toss a few more times to distribute. Allow the popcorn to cool completely in the bowl, about 15 minutes.

Immediately store the popcorn in an airtight container or zip-top plastic bag; it will keep at room temperature for up to 1 week.

JEN SAYS: If you can't find a big enough bowl, you can fake it by inviting a friend over and dividing the popcorn evenly between two large bowls. When the caramel mixture is done, pour half over each bowl of popcorn and toss immediately.

MODERATE

PECAN TURTLE CARAMEL CORN

MAKES ABOUT 20 CUPS, 8 TO 10 SERVINGS

This recipe sprang fully formed from the genius mind of Liz! (And by that we mean Liz made up a recipe, and Jen fixed it so that it tasted better. Well played, Jen.)

In all honesty, we're shocked we hadn't thought of it before. It's a mash-up of several of our favorite things: caramel corn, Turtles (page 137), and pecan pralines. Think crunchy, a little salty, with nice toasty pecans and a drizzle of dark chocolate. Now stop thinking and make it! You can thank us later.

INGREDIENTS

Cooking spray or vegetable oil

18 cups popped popcorn (about ⅔ cup/65 g unpopped kernels)

8 tablespoons (1 stick/110 g) unsalted butter

¾ cup (150 g) granulated sugar

¾ cup (165 g) firmly packed light brown sugar

½ cup (165 g) dark corn syrup

1 teaspoon (6 g) baking soda

1½ cups (165 g) toasted pecan pieces (see Note)

2 teaspoons (10 g) kosher salt

¾ cup (5 ounces/140 g) chopped dark chocolate, or ¾ cup (5 ounces/140 g) chopped dark chocolate and 2 tablespoons (20 g) mild vegetable oil, for drizzling

SPECIAL EQUIPMENT

- 2 heatproof spatulas and/or wooden spoons
- Extra-large (6- to 8-quart) bowl (with enough room to toss the popcorn)
- Candy thermometer
- 2 large (13" x 18") rimmed baking sheets

1. Lightly coat one of the heatproof spatulas and the bowl with cooking spray. Place the popped popcorn in the bowl, and set it aside.
2. Melt the butter in a medium-size (4-quart) saucepan over medium-high heat. Add the sugars and corn syrup, and using the other heatproof spatula, stir to combine. Bring to a boil, and then insert the candy thermometer. Stirring often, cook the mixture to 300°F/150°C (hard crack stage), 5 to 8 minutes.
3. Remove the caramel mixture from the heat. Gently add the baking soda and pecan pieces, making sure not to splatter, and stir thoroughly. This will cause the mixture to foam slightly.
4. *Carefully* pour the caramel evenly over the popcorn and, using the spatulas, toss gently but constantly—like tossing a salad—until all the popcorn is coated with caramel, 8 to 10 minutes. (The more you toss, the less the popcorn will clump and the more even the coating will be.)
5. When the popcorn is coated but still warm, spread it out on the baking sheets and sprinkle the salt evenly over it. Allow the popcorn to cool completely, about 15 minutes.
6. Meanwhile, temper the ¾ cup chocolate according to the instructions on page 26, or use the ¾ cup chocolate and 2 tablespoons oil to make the Cheater's Chocolate Coating as directed on page 32. Drizzle the chocolate over the cooled popcorn and allow it to set, about 15 minutes.

Immediately store the caramel corn in an airtight container or zip-top plastic bag; it will keep at cool room temperature for up to 1 week.

NOTE: To toast raw pecans, spread them out in an even layer on a rimmed baking sheet and bake at 275°F, stirring occasionally, until crunchy and fragrant, about 20 minutes. Let them cool on the baking sheet before using.

LIZ SAYS: Hard-crack sugar is a B-I-T-C-I-minus-one to clean off of, well, pretty much anything. Once you're finished scraping the caramel out of the pot, immediately put the pot in the sink (away from anything meltable), fill it with hot water, and let it sit for a while. The hot water dissolves the hardened sugars, so by the time you're ready to clean the pot (10 to 20 minutes later), most of the sugar will already be dissolved. Get rid of any more sugar by rubbing it with a scrubby sponge under hot running water.

EASY

CAKE AMAZEBALLS

MAKES ABOUT 60 ONE-AND-A-HALF-INCH BALLS

Remember when cake balls were supposed to be "the next cupcakes"? Before everyone realized there would never be "the next cupcakes" because apparently people are totally obsessed with cupcakes all the time, for ever and ever? Yeah, so do we. Most recipes you'll find for cake balls call for a box of cake mix and a tub of ready-made frosting; we think cake balls deserve better. Sure, it might seem a little silly to bake an entire cake and whip up some frosting, only to demolish the cake and mash it all together. But—seriously?—if you make these for your kid's (or mom's, or brother's, or girlfriend's, or postal carrier's) next birthday party, you're gonna be the toast of the town.

We make these in a few different combos: red velvet cake with cream cheese frosting and white chocolate coating; yellow birthday cake with vanilla frosting and white chocolate coating; and sour cream chocolate cake with fudge frosting and dark chocolate coating. Feel free to mix and match!

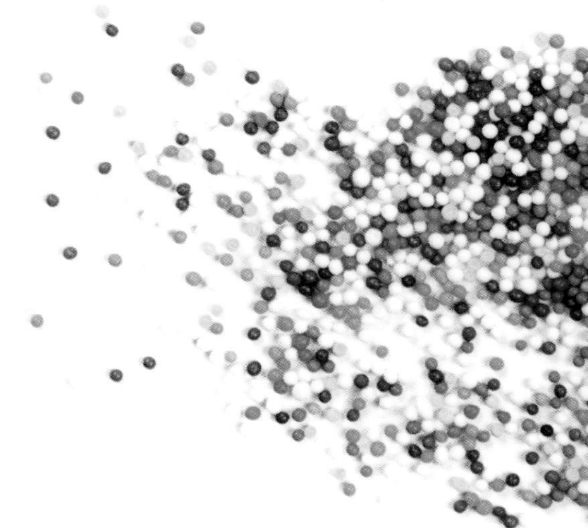

SPECIAL EQUIPMENT

- Stand mixer fitted with paddle attachment, or electric mixer and large bowl
- 2 large (13" x 18") rimmed baking sheets, lined with parchment paper
- Dipping or regular dinner fork

INGREDIENTS

1 recipe cake (see pages 234 to 239), equal to about 9 cups cake crumbs

1 recipe frosting (see pages 235 to 240), equal to 1½ cups frosting

3 cups (19 ounces/540 g) chopped milk, dark, or white chocolate, for coating (see headnote)

White or rainbow nonpareil sprinkles or jimmies, unsweetened cocoa powder, confectioners' sugar, or extra cake crumbs, for decoration (optional)

1. Crumble the cake into the mixer bowl. Add the frosting and beat on medium speed until thoroughly combined, 2 to 3 minutes. Cover with plastic wrap and refrigerate overnight.

2. To form the cake balls, scoop up rounded tablespoons of the cake mixture, roll them into 1½-inch balls with your hands, and transfer the finished balls to one of the lined baking sheets. Once all the balls are rolled, place the baking sheet in the fridge to chill them.

3. While the cake balls are chilling, temper the 3 cups chocolate according to the instructions on page 26, or melt it as directed on page 24.

4. Dip the cake balls one by one in the chocolate, using the fork-dipping method on page 33. Place the balls on the second lined baking sheet. Pause every 5 cake balls or so, before the chocolate sets up, to decorate each with the sprinkles.

5. Allow the cake balls to set up completely until the chocolate is firm to the touch, 10 to 15 minutes.

Store the cake balls, layered between parchment or wax paper, in an airtight container in the fridge for up to 3 days.

EASY

RED VELVET CAKE

MAKES ABOUT 9 CUPS CAKE CRUMBS; SERVES 6 TO 8

Red Velvet Cake: rich and cocoa-y, wonderfully colorful, and divisive as all get-out. Some say the color should come from the reaction of the cocoa to the acid in the buttermilk; others say bring on the food coloring; still others say that beet juice should be involved. We don't like to get political with our cakes; we just get scrumtrulescent*. To that end, we give you a tried-and-true recipe adapted from Jen's cookbook vault. (But hey, if Gamma Rose's Red Velvet is how you wanna go, don't let us get in your way.)

SPECIAL EQUIPMENT

- 2 round (9") cake pans, or one large (9" x 13" x 3") baking pan
- Electric mixer with large bowl, or stand mixer fitted with whisk attachment
- Wire cooling rack (see Nice Rack!, page 107)

INGREDIENTS

Unsalted butter, for greasing the pan(s)

2 cups minus 2 tablespoons (185 g) all-purpose flour, plus extra for flouring the pan(s)

¾ teaspoon (3 g) baking soda

¾ teaspoon (3 g) baking powder

¾ teaspoon (3 g) kosher salt

¼ cup (50 g) Dutch-process cocoa powder

½ cup (100 g) vegetable oil

1 cup (200 g) granulated sugar

1 large egg yolk

2 large eggs

¾ cup (175 g) buttermilk

1 small bottle (about 2½ tablespoons/4 g) red food coloring

1 teaspoon (5 g) pure vanilla extract

1. Preheat the oven to 350°F/175°C. Butter and flour the cake pan(s), and set them aside.

2. In a medium-size bowl, sift together the flour, and the baking soda, baking powder, salt, and cocoa powder. Set aside.

*All due credit to Mr. Will Ferrell.

3. Combine the oil, sugar, egg yolk, and eggs in the mixer bowl. Whip on medium-high speed until light yellow and slightly thickened, about 3 minutes.

4. Add the buttermilk, food coloring, and vanilla and mix on medium speed until combined, about 1 minute. Reduce the speed to low, and add the flour mixture to the egg mixture in a slow, even stream. Mix until well combined, 30 to 60 seconds.

5. Pour the batter into the prepared cake pan(s), and bake until a toothpick inserted in the center comes out clean, about 45 minutes. Let the cake cool completely in the pan(s), and then turn it out of the pan(s) onto the wire rack.

Store the cake, tightly wrapped in plastic wrap, for up to 3 days in the fridge or up to 1 month in the freezer.

LIZ SAYS: No buttermilk? No problem! Stir 2 teaspoons of distilled white vinegar or strained fresh lemon juice into 3/4 cup regular milk. Allow it to sit for 5 minutes, and there you go! Instant buttermilk substitute.

EASY

CREAM CHEESE FROSTING

MAKES 1½ CUPS FROSTING

If there's one thing we do know about Red Velvet, it's that cream cheese frosting is the only way to go. Here's a super-duper simple and tasty recipe that works on pretty much any cake and adds that extra tang to the cake balls.

SPECIAL EQUIPMENT

- Electric mixer with large bowl, or stand mixer fitted with paddle attachment

INGREDIENTS

4 ounces (115 g) cream cheese, at room temperature

4 tablespoons (½ stick/60 g) unsalted butter, at room temperature

1½ cups (200 g) confectioners' sugar, sifted

½ teaspoon (3 g) pure vanilla extract

Place all of the ingredients in the mixer bowl, and mix on low speed to combine, 1 minute. Increase the speed to medium-high and beat until light and fluffy, 3 to 5 minutes.

Store the frosting in an airtight container in the fridge for up to 2 weeks.

EASY

YELLOW BIRTHDAY CAKE

MAKES 9½ CUPS CAKE CRUMBS; SERVES 6 TO 8

This is adapted from a recipe by Joanne Chang, owner of the fantastic Boston bakery Flour, of whom (and which) we are enormous fans. (Best egg sandwich *EVER*. And we, as New Yorkers, do not throw that kind of praise around lightly.) It's the best yellow cake recipe we've come across—period. Think of it this way: Remember that boxed-mix birthday cake your mom made you, with the store-bought tub icing and rainbow sprinkles and everything? Remember how wonderfully vanilla-y and perfectly tender and moist that cake was? Well, this is the same thing. Only much, much better.

SPECIAL EQUIPMENT

- 2 round (9") cake pans or 1 large (9" x 13" x 3") baking pan
- Electric mixer with large bowl, or stand mixer fitted with paddle attachment
- Wire cooling rack (see Nice Rack!, page 107)

INGREDIENTS

1½ cups (3 sticks/350 g) unsalted butter, at room temperature, plus extra for greasing the pan(s)

3 cups (275 g) cake flour, plus extra for flouring the pan(s)

1 teaspoon (4 g) baking powder

½ teaspoon (2 g) baking soda

½ teaspoon (2 g) kosher salt

2 cups (385 g) granulated sugar

3 large egg yolks

3 large eggs

1 teaspoon (5 g) pure vanilla extract

1 cup (250 g) buttermilk

¾ cup colored sprinkles (aka jimmies—the longish, softish kind)

1. Preheat the oven to 350°F/175°C. Butter and flour the cake pan(s) and set them aside.

2. In a medium-size bowl, sift together the 3 cups flour and the baking powder, baking soda, and salt. Set aside.

3. Combine the 1½ cups butter and the sugar in the mixer bowl. Cream them together on medium speed, scraping the bowl down with a rubber spatula once or twice, until the mixture is light and fluffy, 3 to 4 minutes.

4. In a small bowl, whisk together the egg yolks, eggs, and vanilla until just combined. With the mixer on low speed, slowly pour the egg mixture into the butter mixture and mix until just incorporated. Scrape down the bowl, and then beat on medium speed for 30 seconds.

5. Reduce the speed to low and add about a third of the flour mixture to the butter mixture; mix until just barely combined. Add about half of the buttermilk and continue to mix on the lowest speed until it is almost thoroughly incorporated. Stop the mixer and scrape the side and bottom of the bowl well. Again on the lowest speed, add about half of the remaining flour mixture and mix until just barely combined. Add the rest of the buttermilk and mix just until combined.

6. At this point, it's best to finish the mixing by hand. Using the rubber spatula, fold in the remaining flour mixture and the sprinkles just until the batter is mixed. Pour the batter into the prepared pan(s), and bake until a toothpick inserted in the center comes out clean, about 45 minutes. Allow the cake to cool completely in the pan(s), and then turn it out of the pan(s) onto the wire rack.

Store the cake, tightly wrapped in plastic wrap, for up to 3 days in the fridge or up to 1 month in the freezer.

Save those extra egg whites for recipes like Classic European Nougat (page 145), Vanilla Marshmallows (page 141), and Snacker Bars (page 256). Store them in an airtight container in the fridge for up to 10 days, or in the freezer for up to a year. Yes, really.

EASY

VANILLA FROSTING

MAKES ABOUT 2 CUPS

This frosting is as fluffy, white, and sweet as a little lamb. But not quite as woolly. And it is most certainly *not* "vanilla" (see page 10).

SPECIAL EQUIPMENT

- Electric mixer with large bowl, or stand mixer fitted with paddle attachment

INGREDIENTS

4 tablespoons (½ stick/60 g) unsalted butter, at room temperature

2 cups (260 g) confectioners' sugar

½ teaspoon (2 g) kosher salt

⅓ cup (80 g) half-and-half

1 teaspoon (5 g) pure vanilla extract

In the mixer bowl, cream the butter on medium speed until smooth, about 1 minute. Add the confectioners' sugar, salt, half-and-half, and vanilla, and mix on medium speed until light and creamy, 3 to 5 minutes.

Store the frosting in an airtight container in the fridge for up to 2 weeks.

EASY

SOUR CREAM CHOCOLATE CAKE

MAKES ABOUT 9 CUPS CAKE CRUMBS; SERVES 6 TO 8

This recipe is adapted from the Sky High cookbook by Alisa Huntsman and Pete Wynne; it's simple and delicious, and the sour cream imparts a moist, tender quality that we're head-over-heels for. If you ever need to make a chocolate cake for non-cake-ball purposes, we highly recommend this recipe as your go-to.

SPECIAL EQUIPMENT

- 2 small round (8") cake pans or 1 large (9" x 13" x 3") baking pan
- Wire cooling rack (see Nice Rack!, page 107)

INGREDIENTS

Unsalted butter, for greasing the pans

2 cups (250 g) all-purpose flour

2½ cups (500 g) granulated sugar

¾ cup (65 g) Dutch-process cocoa powder

2 teaspoons (9 g) baking soda

1 teaspoon (6 g) fine sea salt

1 cup (225 g) vegetable oil

1 cup (230 g) sour cream

1½ cups (355 g) water

2 tablespoons (30 g) distilled white vinegar

1 teaspoon (5 g) pure vanilla extract

2 large eggs

1. Preheat the oven to 350°F/180°C. Butter the bottom and sides of the cake pan(s). Cut pieces of parchment paper to fit the pan(s), and use them to line the bottom(s).
2. Sift together the flour, sugar, cocoa powder, baking soda, and salt into a large bowl. Stir with a whisk to combine well.
3. Add the oil and sour cream to the flour mixture, and whisk until just blended. Add the water in a thin stream, whisking to incorporate it. Then add the vinegar and vanilla, and stir gently with the whisk until combined.
4. Whisk the eggs in a small bowl, and add them to the flour mixture, stirring until they are well blended, making sure there are no lumps or errant clumps of flour. Scrape down the side of the bowl with a rubber spatula, and divide the batter equally among the prepared cake pans (or pour it all into the prepared rectangular pan).
5. Bake until a cake tester or wooden toothpick inserted in the center comes out almost clean, 30 to 35 minutes if you're using 2 pans; about 45 minutes for 1 pan. Let the cake cool in the pan(s) for about 20 minutes. Then invert onto the wire rack, carefully peel off the paper liner(s), and let cool completely.

Store the cake tightly wrapped in plastic wrap, for up to 3 days in the fridge or up to 1 month in the freezer.

EASY

EASY CHOCOLATE FROSTING

MAKES ABOUT 4 CUPS

This is an adaption of a Martha Stewart recipe we just love. It's a little tangy, a lot chocolaty, and easier than something so delicious has any right to be. The recipe yields more than you'll need for the Amazeballs (page 232), but you can spread the extra on some brownies or just eat it with a spoon—we won't tell.

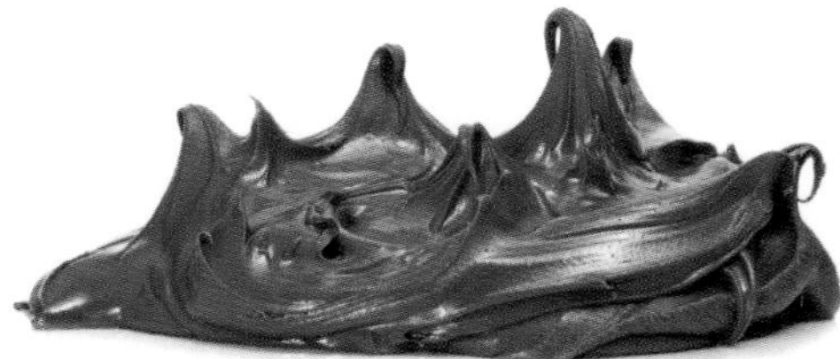

SPECIAL EQUIPMENT

- Electric mixer with large bowl, or stand mixer fitted with whisk attachment

INGREDIENTS

2¼ cups (270 g) confectioners' sugar

¼ cup (25 g) unsweetened cocoa powder

Pinch fine sea salt

12 tablespoons (6 ounces/170 g) cream cheese, at room temperature

12 tablespoons (6 ounces/170 g) unsalted butter, at room temperature

9 ounces (225 g) dark chocolate, melted and cooled slightly (see page 24)

¾ cup (175 g) crème fraîche or sour cream

1. Sift together the sugar, cocoa powder, and salt in a medium-size bowl, and set it aside.
2. Combine the cream cheese and butter in the mixer bowl, and beat on medium-high speed until smooth, 2 to 3 minutes.
3. Reduce the speed to medium-low; gradually add the sugar mixture, and beat until combined, about 1 minute.
4. With the beaters still running, add the chocolate in a slow, steady stream down the side of the bowl. Stop the beaters, add the crème fraîche, and beat on medium speed until combined, 30 seconds.

Store the frosting in an airtight container in the fridge for up to 2 weeks.

EASY

BUTTERSCOTCH SAUCE

MAKES 1¼ CUPS (ABOUT4 GENEROUS POURS OVER ICE CREAM)

When we sent this recipe to our intrepid testers, we got back a few unprintable responses. As in, "Holy ____, this is so ____ing good I ate it all with a spoon." (True story.) Stir it into some Chocolate Ganache, white chocolate edition (see page 36), and make unbelievably tasty butterscotch truffles; or just eat it by itself. It's a win-win.

SPECIAL EQUIPMENT

- Heatproof spatula
- Candy thermometer

1½ cups (300 g) packed dark brown sugar

¼ cup (70 g) light corn syrup

¼ cup (55 g) water

8 tablespoons (1 stick/113 g) unsalted butter

½ cup (135 g) heavy (whipping) cream

¼ cup (45 g) whiskey

½ vanilla bean, split open and seeds scraped out, pod reserved; 1 teaspoon pure vanilla extract; or ½ teaspoon vanilla paste (see pages 10–11)

¾ teaspoon (5 g) fine sea salt

1. Combine the sugar, corn syrup, water, and butter in a small (2-quart) saucepan, and cook over medium-low heat until the butter melts. Insert the candy thermometer, raise the heat to medium-high, and cook, stirring occasionally with the spatula, to 245°F/118°C (firm ball stage), about 7 minutes.

2. Add the cream, whiskey, vanilla bean and seeds (or extract or paste), and salt, and continue to cook over medium-high heat, stirring frequently, for 4 minutes.

3. Remove the sauce from the heat and let it cool for 10 minutes. Fish the vanilla bean (if you used one) out with a slotted spoon and set it aside (you can reuse it; see page 11). Stir the sauce well with the spatula, and go ahead and spoon it up.

Store the butterscotch sauce in an airtight container in the refrigerator for up to 2 months. Reheat it in a microwave in 20-second intervals on High or in a bowl over simmering water, stirring occasionally, for about 10 minutes.

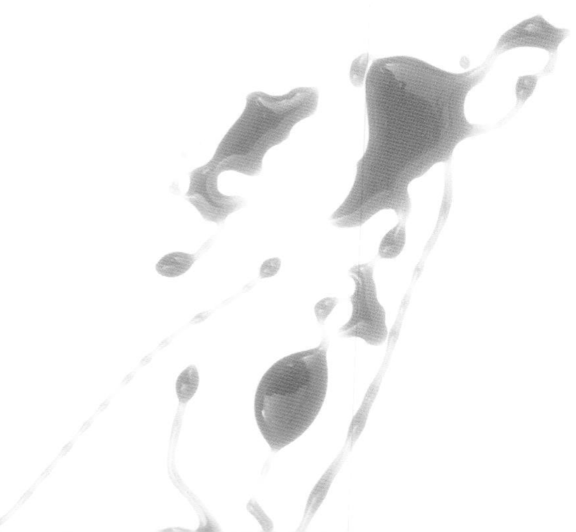

THE BEST HOT FUDGE SAUCE

MAKES ABOUT 2½ CUPS (ABOUT 8 GENEROUS POURS OVER ICE CREAM)

Yup, we'll go ahead and say it: It's the best. It has the gooey texture of the fresh-out-of-the-jar kind that we love—but none of the fakey stuff—and all the rich flavor of dark chocolate, with just a hint of salt. It pours on nice and thick, and firms up to that perfectly fudgy state on cold ice cream. It's also great drizzled on pound cake or used as a dip for fresh fruit—if you don't just eat it out of the jar. But who would do such a thing, right? ;-)

SPECIAL EQUIPMENT

- Heatproof spatula

INGREDIENTS

5 ounces (140 g) dark chocolate, chopped (about ¾ cup)

8 tablespoons (1 stick/115 g) unsalted butter

½ cup (120 g) water

½ cup (100 g) granulated sugar

¼ cup (45 g) packed light brown sugar

¼ cup (70 g) light corn syrup

2 tablespoons (15 g) unsweetened cocoa powder

½ teaspoon (3 g) pure vanilla extract

¼ teaspoon (1 g) fine sea salt

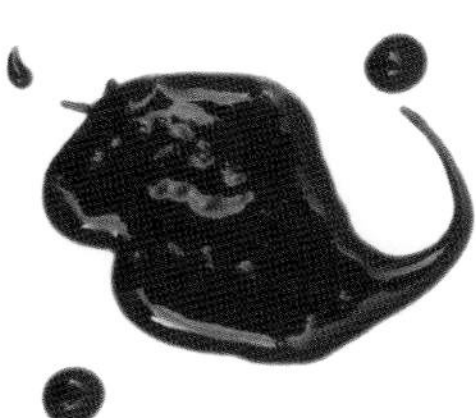

1. Melt the chocolate and butter in a small (2-quart) saucepan over medium-low heat. Add the water, sugars, and corn syrup, and bring to a boil over medium-high heat. Reduce the heat to medium and cook, stirring occasionally, until the mixture has thickened and looks like chocolate syrup, 7 minutes. Turn off the heat.

2. Add the cocoa powder, vanilla, and sea salt, and stir well with the heatproof spatula until combined and smooth. Allow the mixture to cool for 10 minutes. Then stir it again with the spatula to even out the temperature, about 1 minute. Now, what in the Sam Hill are you waiting for? Go ahead and spoon it over some ice cream! (If the sauce is too thick, add a tablespoon of warm water and whisk well until the desired consistency is reached.)

Store the fudge sauce in an airtight container in the fridge for 2 to 3 months.

NOTE: Since there aren't any stabilizers in the sauce, it might get slightly grainy over time; the graininess should disappear once you reheat it in a bowl set over a pan of simmering water, or zap it in the microwave for a few seconds on half power, and whisk it a bit.

Variations

THE GRANDPAPPY SPECIAL Replace the dark chocolate with 100 percent (unsweetened) chocolate, and add a tablespoon of whiskey along with the cocoa, vanilla, and salt.

PB&C Stir in 2 to 4 tablespoons (to taste) of creamy commercial peanut butter, such as Skippy, after the cocoa, vanilla, and salt have been added.

REDEYE Replace the cocoa powder with good-quality instant espresso powder.

SPICE IT UP Add 1 teaspoon of your favorite ground spice along with the water, corn syrup, and sugars; we like cardamom, cinnamon, or gingerbread spice.

CHOCOMALLOW COOKIES
PAGE 287

S'MORES BARS
PAGE 271

THE DORIE BAR
PAGE 279

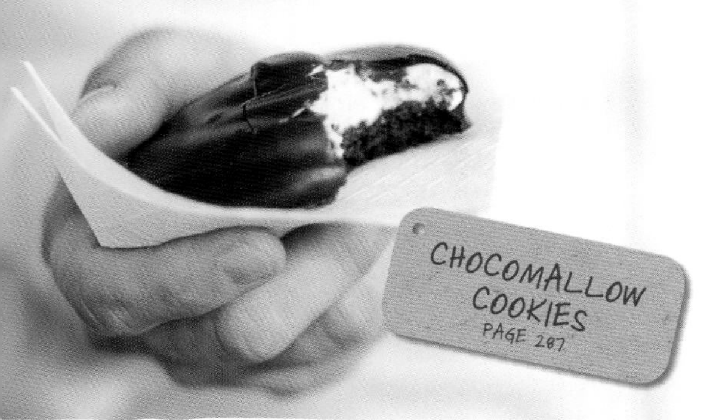

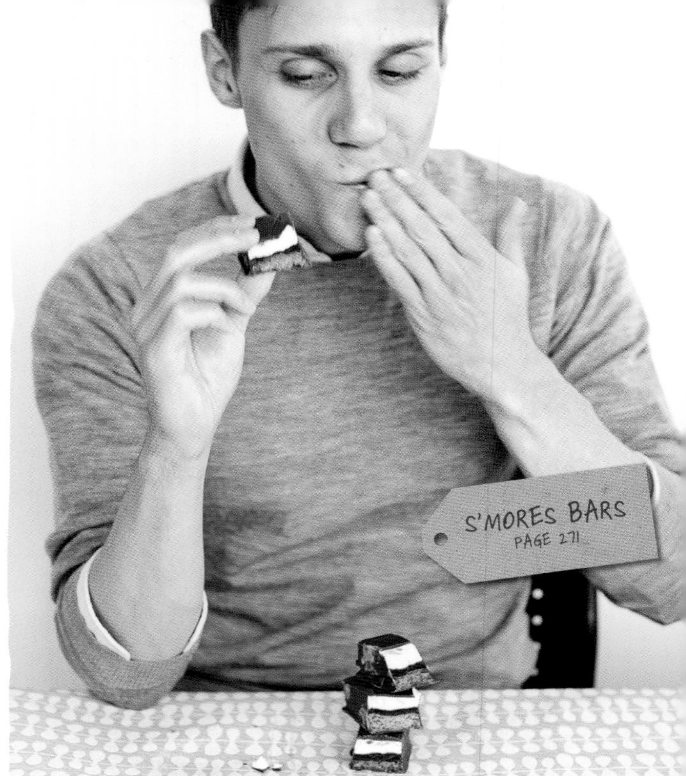

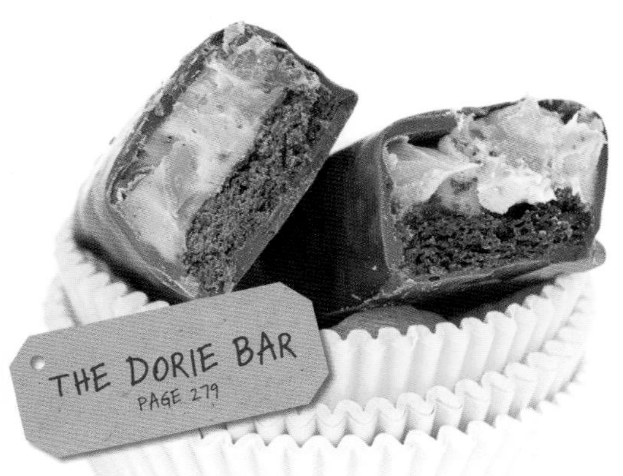

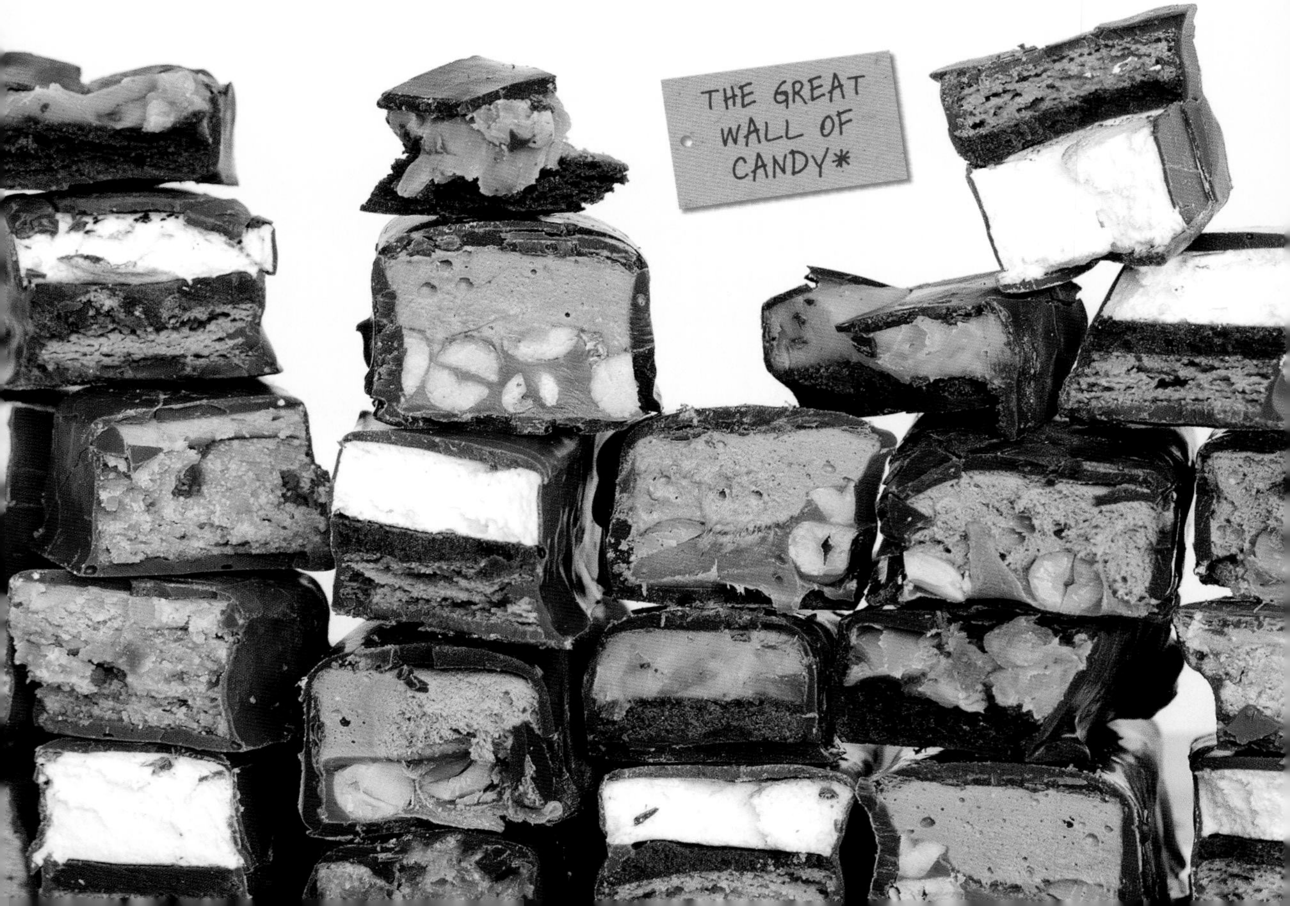
THE GREAT WALL OF CANDY*

Chapter Seven

CANDY WALKS INTO A BAR . . .

*You can see it from space!

Wow! Have you ever got the basics down. You know how to make a gorgeous ganache (page 36); your marshmallow (page 141) is as fluffy as cloud nine; and you beefed up your piping skillz making Nonpareils (page 77). But what happens next?

MAGIC, that's what! Or at least tons of fun. When we started Liddabit, it was with the classic American candy bar in mind. We figured that since we knew how to make all the components, we should be able to stitch them together fairly easily and dunk 'em in chocolate. Right?

Well, yes, and no. It is true that component A + component B + component C + chocolate = bar; however, you definitely have to use some finesse to make the equation work. Sometimes the components don't want to stick together (see page 252); or they get *too* sticky (see page 251); or the cookie crumbles when you cut it (see opposite page). We'll give you as much information as we can within each recipe so that you should have some recourse no matter what happens, but there are also some general things you should know beforehand. Consider what follows your primer in Candy Bar Theory, or the Physics of Deliciousness for beginners. Don your tinfoil thinking caps and read on.

WHAT'S IN A BAR?

(A BAR BY ANY OTHER NAME WOULD TASTE AS SWEET)

In theory, anything you like can go into a candy bar: Layer caramel with marshmallow, spread ganache on a cookie, or just dip a big ol' bar of nougat. It's totally your call. Just keep in mind that different types of layers—gooey, chewy, crunchy—behave differently and have their own care and handling needs. Good to know when you're combining a variety of tastes and textures to assemble your next Nobel-worthy creation.

All Your Cookie Base Are Belong to Us*

The cookie layer of a bar is often the trickiest to deal with, particularly when you start to cut the bars. You have everything stacked and stuck just so, and then you start slicing and—nononoNONO—the cookie crumbles. It's a problem we all run into from time to time (the brown-butter cookie that forms the base of the King Bars on page 267 tends to be particularly crumbly). Which is why, when preparing a cookie base for a bar, generally you want to slightly underbake it. It shouldn't be wet-looking or sticky, but it shouldn't be too well baked (i.e., crispy/crumbly) either. We account for this in the baking times listed in the recipes, but every oven is different! So, we strongly recommend investing in an oven thermometer (you'd be shocked at how many ovens don't heat to the temperature you set them to), rotating the baking sheet halfway through the baking time, and checking the cookie at the low end of the recommended time—for example, if we say it'll take 10 to 15 minutes to bake, check it at 10. Remember that it's going to be cooling to room temperature on the hot baking sheet, too, which will continue to cook it slightly even after it comes out of the oven. When in doubt, take it out.

Pour Some (Caramelized) Sugar on Me

Caramel's a very straightforward layer to make. All you need to keep in mind is that caramel is *very hot* when you pour it out, so if you pour it on top of something

*Don't get this? Google it (skip the word "cookie").

that can melt—say, nougat—you will deflate the nougat and end up with a very sad-panda candy bar. That's why, for bars like the Snacker (page 256), you want to compose the caramel first and then make the nougat and pour it over the cooled caramel. Cookie is much sturdier, and so for something like the Twist Bars (page 260), you can pour the hot caramel right on top. Here's a handy can-it-stand-up-to-caramel chart covering most of the candy categories in this book:

STUFF ONTO WHICH YOU *CAN* POUR HOT CARAMEL	STUFF ONTO WHICH YOU *CANNOT* POUR HOT CARAMEL
Cookie	Nougat
Other caramel	Ganache
Asphalt	Gummi/jelly candy
Nuts/dried fruit	Baby bunnies
Honeycomb Candy	Marshmallow
Coconut-Lime layer	Fondant
Note: Only a few of these things are combined with caramel in this book; these are just examples for when you want to get crazy.	

If you're in doubt, or just want to make the separate components ahead of time, caramel can *always* be made separately and layered on once it's cool. (Not the case with fragile stuff like Fluffy Peanut Butter Nougat, page 172.)

Spreading the ~~Love~~ Ganache

The best way to layer ganache in a bar is to spread it directly onto the layer beneath. Just make sure that whatever it's touching has cooled completely (so the ganache doesn't melt), and apply the ganache when it's cool but still soft enough to spread easily. (If it's been stored in the fridge, allow it to come back to room temperature; you might need to rewarm it slightly in 5-second bursts on High in the microwave or over a pan of simmering water to get it back to the right consistency.)

Keep in mind that when you layer ganache directly onto something dry like a cookie, there will be a moisture exchange: The ganache will become firmer as its moisture seeps into the cookie, softening it. If the idea of this bothers you,

you can use a pastry brush to coat the top of the cookie with a very thin layer of melted chocolate or cocoa butter, which will effectively seal it to keep it crispy longer (though a soft cookie isn't necessarily a terrible thing). Melt cocoa butter the same way you would chocolate; see the instructions on page 24.

Here, Fluffy!

With fluffy things like nougat or marshmallow, you generally want to pour and spread them directly onto the layer below. Why? Well, these candies are temperamental. Consider the Fluffy Peanut Butter Nougat (page 172), which is especially delicate and difficult to handle without breaking; and the Snacker nougat (page 256) and the S'mores marshmallow (page 271), which are just downright sticky. Both of these properties mean that you want to handle those nougs/marshies as little as possible to avoid damaging the entire candy slab and/or making a ginormous mess.

One potential snag can arise when you assemble the S'mores Bars: warm marshmallow + delicate ganache = disaster, right? Not so if you chill the ganache-covered slab beforehand to make sure it's set and will properly support the marshmallow. And be sure to allow the marshmallow to whip until the mixing bowl is just barely warm to the touch. A quick hand while spreading will complete the bar disaster-free. Here are some more general tips for working with fluffy stuff:

- Oil your non-dominant hand. If you're going to be scraping and spreading and evening out something really sticky like marshmallow or nougat, it helps to have one stick-proofed hand to assist.

- Let it cool completely, and then work quickly. The cooler it is, the less chance you have of melting a delicate layer beneath—but make sure to work speedily, or it'll set up before you get a chance to spread it all out.

- If it's flexible, you can make it ahead of time. This means that for marshmallow and Snacker nougat, you can treat it as you would a cooled caramel layer: Just turn it out of its pan and slap it on the layers below. The main obstacle you run into with this technique reveals itself when the layers just refuse to stick together. Not to worry—we have something for that (keep reading)!

Sticking the Landing

Sometimes, layers won't want to stick together. You have a few options:

FEEL THE HEAT. Warming ganache with a hair dryer on low will help soften it up. Simply hold the dryer 6 to 8 inches from the surface and make slow, sweeping motions until the ganache is soft and feels tacky.

HUMIDIFY. Nougat and caramel can be very, very lightly dampened to promote adhesion: Moisten a paper towel or clean dish towel and gently blot it on the surface of the layer you want to make sticky.

WEIGHT IT OUT. If you have a little time, you can place a piece of parchment or wax paper on top of the layered slab, still in the sheet pan; then put another sheet pan or a cutting board on top of the parchment, and let gravity do the work for you (20 to 30 minutes should do it—they don't need to be permanently epoxied together, just sticky enough to survive the enrobing process).

A Robe of Chocolate

When it comes to coating candy bars in chocolate, you have the choice of dipping them or pouring the chocolate over them. For full-size candy bars, we recommend using the pour-over method that follows, just because it's a much easier way to tackle a big batch and wrangle larger pieces. But dipping 'em individually works too, and is actually a good idea with any bars that you've cut into bite-size pieces; for those little guys, you can use the technique described on pages 33 and 34.

If the bars contain something sticky like caramel or nougat, be sure to lightly oil the knife before cutting the candy slab into pieces.

WORTH IT

ENROBING CANDY BARS: THE POUR-OVER METHOD

SPECIAL EQUIPMENT

- Cutting board
- Large bowl of tempered chocolate or Cheater's Chocolate Coating (specific amount called for in the recipe)
- Large and small metal offset spatulas
- Ruler
- 2 large (13" x 18") rimmed baking sheets, lined with parchment paper
- Wire cooling rack or icing screen (see Nice Rack!, page 107)

Turn the assembled slab of candy out of its baking sheet:

1. For the more delicate bars, like the King (page 267), run a knife around the edge of the pan first so that it'll slide right out. Place a sheet of parchment on top of the candy slab. Grasp the parchment and baking sheet on both ends, holding everything together like a giant sandwich. Keeping the parchment as taut as possible, turn "the sandwich" over with one swift, smooth motion onto the cutting board. Remove the baking sheet and peel off any lining. The slab should be upside down; you'll first be coating what will end up as the bottom of the bars.

Coat top and bottom with chocolate:

2. Pour about ¾ cup of the prepared chocolate on top of the slab, and use the large offset spatula to spread it over the surface in an even layer, adding more if needed to cover the entire surface (it's okay if some drips down the sides; you'll be trimming them anyhow). Allow the chocolate to set until it is no longer wet but is still soft, about 5 minutes. Meanwhile, set aside the bowl of chocolate; you'll retemper/reheat it in step 4.

3. While the chocolate layer is still slightly soft, flip the slab of candy so it is chocolate side down, and trim the edges with a sharp chef's knife so that they're more or less straight (if the slab contains sticky layers, oil the knife first). Using the ruler and the knife, measure and score 1- by 4-inch bars or 1- by 1-inch bite-size pieces; then press down with a firm hand to cut along the score lines. Set the cut bars, chocolate side up, on a lined baking sheet, and let the chocolate set completely, about 15 minutes.

4. Meanwhile, retemper the chocolate, or warm the chocolate coating over a pan of simmering water until it's body temperature (test it on your lip; see page 28).

5. Set the wire cooling rack over the second lined baking sheet, and arrange the bars, chocolate side down on the rack, about ½ inch apart. Ladle the warmed chocolate over each bar, pouring long-ways while making small side-to-side motions; coat as much of each bar as possible (if there are a few small gaps that remain uncoated, you can fix them later). Tap the tray against the counter to even out the chocolate.

6. Immediately run a small offset spatula or butter knife underneath each bar to loosen it from the rack. Don't be afraid to scrape along the wires of the rack; you can't do any damage to it, and you want to keep as much chocolate on the bars as possible. Use the spatula to transfer the loosened bars to the first lined baking sheet.

7. Scrape off any excess chocolate on the rack into the pool of chocolate in the baking sheet. Gently pour the chocolate on the baking sheet back into the bowl, and stir it a little to even out the consistency. Using the small offset spatula, cover with chocolate any holes that may be left in the coated bars. Allow the bars to set completely, about 20 minutes.

Coated candy bars will keep, stored in an airtight container, for 3 to 8 weeks (bars with ganache and/or a cookie base will last 3 to 4 weeks; nougat and caramel, 6 to 8).

JEN SAYS: Any time you need to invert a slab of candy onto a lined cutting board—for Hip-to-Be Squares on page 99, say, or Snacker Bars on page 256—there's a really easy way to do it. Simply run a knife around the pan to loosen the candy if necessary, and lay a piece of wax or parchment paper over it. Place a cutting board on top of that, place your thumbs on the cutting board, and get your other fingers underneath the pan that's holding the candy. Grip firmly, and, in a swift, smooth, graceful-like-a-gazelle motion, turn the whole kit 'n' caboodle upside down. When you remove the pan, your candy should be sitting pretty on the lined board.

ENROBING CANDY BARS

1. Invert the candy slab onto a lined cutting board and remove any lining from the slab.

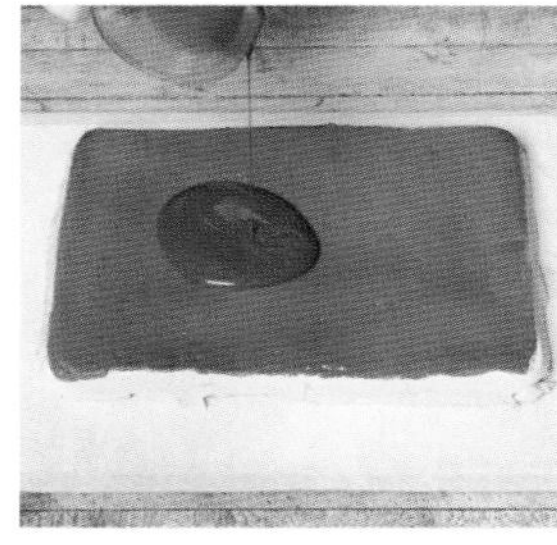

2. Pour some chocolate onto the slab (this will become the bottom of the bars).

3. Spread the chocolate with a large offset spatula.

4. Let the chocolate set up a bit.

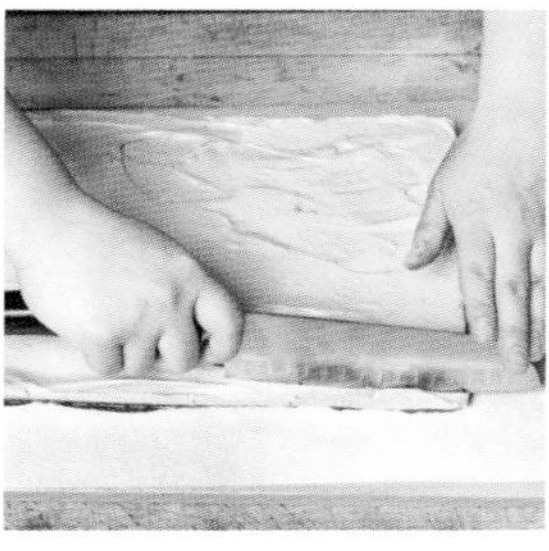

5. Flip the slab over again and trim away the edges.

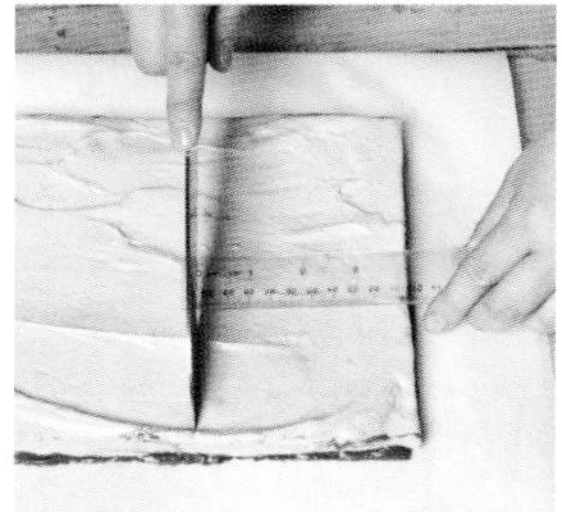

6. Measure and score the bars.

7. Cut the bars along the score lines.

8. Set the bars chocolate side down on the rack.

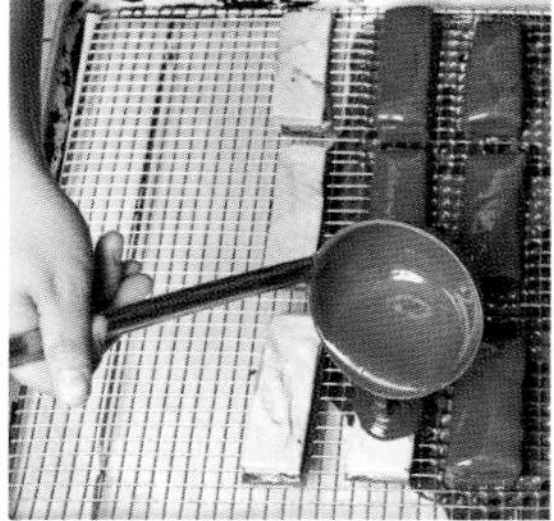

9. Ladle chocolate over the bars.

10. Run a small offset spatula under the bars to loosen them, then move them to the baking sheet.

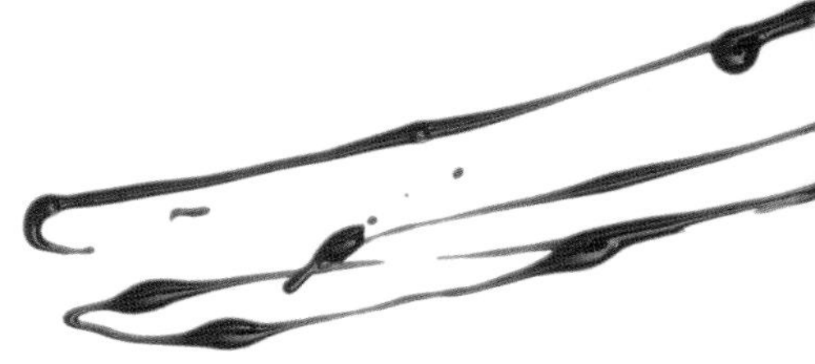

WORTH IT

SNACKER BARS

MAKES ABOUT 35 ONE- BY FOUR-INCH BARS OR 160 ONE-INCH SQUARES

This is the candy bar that started it all. When we finished pastry school, we racked our brains to try and figure out something we could make that would be delicious, yet unique; high-quality, but fun. New York City is awash in bonbons, so we turned to a more American invention: the candy bar. The way we saw it, we knew how to make nougat, we knew how to make caramel . . . how hard could it be?

A few *enormous* prototypes later, we had our own stand at the Brooklyn Flea Market—and the rest, as they say, is history. This candy bar can be a bit tricky to make (mostly the nougat); it's definitely a project, and it makes enough to keep several gaggles of children on a nonstop sugar high for a fortnight. But you can make either (or both) layer(s) ahead of time—they last for a while—and taste-wise, it's extremely forgiving. No matter how un-pretty either layer turns out, the combination of chewy, golden caramel, salty, crunchy peanuts, and creamy chocolate nougat is a surefire winner. We hope you'll try it at least once; it really is worth it.

SPECIAL EQUIPMENT

- Large (13" x 18") rimmed baking sheet
- Candy thermometer
- Heatproof spatula
- Stand mixer fitted with whisk attachment
- Cutting board, lined with parchment paper

INGREDIENTS

FOR THE CARAMEL

Cooking spray or vegetable oil

1¾ cups (340 g) granulated sugar

1½ cups (12 ounces/375 g) evaporated milk

⅔ cup (160 g) heavy (whipping) cream

1 vanilla bean, split open and seeds scraped out, pod reserved; ½ teaspoon vanilla paste (see page 11); or 1 teaspoon pure vanilla extract

¾ cup plus 2 tablespoons (300 g) light corn syrup

3 tablespoons plus 2 teaspoons (scant ½ stick/50 g) unsalted butter

1 tablespoon (18 g) coarse sea salt

2 cups (300 g) roasted and salted peanuts

FOR THE NOUGAT

3 tablespoons (¾ ounce/20 g) unflavored powdered gelatin

½ cup (120 g) cold water

4 large egg whites

3¾ cups (1.3 kg) light corn syrup

2⅓ cups (435 g) granulated sugar

1 cup (235 g) water

12 ounces (340 g) dark chocolate, melted (see page 24) and cooled slightly to lukewarm (about 1½ cups)

1 tablespoon (45 g) pure vanilla extract

FOR ENROBING THE BARS

13 cups chopped dark chocolate (about 5 pounds/2.25 kg), or 13 cups chopped dark chocolate (about 5 pounds/2.25 kg) and 2 cups (450 g) mild vegetable oil

Make the caramel:

1. Coat the baking sheet with cooking spray, and set it aside on a heatproof surface.

2. Combine the sugar, evaporated milk, heavy cream, and vanilla bean and seeds (if using) in a large (6- to 8-quart) saucepan. Bring the mixture to a boil over medium-high heat, uncovered and without stirring.

3. Insert the candy thermometer. Add the light corn syrup, and stir gently with the heatproof spatula until everything is mixed well. Reduce the heat to medium-low and cook, stirring often and making sure to scrape the bottom of the pot to keep the mixture from burning, until it reaches 230°F/110°C (thread stage), about 30 minutes.

4. Add the butter and the vanilla paste or extract (if using). If you used a vanilla bean, fish it out with a slotted spoon. Stirring continuously, continue to cook the caramel until it reaches 241°F/116°C (low firm ball stage), 15 to 20 minutes. The caramel will be a deep golden brown, smell nice and toasty, and have rolling bubbles in the middle. Remove the caramel from the heat and stir in the salt and peanuts, making sure to mix well so that they're distributed evenly.

5. Carefully pour the caramel onto the prepared baking sheet, and spread it into an even layer with the spatula. Allow it to set up until it is cool to the touch, about 2 hours.

Make the nougat:

6. Mix the gelatin and the cold water together in a small bowl and let it set until softened, about 5 minutes.

7. Place the egg whites in the mixer bowl.

8. Combine the light corn syrup, sugar, and water in a medium-size (4-quart) saucepan and bring to a boil over high heat. Insert the candy thermometer, reduce the heat to medium-high, and cook the syrup, uncovered and without stirring, until the syrup reaches 250°F/120°C (firm ball stage).

9. Start whipping the egg whites on medium speed until they become foamy and soft peaks form, 5 to 7 minutes. At this point, the syrup should have reached 265°F/130°C (hard ball stage); if it hasn't reached the proper temperature, just stop the mixer until the syrup catches up.

10. When the syrup comes to temperature, remove it from the heat. With the mixer on low speed, slowly and carefully pour the hot syrup down the inside of the mixing bowl (if the syrup is poured directly onto the moving whisk, it will splatter, which could mean severe pain for you). Once all the syrup has been added, add the softened gelatin and increase the speed to medium-high and whip until the mixture is very thick and looks like a skin has developed on top, 10 minutes.

11. Pour in the melted chocolate and the vanilla extract, and mix for another 10 to 15 seconds to incorporate. Remove the bowl from the mixer and scrape the bottom with the spatula, folding the mixture to evenly distribute the chocolate. Once the chocolate

is fully incorporated, pour the nougat onto the caramel. Spread it into an even layer with the spatula and allow it to set up until it is cool to the touch, about 30 minutes.

Assemble the bars:

12. Temper the 13 cups chopped dark chocolate according to the instructions on page 26, or use the 13 cups chopped dark chocolate and 2 cups oil to make the Cheater's Chocolate Coating as directed on page 32.

13. Enrobe and cut the bars following the directions on page 253 (you want the caramel to end up on the bottom of the bars).

Store the bars, layered with parchment or wax paper, in an airtight container at cool room temperature for up to 8 weeks.

Variation

TRILLIAN BARS With just a few adjustments to the recipe, you can make a creamy, gooey bar that's a lot like a Milky Way (but way cooler, since it's named after the badass leading lady in Douglas Adams's *Hitchhiker's Guide* series): In the nougat, replace the dark chocolate with white chocolate and the seeds of 1 vanilla bean. And you can simply leave the peanuts out of the caramel if you like, or, as we prefer, replace it altogether with the one called for in the Twist recipe (page 260); it has a darker, richer taste that contrasts really nicely with the less assertive white chocolate nougat.

JEN SAYS: Although the recipe calls for five pounds of chocolate (we know it sounds like a lot), you don't need to use every last drop—there will be lots left over once the bars are dipped, which can be reused for dipping later!

WORTH IT

TWIST BARS

MAKES ABOUT 30 ONE- BY FOUR-INCH BARS

This recipe was inspired by a well-known candy bar that shall not be named. We wanted to make a version that wasn't so sugary but that maintained the delicious simplicity of the original: a crunchy, not-too-sweet cookie topped with a layer of chewy caramel and enrobed in chocolate. (Know which candy bar we're talking about now? *Riiight*, that one.) Our original cookie recipe was tasty indeed, but so crumbly that it elicited some R-rated language once cutting and dipping time came around. Our new improved version is much more family-friendly.

The caramel we use here is adapted from an Ina Garten recipe (thanks, Ina!) and is a bit different from the Sea Salt Caramels on page 123; it's got a ton of fresh dairy and no evaporated milk, which gives it a really sumptuous, rich, buttery flavor. The method is also different: You make a dark golden caramel first, using only the sugars and some water, then add the dairy and continue to cook to temperature. The advantage of this method is that it gives you a little more control over the color; darker caramel = more robust flavor. But be careful not to let it burn—truly burnt sugar has an unpleasantly bitter taste and is a royal pain in the derrière to clean up.

If you want to make the cookie base ahead of time, you can: Baked, it will keep at cool room temperature, tightly wrapped in plastic wrap, for 2 to 3 days. If you want to make the dough *way* ahead of time but don't want to bake it right away, you can wrap it tightly in plastic wrap and freeze it for up to 1 month (you may need to bake it for a few minutes extra).

SPECIAL EQUIPMENT

- Stand mixer fitted with paddle attachment, or electric mixer with large bowl
- Rolling pin
- Large (13″ x 18″) rimmed baking pan
- Candy thermometer
- Cutting board, lined with parchment or wax paper

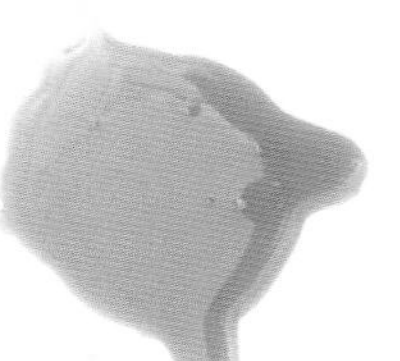

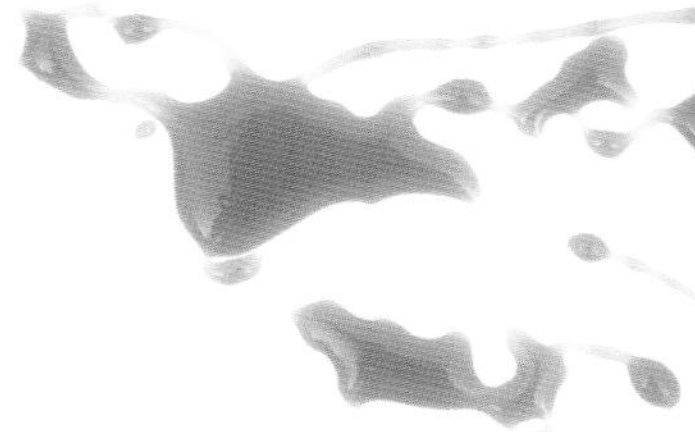

INGREDIENTS

FOR THE COOKIE BASE

½ pound (2 sticks/225 g) unsalted butter, at room temperature

⅔ cups (132 g) granulated sugar

2 large egg yolks

½ teaspoon (3 g) salt

2⅓ cups (290 g) all-purpose flour, plus extra for rolling out the dough if not using a silicone mat

1 teaspoon (5 g) pure vanilla extract

FOR THE CARAMEL

3 cups (600 g) granulated sugar

1 cup (350 g) light corn syrup

½ cup (120 g) cold water

2 cups (485 g) heavy (whipping) cream

10 tablespoons (140 g) unsalted butter

1 vanilla bean, split open and seeds scraped out, pod discarded; or 1 teaspoon pure vanilla extract

2½ teaspoons (13 g) Maldon or other flake-type sea salt

FOR ENROBING THE BARS

Cooking spray

13 cups chopped dark chocolate (about 5 pounds/2.25 kg), or 13 cups chopped dark chocolate (about 5 pounds/2.25 kg) and 2 cups (450 g) mild vegetable oil

Make the cookie base:

1. Put the butter and sugar in the mixer bowl, and beat on medium-high speed until the mixture becomes creamy and the color lightens, 2 to 3 minutes.

2. With the mixer running, add the egg yolks one at a time, and beat on high speed until well blended.

3. Add the salt, and then slowly add the 2⅓ cups flour, 1 cup at a time, while beating on medium speed until the mixture is well combined. Add the vanilla extract and mix until just blended.

4. Cut a piece of parchment paper to fit the bottom of your baking sheet. Using this as a guide, dust the rolling pin with flour and roll out the dough on top of the paper to fit it. (You can trim the edges and reattach the scraps to fill any holes.) Gently slide the dough, on the parchment, onto the baking sheet. Chill the dough in the fridge or freezer for 30 minutes.

5. Preheat your oven to 350°F/177°C.

6. Put the chilled dough straight in the oven and bake until the edges are barely golden brown, 20 to 25 minutes. Let the cookie cool completely in the baking sheet.

Make the caramel:

7. Combine the sugar, light corn syrup, and cold water in a medium-size (4- to 6-quart) saucepan, and bring to a boil, uncovered, over medium-high heat. Insert the candy thermometer and cook until the syrup is a medium to dark amber color and reads 300° to 305°F/150° to 152°C (hard crack stage). While it is heating, keep an eye on it and proceed with the next step.

8. Combine the heavy cream, butter, and vanilla scrapings or extract in a microwave-safe bowl and heat on High for 30 seconds and then in 10-second intervals until the butter is melted and the cream is hot but not boiling. (Alternatively, place the mixture in a small, 2-quart, saucepan over medium heat and cook for about 7 minutes, stirring occasionally.) Set aside.

9. When the caramel has reached the desired color and temperature, remove the thermometer and *slowly* pour in the hot cream mixture while stirring with a heatproof spatula or wooden spoon. The mixture will bubble and steam, so make sure your face isn't all up in the saucepan. Stir until all the caramel is dissolved, and then reinsert the candy thermometer.

10. Continue to cook the mixture over medium-high heat, stirring frequently, until the caramel comes to 248°F/120°C (firm ball stage), 15 to 20 minutes.

Assemble and enrobe the bars:

11. Remove the caramel from the heat. Carefully pour it over the cooled cookie base, spread it out evenly, and sprinkle the salt over the surface. Allow it to sit until it is cool and firm to touch, at least 2 hours but preferably overnight.

12. Lightly coat a paring knife with cooking spray, run it around the edges of the baking sheet to loosen the caramel, and turn the caramel out onto the lined cutting board.

13. Temper the 13 cups chopped dark chocolate according to the instructions on page 26, or use the 13 cups chopped dark chocolate and 2 cups oil to make the Cheater's Chocolate Coating as directed on page 32.

14. Enrobe and cut the bars following the directions on page 253. Allow the bars to set up at room temperature for at least 1 hour.

Store the bars in an airtight container at cool room temperature for up to 4 weeks.

LIZ SAYS: To make these bars in half the time, you can buy some good-quality shortbread from your local bakery or grocery store—enough to cover the bottom of your baking sheet. (This means about 80 of the "finger"-size cookies. If you use Walker's, our go-to brand, you'd need 7 packages of the 12-piece, 8.8-ounce "finger" boxes. It'll set you back around $40, so make sure whoever is getting these bars as a gift bows down and shows the proper obeisance.) Simply line the cookies up on the parchment-lined baking sheet to cover as much of it as possible, and pour the caramel over them. Once the caramel is set, flip the slab over and use an oiled knife to cut the caramel-coated cookies apart. Coat them as you would the from-scratch bars.

MODERATE

NUTTY BARS

MAKES ABOUT 35 ONE- BY FOUR-INCH BARS

Sometimes, simple is the best way to go. It's hard to mess up with caramel and peanuts, but any nut will do here, really. This bar is about as simple as it gets: caramel, with peanuts mixed in, dipped in chocolate. There's very little in the way of arguments that can be made against this combination, assuming that you're not allergic to nuts. If you are, we bet CornNuts would be damn delicious, too, because the extra crunch and salty kick really make this bar. If you don't feel like dipping the bars in chocolate, you can cut them into bite-size pieces and wrap them in wax twisting paper—they're just as tasty solo (though they'll only last for two weeks).

SPECIAL EQUIPMENT

- Large (13" x 18") rimmed baking sheet
- Candy thermometer
- Heatproof spatula
- Cutting board, lined with parchment or wax paper

INGREDIENTS

Cooking spray

1¾ cups (340 g) granulated sugar

1½ cups (12 ounces/375 g) evaporated milk

⅔ cup (160 g) heavy (whipping) cream

1 vanilla bean, split open and seeds scraped out, pod reserved; ½ teaspoon vanilla paste (see page 11); or 1 teaspoon pure vanilla extract

¾ cup plus 2 tablespoons (300 g) light corn syrup

3 tablespoons plus 2 teaspoons (scant ½ stick/50 g) unsalted butter

1 tablespoon (18 g) coarse sea salt

6 cups (800 g) roasted and salted peanuts

13 cups chopped dark chocolate (about 5 pounds/2.25 kg), or 13 cups chopped dark chocolate (about 5 pounds/2.25 kg) and 2 cups (450 g) mild vegetable oil, for enrobing the bars

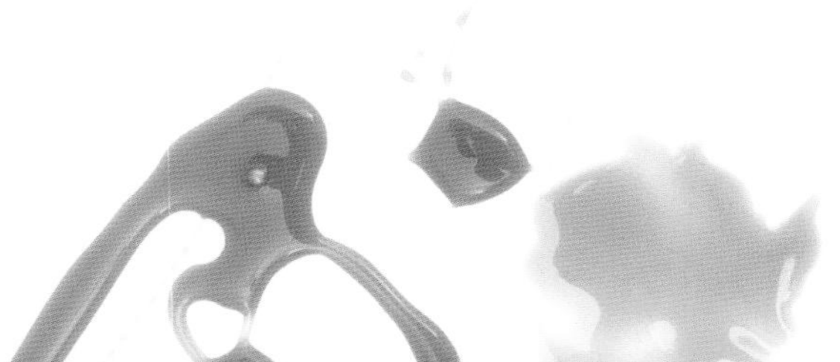

1. Coat the baking sheet with cooking spray, and set it aside.

2. Combine the sugar, evaporated milk, heavy cream, and vanilla bean and seeds (if using) in a large (6- to 8-quart) saucepan. Bring to a boil over medium-high heat, uncovered and without stirring.

3. Once the mixture has come to a boil, insert the candy thermometer. Add the light corn syrup, and stir gently with the heatproof spatula until everything is mixed well. Reduce the heat to medium-low and cook, stirring often and scraping the bottom of the pot to keep the mixture from burning, until it reaches 230°F/110°C (thread stage), about 30 minutes.

4. Add the butter and the vanilla paste or extract (if using). If you used a vanilla bean, fish it out with a slotted spoon. Stirring continuously, cook the caramel until it reaches 241°F/116°C (firm ball stage), 15 to 20 minutes. The caramel will be a deep golden color, have a toasty caramel smell to it, and have rolling bubbles in the middle. Remove it from the heat, and stir in the salt and peanuts, making sure to mix well so that they're distributed evenly.

5. Pour the caramel onto the prepared baking sheet, and spread it into an even layer with the spatula. Allow it to cool until set, 2 to 3 hours, or overnight.

6. Lightly coat a sharp chef's knife with cooking spray and run the tip of the knife around the edge of the caramel to loosen it, if necessary. Gently turn the caramel out onto the prepared cutting board, and cut it into one- by four-inch bars.

7. Temper the 13 cups chopped dark chocolate according to the instructions on page 26, or use the 13 cups chopped dark chocolate and 2 cups oil to make the Cheater's Chocolate Coating as directed on page 32. Then enrobe the bars, following the directions on page 253. Allow the bars to set up at room temperature for at least 1 hour.

Store the bars, layered with wax paper, in an airtight container at room temperature for up to 6 weeks.

Variation

CRAZY GO NUTS BARS Skip the chocolate and instead roll the bars in 1 cup crushed roasted and salted peanuts. Cha-ching—Pay Day!

KING BARS

MAKES ABOUT 30 ONE- BY FOUR-INCH CANDY BARS

The King Bar is another one of Liddabit's cornerstones (along with the Sea Salt Caramels, page 123, the Beer and Pretzel Caramels, page 133, Honeycomb Candy, page 197, and Snacker Bars, page 256). The idea was simple enough: Jen wanted to pay tribute to Elvis Presley himself by doing a candy bar version of his famous favorite sandwich, the fried peanut-butter-and-banana (no bacon for us, thankyouverymuch).

The crumbly brown-butter dough—inspired by a recipe from one of our favorite blogs, Smitten Kitchen—incorporates the lovely caramelized-butter flavor of a true fried sandwich; the Fluffy Peanut Butter Nougat was a shoo-in for the peanut butter role. And playing the part of fresh bananas: fresh bananas, mixed into white chocolate ganache. It makes sense when you break it down, but melded together and enrobed in milk chocolate, it's . . . spectacular? Ethereal? We would go so far as to say, inasmuch as anything can bear this label: perfect.

SPECIAL EQUIPMENT

- Heatproof spatula
- Stand mixer fitted with paddle attachment, or electric mixer with large bowl
- Rolling pin
- Large (13" x 18") rimmed baking sheet
- Candy thermometer

INGREDIENTS

FOR THE COOKIE BASE

1 cup (2 sticks/225 g) unsalted butter

¾ cup tightly packed (145 g) dark brown sugar

¾ teaspoon (3 g) coarse sea salt

2¾ cups (275 g) all-purpose flour, plus extra as needed

¾ teaspoon (4 g) pure vanilla extract

FOR THE NOUGAT

5 large egg whites (150 g)

3⅔ cups (730 g) granulated sugar

1 cup (240 g) water

2¼ cups (580 g) creamy commercial peanut butter, such as Skippy

1 tablespoon (18 g) coarse sea salt

FOR THE BANANA GANACHE

16 ounces (450 g) white chocolate, chopped (about 2½ cups)

½ cup (120 g) heavy (whipping) cream

¼ cup (85 g) light corn syrup

½ cup (130 g) pureed very ripe banana (from about 1 medium-size banana)

½ teaspoon (3 g) kosher salt

FOR ENROBING THE BARS

13 cups chopped dark chocolate (about 5 pounds/2.25 kg), or 13 cups chopped dark chocolate (about 5 pounds/2.25 kg) and 2 cups (450 g) mild vegetable oil

Cooking spray

Make the cookie base:

1. Melt the butter in a small (2-quart) saucepan over medium heat. Reduce the heat to low and cook, stirring frequently with a heatproof spatula, until the butter has turned golden brown and smells fragrant and nutty, about 8 minutes. *Immediately* remove it from the heat and allow it to cool to lukewarm in the saucepan, about 1 hour.

2. Pour the butter into the mixer bowl. Add the brown sugar and sea salt, and mix on medium-high speed until combined, 3 minutes.

3. Add the flour and vanilla extract, and mix on low speed until just combined. The dough will be very soft; if it's too sticky to handle, add more flour, a teaspoon at a time, and mix until it's just firm enough to handle. Turn the dough out onto a piece of

plastic wrap. Form it into a flat rectangle, wrap it tightly, and refrigerate it until firm, about 3 hours (or you can freeze it for up to 2 months).

4. When you're ready to roll out the dough, cut a piece of parchment paper to fit the bottom of your baking sheet. Using this as a guide, dust a rolling pin with flour and roll out the dough on top of the paper to fit it. (You can trim the edges and reattach the scraps to fill any holes.) Gently slide the trimmed dough, on the parchment, onto the baking sheet. Refrigerate it for 30 minutes.

5. Preheat the oven to 350°F/175°C.

6. Place the baking sheet on the middle rack of the oven and bake the dough, rotating the sheet once, until it's dry to the touch and bubbling around the edges, 10 to 12 minutes. Remove it from the oven and allow to cool on the baking sheet.

Make the nougat:

7. Clean and dry the mixer bowl. Place the egg whites in it and set it aside.

8. Combine the sugar and water in a small (2-quart) saucepan. Place the mixture over high heat, and bring to a boil while stirring with the spatula to dissolve the sugar. Once the syrup has boiled, insert the candy thermometer. Turn the heat to medium-high and cook, uncovered and without stirring, until it reaches 240°F/115°C (soft ball stage), about 10 minutes. Meanwhile, work on the next step.

9. While the syrup is cooking, put the peanut butter in a microwave-safe bowl and heat it on High in bursts of 5 to 10 seconds until it is warm and slightly liquid. (Alternatively, gently heat it in a small bowl set over a saucepan of simmering water.)

10. When the syrup reaches 240°F/115°C (soft ball stage), begin whipping the egg whites on medium speed. Continue to cook the syrup to 255°F/125°C (hard ball stage), about 10 minutes. This is the trickiest part of the recipe, but it's all in the timing. You want the whites to be around soft peak stage—thick and fluffy but still soft—when the syrup has reached 255°F/125°C, about 6 minutes. If you need to stop beating the egg whites to let the syrup catch up, that's fine; if you need to turn the heat down on the syrup so you can whip the whites a little more, that's fine, too.

11. When the syrup has reached 255°F/125°C (hard ball stage), put on oven mitts and remove it from the heat. Turn the mixer speed down to low, then carefully pour the hot syrup into the egg whites while they're whipping (don't pour it directly on the beaters—it will splatter!).

12. Increase the speed to medium-high, and continue beating until the bowl has cooled so that it is warm—not hot—to the touch, about 10 minutes. Stop the mixer. Using the spatula, quickly fold the peanut butter and salt into the egg whites until just combined; there should be no more white streaks.

13. Spread the nougat directly on top of the cooled cookie base. Allow it to set for at least 1 hour, or as long as overnight.

Make the banana ganache:

14. Fill a small (2-quart) saucepan about one-third of the way (to a depth of about 2 inches) with hot water and bring it to a simmer over medium heat. Put the white chocolate in a medium-size heatproof bowl, place the bowl over the simmering water, and melt the chocolate, stirring occasionally to prevent it from burning.

15. Meanwhile, combine the cream, light corn syrup, pureed banana, and salt in a medium-size microwave-safe bowl, and microwave on High for 30 seconds, stirring halfway through. (Alternatively, place the bowl over another pan of simmering water and heat, stirring occasionally, for about 10 minutes.) Once the banana mixture is hot to the touch and steaming, set it aside.

16. As soon as the white chocolate is completely melted, remove it from the heat (don't let it overheat!). Add the banana mixture and stir gently with the spatula until combined and uniform, about 3 minutes.

17. Allow the ganache to cool until it's no longer hot but still liquidy, 15 to 20 minutes. Pour it over the nougat and spread it in an even layer. Allow it to set until it's no longer wet but still slightly soft to the touch, at least 30 minutes at room temperature, and up to overnight. (You can speed up the set by placing it in the fridge for no more than 15 minutes.)

Enrobe the bars:

18. Temper the 13 cups chocolate according to the instructions on page 26, or use the 13 cups chocolate and 2 cups oil to make the Cheater's Chocolate Coating as directed on page 32.

19. Lightly spray the top of the banana ganache with cooking spray, then turn the candy slab out of the pan. Enrobe and cut the bars following the directions on pages 253–255.

The bars will keep, stored in an airtight container at cool room temperature, for up to 3 weeks.

JEN SAYS: The brown butter dough makes delicious cookies that go great with tea: Cut the dough into 2-inch rounds with a cutter or a floured drinking glass, carefully transfer the rounds to a parchment-lined baking sheet, leaving at least 2 inches between them (the cookies spread out a lot), chill in the refrigerator for 20 minutes, and bake at 350°F/175°C until golden brown around the edges and completely dry-looking, 5 to 7 minutes.

WORTH IT

S'MORES BARS

MAKES ABOUT 30 ONE- BY FOUR-INCH BARS

There are many s'mores candies out there. Most of them involve a graham cracker and a layer of marshmallow dipped in chocolate. Graham + marshmallow + chocolate = s'more. Right? Well, that's not good enough for us. We came at our version from the s'mores-eater's point of view. What are the classic characteristics of a s'more? Crispy graham cracker; that's a given. But what about the chocolate? It melts and gets soft—a ganache mimics that texture. And the marshmallow is toasted, and maybe a little smoky from the bonfire—so we infused the ganache with smoked tea and took a torch to the mallow (don't worry, we're bypassing that step here). This bar has slowly but steadily gained a rabid fan base since we started; when you get around to making it, you'll quickly see why.

The graham cracker base is more like a hearty cookie than a cracker, adapted from a (naturally) sublime recipe from the incomparable Deb over at the blog Smitten Kitchen.

For the ganache, we use Lapsang Souchong tea; it lends a really lovely mellow smokiness to the ganache that brings us right back to that bonfire. Lapsang Souchong is available at some high-end groceries and specialty stores, as well as online at Amazon; several well-known brands, like Twinings and Republic of Tea, have their own versions.

Heads-up that the marshmallow recipe makes twice as much as we use for the bars. It's not possible to make half of this particular recipe (trust us, we've tried), so you can either pour half of the marshmallow into a separate greased 9- × 13-inch pan, to cut up and enjoy later, or just double up on mallow in the bar and make them tall like supermodels.

SPECIAL EQUIPMENT

- Stand mixer
- Large (13″ x 18″) rimmed baking sheet
- Rolling pin
- Heatproof spatula
- Candy thermometer
- Rubber spatula or metal offset spatula
- Small (9″ x 13″) baking sheet, lightly coated with cooking spray

INGREDIENTS

FOR THE GRAHAM CRACKER BASE

1½ cups (185 g) all-purpose flour, plus extra for dusting

1 cup plus 2 tablespoons (135 g) whole wheat flour

1 cup (175 g) light brown sugar

1¼ teaspoons (6 g) baking soda

1 teaspoon (6 g) kosher salt

8 tablespoons (1 stick/110 g) unsalted butter, cut into 1-inch pieces and chilled

⅓ cup (115 g) mild honey, such as clover

5 tablespoons (80 g) whole milk

2 tablespoons (30 g) pure vanilla extract

FOR THE SMOKED TEA GANACHE

22 ounces (630 g) dark chocolate, chopped (about 4½ cups)

1 cup (255 g) heavy (whipping) cream

2½ tablespoons (50 g) light corn syrup

1 teaspoon (2 g/2 individual bags) Lapsang Souchong tea leaves

¾ teaspoon (3 g) kosher salt

FOR THE MARSHMALLOW LAYER

1¼ cups (300 g) cold water, divided into ¾ cup (175 g) and ½ cup (125 g)

4 tablespoons plus 1 teaspoon (32 g) unflavored powdered gelatin

2¾ cups (550 g) granulated sugar

¾ cup (255 g) light corn syrup

3 large egg whites, at room temperature

1 vanilla bean, split open and seeds scraped out, pod reserved; or 1 teaspoon pure vanilla extract

FOR ENROBING THE BARS

13 cups chopped milk chocolate (about 5 pounds/2.25 kg), or 13 cups chopped milk chocolate (about 5 pounds/2.25 kg) and 2 cups (450 g) mild vegetable oil

Cooking spray

Make the graham cracker base:

1. Combine the flours, brown sugar, baking soda, and salt in a large bowl or the bowl of a stand mixer fitted with the paddle attachment, and mix on low speed to blend.

2. Add the butter and mix on low speed, until the mixture resembles coarse meal.

3. Whisk together the honey, milk, and vanilla extract in a small bowl. Add the honey mixture to the flour mixture and mix on low speed until the dough just comes together—it will be very soft and sticky.

4. Lay out a large piece of plastic wrap and dust it lightly with flour. Scrape the dough out onto it and pat it into a rectangle about 1 inch thick. Wrap it up in the plastic wrap and refrigerate it until it is cold and firm to the touch, 2 hours or overnight.

5. Remove the dough from the fridge, and preheat the oven to 350°F/175°C.

6. Cut a piece of parchment paper to fit the bottom of your baking sheet. Using this as a guide, dust the rolling pin with flour and roll out the dough on top of the paper to fit it. (You can trim the edges and reattach the scraps to fill any holes.) Gently slide the dough, on the parchment, onto the baking sheet.

7. Bake the cookie until it is lightly browned all over, 12 to 15 minutes. Allow it to cool completely in the baking sheet.

Make the smoked tea ganache:

8. Place the dark chocolate in a medium-size bowl. Set it aside.

9. Combine the heavy cream and corn syrup in a small (1-quart) saucepan, and place it over high heat. Bring the mixture just barely to a boil and then turn off the heat. Add the tea leaves, cover the pan, and steep for 20 minutes.

10. Pour the cream through a strainer to remove the tea leaves. Return the cream to the saucepan and bring it just to a boil again over medium heat. Immediately pour the cream over the chocolate in the bowl, and allow it to sit until the chocolate is melted, about 5 minutes.

11. Using the spatula, stir gently in the center of the bowl. The ganache will start to come together around the spatula. Resist the urge to scrape the side of the bowl—keep stirring in the center. After 2 to 3 minutes the ganache will be almost completely emulsified. Sprinkle in the salt and give a few thorough but gentle stirs until all the cream and salt are incorporated.

12. Allow the ganache to cool, stirring it occasionally, until it is thickened and no longer warm, 10 to 15 minutes. Pour the ganache over the cooled graham cracker base (still in the baking sheet) and allow it to set until firm, about 1½ hours.

Make the marshmallow layer:

13. Place ¾ cup of the cold water in a small bowl, sprinkle the gelatin over it, and stir to combine. Set it aside to soften, at least 5 minutes.

14. Place the remaining ½ cup water, the sugar, corn syrup, and vanilla bean and seeds in a medium-size (4-quart) saucepan, and stir with the heatproof spatula to combine. Bring the mixture to a boil, without stirring, over medium-high heat. Then insert the candy thermometer and cook, uncovered, until it reaches 240°F/116°C (firm-to-hard ball stage), about 10 minutes.

15. Place the egg whites in the bowl of the stand mixer fitted with the whisk attachment, and beat at medium speed until they hold soft peaks, 4 to 6 minutes. Turn the speed down to low; with the mixer still running, proceed to the next step.

16. Once the syrup reaches 250°F/121°C (firm-to-hard ball stage), remove it from the heat and use a slotted spoon to fish out the vanilla bean. Carefully pour the hot syrup down the inside of the

bowl containing the egg whites. Add the softened gelatin and turn the speed up to high, beating until the mixture is white, thick, and almost tripled in volume, about 6 minutes.

17. If using the vanilla extract, add it, and beat until just combined.

18. Pour half of the warm marshmallow onto the ganache layer and spread it quickly and evenly with a rubber spatula or metal offset spatula. Allow it to set until it springs back to the touch, about 30 minutes.

Enrobe the bars:

19. Temper the 13 cups chopped milk chocolate according to the instructions on page 26, or use the 13 cups chopped milk chocolate and 2 cups oil to make the Cheater's Chocolate Coating as directed on page 32.

20. Coat the top of the marshmallow lightly with cooking spray. Enrobe and cut the bars, following the directions on page 253.

Store the bars, layered with parchment or wax paper, in an airtight container at room temperature for up to 3 weeks.

LAYERING THE MARSHMALLOW

1. Pour half of the marshmallow onto the ganache layer. (Reserve the rest for other fun.)

2. Spread the marshmallow quickly and evenly across the top. Allow it to set for 30 minutes.

Don't toss that leftover marshmallow! Set it up, cut it, and dip it in chocolate (see page 33) or drop it into mugs of hot cocoa.

MODERATE

PASSION SPICE CARAMEL BARS

MAKES ABOUT 25 ONE- BY FOUR-INCH BARS, OR 120 ONE-INCH PIECES

These bars make an appearance at Liddabit for special occasions—Valentimes* in particular—though they have a very loyal (and vocal) contingent that's constantly asking us why we don't offer them year-round. The frustrating-parent answer we always give is, "Well, then they wouldn't be special, would they?" Just between you and us, these are special any time of year, whenever you decide to make them. The pucker of the passion fruit, the slow burn of the spice, the buttery chew of the caramel, and the subtle crunch of the crisped rice . . . well, you can see why we save it for Valentimes.**

*We are aware it's not actually spelled like that.

**Yup, still aware.

SPECIAL EQUIPMENT

- Small (9″ x 13″) rimmed baking sheet
- Silicone mat or parchment paper
- Heatproof spatula
- Candy thermometer

INGREDIENTS

Cooking spray

3 cups (700 g) heavy (whipping) cream

3 cups (600 g) granulated sugar

⅓ cup plus 1 tablespoon (140 g) light corn syrup

6 tablespoons (¾ stick/90 g) unsalted butter

1½ teaspoons (8 g) fine sea salt

1½ teaspoons (3 g) ground cayenne pepper or chile powder

⅓ cup (70 g) unsweetened passion fruit puree (see Note)

3½ cups (75 g) crisped rice cereal

13 cups chopped dark chocolate (about 5 pounds/2.25 kg), or 13 cups chopped dark chocolate (about 5 pounds/2.25 kg) and 2 cups (450 g) mild vegetable oil, for enrobing the bars

1. Lightly coat the baking sheet with cooking spray, line it with the silicone mat, and set it aside.

2. Combine the heavy cream, sugar, corn syrup, butter, sea salt, and cayenne pepper in a large (6-quart) saucepan or stockpot. Bring to a boil over medium-high heat. When the sugar has dissolved, insert the candy thermometer.

3. Cook the syrup over medium-high heat, stirring occasionally with the heatproof spatula, until the mixture has reached 240°F/115°C (soft ball stage). Slowly add the passion fruit puree (be careful—it may spatter) and cook, stirring frequently, until the temperature reaches 250°F/120°C (firm ball stage).

4. Remove the passion fruit caramel from the heat and stir in the rice cereal. Pour the caramel onto the prepared baking sheet and allow it to cool completely, 2 to 3 hours.

5. Temper the 13 cups chopped dark chocolate according to the instructions on page 26, or use the 13 cups chopped dark chocolate and 2 cups oil to make the Cheater's Chocolate Coating as directed on page 32.

6. Enrobe and cut the bars, following the directions on page 253.

Store the bars in an airtight container at cool room temperature for up to 6 weeks; in the refrigerator, up to 3 months.

NOTE: Passion fruit puree is available online from Amazon. If you can't get your hands on any, you can often find passion fruit juice at specialty or health food stores. When using juice, increase the amount to 1 cup and add 1 tablespoon freshly squeezed lemon or lime juice (the juice boils down in the candy while it cooks).

WORTH IT

THE DORIE BAR

MAKES ABOUT 35 ONE- BY FOUR-INCH BARS

This lovely, magical candy bar is named for our lovely, magical friend and mentor, Dorie Greenspan. We could think of no better tribute to Dorie, a renowned cookbook author herself, than to include the bar that she inspired. It's a combination of all our favorite flavors and textures: the crispness and deep, dark flavor of the chocolate cookie (adapted from one of Thomas Keller's recipes, no less—see page 280); the lush, melt-in-your-mouth salted caramel ganache; the chewy dried apricots and tart lemon; and the surprising zip of black pepper. "More than the sum of its parts" doesn't even begin to describe it. Give it a go—it's almost as nice as hanging out with the lady herself! *(Almost.)*

Before you begin, note that you're making a dry caramel for the ganache recipe—it wouldn't do you any harm to read up on the dry caramel technique on page 50.

Both the ganache and the cookie can be made ahead of time. The ganache, minus the apricots, can be stored in an airtight container in the refrigerator for up to 1 week. Before using it, allow it to come to room temperature and then warm it in 5-second intervals on half power in the microwave, or over a pot of simmering water, until it is soft and spreadable like peanut butter. Mix in the apricots before spreading. The cookie dough, tightly wrapped in plastic wrap, can be kept in the refrigerator for up to 1 week or in the freezer for up to 2 months. The cookie can also be baked up to 2 days ahead of time, as long as it is kept, wrapped tightly in plastic wrap, at cool room temperature. So in other words: There may be lotsa steps here, but you can tackle 'em in stages if you like.

SPECIAL EQUIPMENT

- Stand mixer fitted with paddle attachment, or electric mixer with large bowl
- Rolling pin
- Large (13" x 18") rimmed baking sheet, lined with parchment paper
- Heatproof spatula
- Large offset spatula

INGREDIENTS

FOR THE COOKIE BASE

2 cups (250 g) all-purpose flour, plus extra for dusting

1 cup (200 g) granulated sugar

1 cup (85 g) unsweetened cocoa powder

¾ teaspoon (4 g) baking soda

2 teaspoons (12 g) fleur de sel or kosher salt

2½ cups (5 sticks/425 g) unsalted butter, very soft

FOR THE SALTED CARAMEL GANACHE

23 ounces (650 g) white chocolate, chopped (3¾ cups)

¾ cup (160 g) granulated sugar

1 tablespoon (20 g) light corn syrup

1½ cups (360 g) heavy (whipping) cream

3 tablespoons plus 2 teaspoons (50 g) unsalted butter, at room temperature

1½ teaspoons (10 g) fleur de sel or fine sea salt

FOR THE LEMON APRICOTS

1 pound (about 4 cups/450 g) dried apricots, diced into ½-inch pieces or smaller

2 tablespoons (30 g) olive oil

Finely grated zest and juice of 1 medium-size (3-inch) lemon

1 tablespoon (5 g) freshly ground black pepper

FOR ENROBING THE BARS

13 cups chopped dark chocolate (about 5 pounds/2.25 kg), or 13 cups chopped dark chocolate (about 5 pounds/ 2.25 kg) and 2 cups mild vegetable oil

Make the cookie base:

1. Put the flour, sugar, cocoa powder, baking soda, and fleur de sel in the mixer bowl and stir together with a rubber spatula. Start the mixer on low speed and begin to add the butter, a couple tablespoons at a time, waiting for each addition to incorporate before adding the next one.

2. Once all the butter is added, mix on medium-low speed until the mixture looks very coarse and dry, like pebbles, about 4 minutes. Stop the mixer and transfer the dough to a cutting board or silicone mat.

3. Gently knead the dough with your hands until it comes together, 2 to 3 minutes. Pat it into a small rectangle, about 1 inch thick, wrap it tightly in plastic wrap, and allow it to rest in the refrigerator for 1 hour.

4. Preheat the oven to 350°F/175°C.

5. Cut a piece of parchment paper to fit the bottom of your baking sheet. Using this as a guide, dust the rolling pin with flour and roll out the dough on top of the paper to fit it. (You can trim the edges and reattach the scraps to fill any holes.) Gently slide the dough, on the parchment, onto the baking sheet.

6 Bake the cookie until the edges are dry but the center still looks underbaked, 10 to 12 minutes. (You don't want to overbake the cookie or the cutting process will be very difficult—less is more.) Allow the cookie to cool completely in the baking sheet, about 30 minutes.

Make the salted caramel ganache:

7 Put the white chocolate in a medium-size heatproof bowl and set it aside.

8 Place a small (2-quart) saucepan (make sure it is absolutely bone-dry!) over medium heat and pour in the sugar, about ¼ cup at a time, allowing the sugar to melt between each addition and gently and occasionally stirring it with the heatproof spatula to prevent any spots from burning (don't stir too much or you'll get lumps!). Cook over low heat until the sugar turns a dark maple-syrup color and smells like the dreams of a thousand rainbow candy unicorns (that is, like rich and toasty caramel).

9 Add the light corn syrup and stir to combine. Then set your spatula aside and pick up a whisk. Add the cream in a slow stream, whisking as you go (the caramel might bubble and steam here, so no French-kissing the hot sugar syrup).

10 Once the cream is incorporated, remove the caramel from the heat and pour it over the white chocolate in the bowl. Allow it to sit for 5 minutes, then start stirring with the whisk in the middle of the bowl, using a gentle circular motion. Continue stirring gently in the center of the bowl until the ganache is emulsified, 5 to 7 minutes. Stir in the butter and salt until completely combined, and allow to cool to room temperature.

Make the lemon apricots:

11 Place the apricots, olive oil, and lemon zest and juice in a small frying pan over medium heat and cook, stirring constantly, until all the liquid has evaporated, about 7 minutes.

12 Remove the apricots from the heat, stir in the black pepper, and let them cool. Add the apricots to the salted caramel ganache, and stir well.

Assemble and enrobe the bars:

13 Scrape the ganache directly onto the cooled cookie, and use the offset spatula to spread it in an even layer. Place the baking sheet in the fridge until the ganache firms up, about 15 minutes. (You can let it cool at room temperature, too; it'll just take longer—1 to 2 hours.)

14 Run a sharp chef's knife around the edges of the baking sheet to loosen the slab of candy.

15 Temper the 13 cups chopped dark chocolate according to the instructions on page 26, or use the 13 cups chopped dark chocolate and 2 cups oil to make the Cheater's Chocolate Coating as directed on page 32.

16 Enrobe and cut the bars following the directions on page 253.

Store the bars, layered between parchment or wax paper, in an airtight container at room temperature for up to 3 weeks—if you don't eat them all before then. (You probably will.)

MODERATE

COCONUT-LIME BARS

MAKES 30 TO 35 ONE- BY FOUR-INCH BARS

This tropical twist of a candy bar—falling somewhere between "moist and chocolaty macaroon" and "awesome"—has been known to convert many a coconut-shy candy lover. We add fresh lime zest and toasted macadamia nuts to the center, as well as a dash of good white or coconut-flavored rum to give it a little extra zing (never fear—the booze cooks off).

SPECIAL EQUIPMENT

- Large (13" x 18") rimmed baking sheet
- Candy thermometer
- Heatproof spatula
- Cutting board, covered with parchment or wax paper
- Ruler (optional)

INGREDIENTS

Cooking spray or vegetable oil

1¾ cups (300 g) toasted macadamia nuts (see Note)

3 medium-size limes (about 2½ inches each), washed and dried

10½ cups (800 g/28 ounces) shredded unsweetened coconut

1½ tablespoons (22 g) fine sea salt

2 cups (400 g) granulated sugar

5 tablespoons (75 g) white or coconut-flavored rum (optional)

½ cup (125 g) water

2½ cups (875 g) light corn syrup

2 cups (225 g) marshmallow creme, such as Marshmallow Fluff

13 cups chopped dark chocolate (about 5 pounds/2.25 kg), or 13 cups chopped dark chocolate (about 5 pounds/2.25 kg) and 2 cups (450 g) mild vegetable oil, for enrobing the bars

1. Generously coat the baking sheet with cooking spray, and set it aside.

2. Crush the macadamia nuts slightly with a rolling pin or the bottom of a jar (you can put them in a plastic baggie first to minimize mess).

3. Finely zest and juice the limes into a large bowl. Add the coconut, salt, and crushed macadamias, and stir to combine.

4. Combine the sugar, rum (if using), water, and light corn syrup in a medium-size (4-quart) saucepan and bring to a boil, uncovered and without stirring, over high heat. Reduce the heat to medium-high, insert the candy thermometer, and cook, uncovered and without stirring, until the syrup reaches 242°F/117°C (firm ball stage), about 10 minutes.

5. Remove the pan from the heat. Carefully pour the syrup over the coconut mixture, add the marshmallow creme, and stir it all together very thoroughly with the spatula until well combined. Spread the

mixture onto the prepared baking sheet in an even layer. (If you're having trouble spreading it, lay a sheet of parchment paper or a silicone mat on the surface, and press with your hands until it's even.) Allow the coconut slab to cool until it has set and is fairly firm to the touch, about 2 hours, or overnight.

6. Carefully turn out the slab of coconut onto the lined cutting board.

7. Wash the previously used baking sheet, and line it with parchment or wax paper.

8. Temper the 13 cups chopped dark chocolate according to the instructions on page 26, or use the 13 cups chopped dark chocolate and 2 cups oil to make the Cheater's Chocolate Coating as directed on page 32.

9. Enrobe and cut the bars following the directions on page 253.

Store the bars, layered with parchment or wax paper, in an airtight container at cool room temperature for up to 6 weeks.

NOTE: If you can only find raw nuts, toast them in a preheated 325°F/165°C oven, stirring them occasionally, until they're golden brown and fragrant, 5 to 10 minutes, then allow them to cool on the baking sheet.

LIZ SAYS: Play around with the flavor components! Don't like macadamia nuts? Almonds or cashews work well, too. Just remember to toast them if they're raw (see Note)—toasted nuts have a deeper flavor and crunchier texture than raw, the better to contrast with the soft coconut.

JEN SAYS: This bar was inspired by the ubiquitous coconut-almond bar you find in any corner store, but we wanted to put our own twist on it while cutting the sweetness. We decided to use unsweetened coconut, and added some citrus and buttery macadamias to balance it all out.

EASY

CHOCOLATE TOFFEE MATZO CRUNCH

MAKES ABOUT 50 TWO-INCH PIECES

*This candy has a lot going for it: It's economical, super-*simple to make, impressive to look at, and—oh, right—we totally almost forgot how irresistibly munchable it is. It's perfect for any kind of potluck or get-together; make it for a dessert swap and watch it magically disappear before your eyes. We use plain, unsalted matzo (we're control freaks, so we like to put in the *exact* amount of salt we want), but use whichever kind you like. It can't help but be delectable. (If you want to fancy this up, add your favorite toppings—we especially like unsweetened coconut, which makes this an alternative to the tooth-jarringly sweet macaroons that are often available on the same shelf as the matzo).

SPECIAL EQUIPMENT

- Large (13″ x 18″) rimmed baking sheet, lined with parchment paper or aluminum foil
- Heatproof spatula

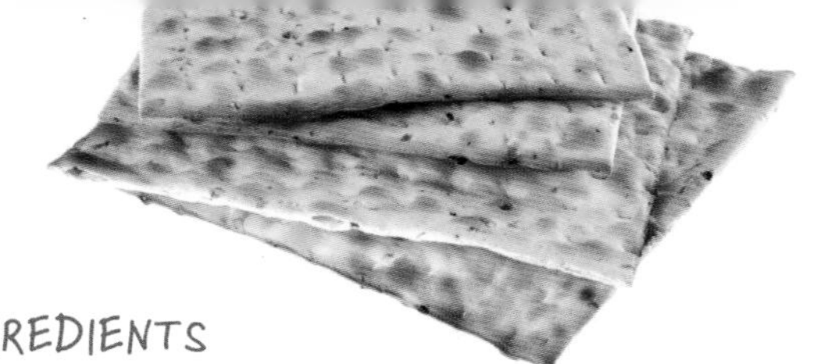

INGREDIENTS

- 4½ sheets unsalted matzo
- 1 cup (200 g) packed light brown sugar
- 14 tablespoons (1¾ sticks/200 g) unsalted butter
- 1½ teaspoons (7 g) fine sea salt
- 6.5 ounces (180 g) dark chocolate, chopped (1 cup)
- 1 tablespoon (18 g) fleur de sel or coarse sea salt, or ⅓ cup toppings such as slivered almonds, or chopped dried cherries, or unsweetened shredded coconut (optional)

1. Preheat the oven to 375°F/190°C.
2. Place the matzo in a single layer on the prepared baking sheet, breaking it into pieces where necessary to fill the pan completely. Set aside.
3. Combine the brown sugar and butter in a medium size (4-quart) saucepan over medium heat. Stirring constantly with the heatproof spatula, bring to a boil, then continue to cook, still stirring constantly, until the mixture has thickened and is just starting to pull away from the side of the pan, about 3 minutes.
4. Remove the mixture from the heat and sprinkle in the fine sea salt, stirring well to incorporate it. Pour it over the matzo in the baking sheet, spreading it in an even layer with the spatula. Place the baking sheet in the oven and immediately turn the heat down to 350°F/175°C.
5. Bake, watching to make sure it doesn't burn, until the toffee bubbles up and turns a rich golden brown, 15 minutes. If it looks like it's starting to burn, turn the heat down to 325°F/163°C.
6. Remove the baking sheet from the oven and immediately sprinkle the chocolate over the hot matzo. Let it sit for 5 minutes, then spread the now-melted chocolate evenly with the spatula and sprinkle with the salt or your favorite toppings while the chocolate is still melted.
7. Allow the matzo to cool completely, 20 to 30 minutes, then break it into smaller (roughly 2-inch square) pieces.

Rumor has it that, stored properly—layered with wax paper, in an airtight container in the refrigerator—this will last a week, but, well, we've never had it last long enough to test the theory.

JEN SAYS: If it's not Passover and/or matzos are hard to come by, you can use unsalted saltine crackers (hello, oxymoron!) instead; but we prefer the flavor and texture of matzo.

MODERATE

CHOCOMALLOW COOKIES

MAKES ABOUT 35 TWO-INCH COOKIES

A couple years ago, we taught our first class at the fantastic home cook's haven that is The Brooklyn Kitchen. They'd just moved into their new digs, and the classroom wasn't finished yet; in fact, it was missing the entire counter. But we taught the class and had a lot of fun; on a whim, we decided to present our take on a Mallomars recipe, since everyone could get their hands dirty piping marshmallow and coating everything in chocolate. They were a huge hit—even *we* were surprised by how much we liked them. And have you heard the news? Marshmallow cookies are the new cupcake. (Just kidding. There's no such thing, because cupcakes will never die.)

The main change we made was replacing the standard vanilla cookie with a salty, deeply cocoa-y one—and it's a Thomas Keller recipe, so you know it has to be amazing. The combination of crumbly cocoa cookie, fluffy sweet marshmallow, and rich chocolate coating is a real crowd-pleaser to keep up your sleeve for special occasions. (For the record, Tuesdays totally count as special occasions.)

This recipe—as with the S'mores Bars on page 271—makes twice as much marshmallow as you need. We recommend pouring half of it out into a greased 9- × 13-inch pan to cut up and enjoy later.

SPECIAL EQUIPMENT

- Stand mixer, or electric mixer with large bowl
- 1½- to 2-inch round cookie cutter or floured drinking glass
- 2 large (13" x 18") rimmed baking sheets, lined with parchment paper or silicone mat
- Heatproof spatula
- Candy thermometer
- Small (9" x 13") baking sheet, lightly coated with cooking spray
- Piping bag or 1-gallon zip-top plastic bag (see page 20)
- Three-tined dipping fork (see page 20) or regular dinner fork

INGREDIENTS

FOR THE COOKIE BASE

2⅓ cups (290 g) all-purpose flour, plus extra for dusting

¾ cup (160 g) granulated sugar

¾ cup plus 2 tablespoons (75 g) unsweetened cocoa powder

½ teaspoon (3 g) baking soda

1½ teaspoons (10 g) coarse sea salt

1 cup (2 sticks/215 g) unsalted butter, at room temperature

FOR THE MARSHMALLOW

1¼ cups (300 g) cold water, divided into ¾ cup (175 g) and ½ cup (125 g)

4 tablespoons plus 1 teaspoon (about 1 ounce/32 g) unflavored powdered gelatin

2¾ cups (550 g) granulated sugar

¾ cup (255 g) light corn syrup

3 large egg whites, at room temperature

1 vanilla bean, split open and seeds scraped out, pod reserved; or 1 teaspoon pure vanilla extract

FOR DIPPING THE COOKIES

13 cups chopped dark chocolate (about 5 pounds/2.25 kg), or 13 cups chopped dark chocolate (about 5 pounds/2.25 kg) and 2 cups (450 g) mild vegetable oil

Make the cookie base:

1. Combine the flour, sugar, cocoa powder, baking soda, and salt in a medium-size bowl or the bowl of a stand mixer fitted with the paddle attachment. With the mixer on low speed, add the butter, a bit at a time, and mix until it comes together into a dough; it will be very sandy and crumbly. Turn the dough out onto a piece of plastic wrap, pat it into a flat rectangle, and wrap it tightly. Refrigerate it until firm, at least 4 hours, or overnight.

2. When you're ready to bake the dough, remove it from the refrigerator and preheat the oven to 325°F/163°C.

3. Lightly dust a cutting board or other work surface with flour. Roll the dough out to about ¼-inch thickness, and cut it into rounds with a cookie cutter or floured drinking glass. Place the rounds on the prepared large baking sheet, spacing them at least 1 inch apart. Bake until the cookies are slightly puffy and dry looking, 7 to 10 minutes. Allow them to cool completely on the baking sheet.

Make the marshmallow:

4. Place ¾ cup of the cold water in a small bowl, sprinkle the gelatin over it, and stir to combine. Set it aside to soften, at least 5 minutes.

5. Place the remaining ½ cup water, the sugar, the corn syrup, and the vanilla bean and seeds (if using) in a medium-size (4-quart) saucepan, and stir with the heatproof spatula to combine. Bring the mixture to a boil, without stirring, over medium-high heat. Then insert the candy thermometer and cook, uncovered, until it reaches 240°F/116°C (firm-to-hard ball stage), about 10 minutes.

6. Place the egg whites in a large bowl or the bowl of a stand mixer fitted with the whisk attachment, and beat at medium speed until they hold soft peaks, 4 to 6 minutes. Turn the speed down to low; proceed to the next step.

7. Once the syrup reaches 250°F/121°C (firm-to-hard ball stage), remove it from the heat and use a slotted spoon to fish out the vanilla bean (if you used one). Pour the hot syrup into the bowl containing the egg whites, pouring down the side of the bowl. Add the softened gelatin and turn the speed up to high, beating until the mixture is white, thick, and almost tripled in volume; about 6 minutes for a stand mixer or 10 to 12 minutes with a handheld mixer.

8. If using the vanilla extract, add it, and beat until just combined. Meanwhile, place the piping bag in a measuring cup and set it aside nearby.

9. Pour half of the warm marshmallow into the piping bag in the cup. Pour the rest into the prepared small baking sheet, spread it evenly with a rubber spatula or metal offset spatula, and set it aside. (When it has cooled, cut it up to store or enjoy later.)

Assemble and dip the cookies:

⑩ Seal the piping bag and snip a hole about ½ inch off the tip. Pipe the marshmallow onto the baked cookies in nice big puffs. Allow the marshmallow to firm up, 2 to 3 hours.

⑪ Temper the 13 cups chocolate according to the instructions on page 26, or use the 13 cups chocolate and 2 cups oil to make Cheater's Chocolate Coating as directed on page 32.

⑫ Dip each marshmallow-topped cookie following the fork dipping directions on page 33, and place them on the remaining lined large baking sheet. Let the chocolate set up, about 15 minutes.

Store the cookies in an airtight container at cool room temperature for up to 1 week.

RESOURCES

HANDY-DANDY KEY
T: Tools
I: Ingredients
P: Packaging

EQUIPMENT

BOWERY KITCHEN SUPPLY (BKS) T

75 9th Avenue, New York, NY 10011, (212) 376-4982; bowerykitchens.com
One of our favorite stores to get lost in, BKS carries all the basics, like metal mixing bowls, rimmed baking sheets, silicone mats, and bench scrapers.

CANDYLAND CRAFTS T/I/P

candylandcrafts.com
Buy your foil candy cups and cellophane wrappers here! It's also another great resource for molds, candy equipment, packaging, and specialty ingredients like flavors and colorings.

HAUSER CHOCOLATIER I

hauserchocolates.com
The only place we can find that sells 1-pound packages of feuilletine (for Hip-to-Be Squares, page 99). They also sell block chocolate and cocoa butter, a good deal if you're planning to make big batches.

INDIA TREE I

indiatree.com
Want natural food colorings, spices, and maple sugar? Go here. Plus they have a bajillion kinds of sprinkles and other garnishes like candied flower petals and sparkle sugar.

JB PRINCE T

36 East 31st Street, New York, NY 10016, (800) 473-0577; jbprince.com
Tons of gorgeous polycarbonate bonbon molds and all sorts of other obscure specialty equipment, like chocolate dipping tools, large metal tweezers, and extra-long-handled heatproof spatulas.

KING ARTHUR FLOUR I

kingarthurflour.com
Specialty ingredients, high-quality extracts and spices, bulk chocolate, nut flours and pastes, and other sundry bits and pieces are available in their online store.

NASHVILLE WRAPS P

nashvillewraps.com
We buy most of our gift packaging from Nashville; their selection can't be beat, and they offer a lot of ecofriendly options as well.

N.Y. CAKE AND BAKE I/P

56 West 22nd Street, New York, NY 10010, (212) 675-CAKE; nycake.com
Another excellent source for molds and smaller quantities of specialty ingredients like sheet gelatin and citric acid, glucose, gel food coloring, and ready-made fondant (for Cherry Cordials, page 85, and Mint Patties, page 164). Plus they have disco dust!

SUGARCRAFT T/I

sugarcraft.com
Every shape and size of candy or chocolate mold imaginable is available on this site, as are lollipop sticks, candy funnels, flavorings, and all kinds of other equipment. They also carry a lot of fun packaging for gifts or events.

WILLIAMS-SONOMA T/I

Various locations nationwide; williams-sonoma.com
A terrific resource for digital thermometers, baking pans, precut parchment sheets, and silicone molds that you can use for chocolate.

WORLD WIDE CHOCOLATE I

worldwidechocolate.com
Offers an excellent variety of chocolate discs (aka pistoles), cocoa powder, cocoa butter, nibs—basically everything chocolate. You don't need to sign up for an account, there are often sales, and they carry all our favorite brands such as Valrhona, Cluizel, and Cacao Barry.

If all else fails . . .

AMAZON T/I/P

amazon.com
Surely you already know this megalithic online retailer; if you don't, Google it—or better yet, Amazon it!

Amazon carries almost everything, though we especially like them for equipment like kitchen scales, thermometers, and mixers, and specialty items like wax twisting paper for wrapping caramels and other small candies. They also have a lot of specialty confectionery ingredients, such as glucose, nut flours, hard-to-find extracts, and fruit puree.

CANDY BOOKS

If you're interested in delving deeper into the sugary sea of candy facts, technique, and lore, the following books are a good place to start:

Brittles, Barks, and Bonbons by Charity Ferreira

Chocolate Desserts by Pierre Hermé by Dorie Greenspan

Chocolates and Confections and *Chocolates and Confections at Home,* both by Peter Greweling and The Culinary Institute of America

Field Guide to Candy by Anita Chu

On Food and Cooking: The Science and Lore of the Kitchen by Harold McGee

The Fundamental Techniques of Classic Pastry Arts by The French Culinary Institute and Judith Choate

Sugar Baby by Gesine Bullock-Prado

The Ultimate Candy Book by Bruce Weinstein

Who Wants Candy? by Jane Sharrock

OTHER INSPIRATION AND STUFF WE LIKE

We're constantly seeking ideas in our everyday lives—these favorite blogs and books never fail to inspire when we need a great recipe or creative boost:

Baking: From My Home to Yours by Dorie Greenspan (plus her blog at doriegreenspan.com)

Cooking Issues blog by Dave Arnold and Nils Norén

Flour by Joanne Chang

Food52, food52.com

The Food Lab by J. Kenji López-Alt on *Serious Eats,* seriouseats.com/the-food-lab

The Great Book of Chocolate by David Lebovitz (plus his blog at davidlebovitz.com)

Michael Laiskonis's blog at michaellaiskonis.typepad.com

Smitten Kitchen blog by Deb Perelman, smittenkitchen.com

INDEX

Page references in *italic* refer to photographs.

D

E

F

G

N

O

P

R

S

ADDITIONAL PHOTOGRAPHY CREDITS

Fotolia: 1999istek p. 98 third from top (right), p. 194 top, p. 196 right; Aaron Amat p. 194 bottom; abcmedia p. 3; aerogondo p. 116, p. 171 bottom, p. 179 top, p. 245 second from bottom; Africa Studio p. 97 top right, p. 98 third from top (left), p. 128, p. 166 top, p. 197, p. 257 bottom, p. 280; Akova p. 17 bottom right; Alexander Petrov p. 279 top; alexlukin p. 86; Artur Synenko p. 17 middle far left; Barbro Bergfeldt p. 251; Bert Folsom p. 17 middle right, p. 61 top; Billy Hoiler p. 268; blueee p. 21 middle left, p. 198; Brad Pict p. 65 bottom; Brooke Becker p. 18 top right, p. 21 bottom left; by-studio p. 161 top; Chariclo p. 138 right; Christian Jung p. 32; Constantinos p. 212 top; Corinna Gissemann p. 179 bottom; Darren Brode p. 16 middle left; Dasha Petrenko p. 141; David Gordon p. 235; Denis Khveshchenik p. 81 second from top; design56 p. 17 middle left; Diana Taliun p. 144 top right, p. 153, p. 259 top right; Dionisvera p. 61 middle, p. 283; Dmitriy Syechin p. 252; FilipHerzig p. 226; fivespots p.138 left; fkruger p. 284; flas100 p. 23 top right, p. 29 bottom right, p. 290; Francesco83 p. 92; Frog 974 p. 116 left; Gresei p. 245 top; Jessica Blanc p. 101 right; Jiri Hera p. 12, p. 123; JJAVA p. 212 middle; Kelpfish p. 245 second; Kimberly Reinick p. 68; Kitch Bain p.14 right; kostrez p. 88 top; Leonid Nyshko p. 286; lonescu Bogdan p. 16 bottom right; Luis Santos p. 132; Marco Mayer p. 129; MarcoBagnoli Elflaco p. 98 second; Marek p. 227 top; margo555 p. 196 left; marilyn barbone p. 10, p. 115; marslander p. 106; mates p. 72, p. 84 middle, p. 98 bottom left; matin p. 65 top, p. 277; Meliha Gojak p. 73, p. 84 bottom, p. 173; Michael Flippo p. 209; Mona Makela p. 22 bottom, p. 81 third from top; Neiromobile p. 98 bottom right; nenovbrothers p. 62, p. 64 bottom; netrun78 p. 217; Nina Morozova p. 18 middle right; nito p. 98 fourth from top, p. 174, p. 211, p. 240; nivana p. 171 second from top; Norman Pogson p. 199; Oleksii Sagitov p. 245 bottom; Patricia Hofmeester p. 194 middle; Pavelis p. 66 bottom; phloem p. 218; photocrew p. 145; picsfive p. 23 top left, p. 29 top left, p. 42 bottom, p. 44, p. 48, p. 108, p. 193, p. 213 right; Popova Olga p. 279 bottom; Predrag Vasilevski p. 257 top; proffelice p. 46; rgbdigital.co.uk p. 17 top left; rimglow p. 188; robynmac p. 144 bottom left, p. 160; Sascha Burkard p. 131; schenkArt p. 100, p. 179 middle, p. 216; Silkstock p. 21 top left; sirogio p. 176, p. 213 left; SLDigi p. 61 bottom; sommai p. 66 top; Stéphane Bidouze p. 84 top; Stockmdm p. 81 bottom; teena137 p. 18 top left; terumin p. 59; tuja66 p. 24 top; UZUMBA p. 107; vadidak p.136, Vidady p. 166 bottom, p. 266; VIPDesign p. 81 top; WavebreakmediaMicro p. 119; Winston p. 259 left; xjbxjhxm p. vii; Zbyszek Nowak p. 98 top; **iStockphoto:** flas100 p. 302, Kathy Dewar p. 93; **Melissa Lucier:** p. 20 right middle, p. 21 right, p. 234, p. 237, p. 238, p. 239, p. 242, p. 262.

BYE!